Globalization and Development

Globalization and Development

Why East Asia Surged Ahead and Latin America Fell Behind

Anthony Elson

First published in 2013 by
PALGRAVE MACMILLAN®
in the United States—a division of St. Martin's Press LLC,
175 Fifth Avenue, New York, NY 10010.

Where this book is distributed in the UK, Europe and the rest of the world,
this is by Palgrave Macmillan, a division of Macmillan Publishers Limited,
registered in England, company number 785998, of Houndmills,
Basingstoke, Hampshire RG21 6XS.

Palgrave Macmillan is the global academic imprint of the above companies
and has companies and representatives throughout the world.

Palgrave® and Macmillan® are registered trademarks in the United States,
the United Kingdom, Europe and other countries.

ISBN: 978–1–137–27474–8

Library of Congress Cataloging-in-Publication Data is available from the
Library of Congress.

A catalogue record of the book is available from the British Library.

Design by Newgen Knowledge Works (P) Ltd., Chennai, India.

First edition: December 2013

10 9 8 7 6 5 4 3 2 1

To
Marjorie Louise Frieder, Amanda Erin Toledano,
and Kerry Mackinnon,
the three special, lovely women
in my life

Contents

Illustrations

Preface

This book, along with *Governing Global Finance: The Evolution and Reform of the International Financial Architecture*, published by Palgrave Macmillan in 2011, constitute what I like to call my "professional biography." The first book was institutionally based and examined a number of international institutions and bodies, such as the International Monetary Fund (IMF), the Bank for International Settlements (BIS), the Financial Stability Forum (now Board), the World Bank, and the G7/20 (that form part of the international financial architecture), with which I became very familiar during a career at the IMF and a period of consulting at the World Bank. The current book is thematic and, obviously, based on country and regions, and deals with a number of countries in East Asia and Latin America with which I worked for many years as a professional staff member of the IMF and World Bank consultant. The operational focus of the IMF provided a unique perspective on the macroeconomic policy and performance of a number of countries across these two regions, while frequent contact with counterparts in the World Bank (along with my work as a consultant) provided a medium- to long-term developmental perspective on these countries to complement my institutional focus at the IMF. This experience provided an important background for framing many of the issues raised in this book.

Following my career at the IMF, I spent an academic year at St. Antony's College (Oxford) and the London School of Economics, where I began to think more intensively about the issues raised in this book. In England, I had the opportunity to interact with a number of prominent development scholars, such as Jeffrey Chwieroth, Paul Collier, Rodrigo Cubero, Valpy Fitzgerald, Sanjaya Lall, Frances Stewart, Rosemary Thorpe, Andrew Walter, and Robert Wade, among others, with whom I was able to test some of my views on comparative development and who, for their part, significantly influenced my thinking about the process of economic development. As a first step toward the production of this book, I developed an academic curriculum on the comparative economic development of East Asia and Latin America, which I have been using, and adapting, for a course I have been teaching at the Johns Hopkins School of Advanced International Studies (SAIS) in Washington, DC and the Duke Center for International Development (DCID) since 2004. A brief discussion of some of the major themes raised in that course (and in this book) was presented in my paper published in the April–June 2006 issue of *World Economics*, and in a shorter form in an issue of *Finance and Development* in that same year.

This book draws directly from many of the issues raised in that course, and in those papers, and follows their interdisciplinary approach. My first debt of thanks for this book, then, is to the academic scholars mentioned above, whose ideas have significantly influenced my thinking on regional and global development issues. My second debt of thanks is to the teams of students at Johns Hopkins SAIS and DCID who have taken my course, and during the evolution of my teaching have both influenced my thinking on certain issues and confirmed it on others. Over time, the generally positive response I have received from these students to my course has influenced my decision to proceed with the preparation of this book.

My interest in Latin America preceded my career at the IMF and was first ignited by a summer tour of the region I made as a college student with my university glee club. Following that tour, I began the study of Portuguese more intensively and started to think about the issues of economic development for the first time, and how, more specifically, for example, one could try to understand why Brazil and the United States, two large, resource-rich countries, had had such different development trajectories since the time of their colonization by European powers. (In effect, I have been thinking about this question for many decades right up to the time of writing this book!) After completing my undergraduate education, I enrolled in Columbia University's School of International and Public Affairs and its Institute for Latin American Studies to pursue in a more focused way my interest in development issues. This two-year degree program was followed by a Fulbright Fellowship to Brazil where I was affiliated with the Instituto Joaquim Nabuco de Pesquisas Sociais, which was founded by Gilberto Freyre in Recife, Pernambuco. Over time, as my academic interest began to focus in a more disciplined way on the contemporary problems of economic development for Brazil and the rest of the Latin American region, I continued my studies at Columbia University in its Department of Economics, where

I completed my PhD with a dissertation on the impact of exchange rate policy on the export development of Argentina.

When I took my first full-time professional job as an economist, I considered, simultaneously, positions at both the IMF and the UN Economic Commission for Latin America, without much appreciation for the history of strong intellectual conflict that had developed between these two institutions, which I write about briefly in chapter 5. I decided to join the IMF because I was offered an opportunity to participate in a special project called the Inflation Study Group, which was a two-year comparative study of the experience of selected countries in East Asia and Latin America dealing with problems of rapid inflation and stabilization, and the implications of that experience for IMF programs of financial assistance. At the time (early 1970s), this project was a relatively uncommon, internal staff review of IMF financial arrangements dealing with a common problem across a range of countries. One of the operational recommendations that emerged from the study was that the Fund needed to frame its support for certain stabilization programs within a medium-term framework, for which a one-year-stand-by arrangement that was the standard instrument at the time may not have been appropriate, in order to assist countries more effectively in dealing with problems of stabilizing rapid inflation, which were endemic in Latin America. In response to a number of concerns at the time, the IMF created the Extended Fund Facility, which supported three-year financial arrangements, in 1974.

This research activity was my first exposure to the comparative economic study of countries in East Asia and Latin America, and was followed by many years of active involvement in the IMF's economic surveillance and financial assistance operations with several countries in Latin America and the Caribbean. This activity was followed by a similar experience of shorter duration with countries in East and Southeast Asia. There are many points of contrast and comparison that are typically considered in the analysis of economic policies and prospects of countries in East Asia and Latin America at institutions like the IMF and World Bank, given that they comprise the bulk of the emerging market economies and have many points of similarity in terms of the challenges they face in dealing with the forces of globalization. As noted earlier, this experience undoubtedly influenced my thinking about the comparative economic development of the two regions, and in particular the discussion of economic policy choices in chapters 5 and 6 of this book. This institutional exposure also placed me on the frontlines of economic reform programs that were identified with the

Washington Consensus during the Latin American debt crises of the 1980s, which I examine in chapters 3 and 10 of this book, as well as the Fund's response to the Asian financial crisis of 1997–1998. In addition, each of the case studies I examine in chapter 9 of the book draws on the direct exposure I had to these countries while working at the IMF and the World Bank.

Typically, a contrast is made in academic studies between the divergent development paths of a developing region and a related advanced region. In the Western Hemisphere, the contrast and comparison in the economic development of North and South America, given their similar dates of encounter with European colonization and settlement, have provided an endlessly intriguing field of analysis for social scientists. I have also been fascinated by this literature, as suggested earlier, some of which I examine in chapter 4. However, my exposure to both East Asia and Latin America at the IMF also ignited my curiosity about the different role that Japan has played within the East Asian region, compared with that of the United States within the Western Hemisphere. As portrayed in this book, Japan has played a decidedly developmental role within the East Asian region (as depicted in the so-called "flying geese" model, which originated in Japan), and has been a strong force promoting economic integration within the region. These regional effects, in fact, have been reinforced by the United States, which has provided an important security umbrella for the region since the end of the Second World War that has allowed these countries to focus, without major distraction from regional conflict, on the challenges of their economic development.

By contrast, the United States has had a more ambiguous and conflictive relationship with Latin America. A similar security umbrella has, in effect, been provided by the United States for the Latin American region, traditionally for nearly two centuries within the terms of the Monroe Doctrine. In addition, flows of foreign direct investment, foreign trade, and official aid from the United States have promoted important economic linkages within the Western Hemisphere region, in particular in the period since the end of WW2. However, inter-American relations have been complicated by the political turmoil that has characterized many countries in Latin America during the second half of the twentieth century, and for a time by an autochthonous strain of international relations theory developed in Latin America, called "dependency theory." This theory, which is examined in chapter 4, posed the United States and Latin America as mutually antagonistic forces within the international economic system, given their marked differences in stage of development and foreign economic interests. While the influence of this theory has withered since the late 1960s, it is interesting to note how it still influences the thinking of some politicians and intellectuals on the left in Latin America. As a result of these differences, one cannot see over time the same process of convergence taking place within the Western Hemisphere as has occurred within East Asia.

What this brief discourse suggests is that Latin America, during the second half of the twentieth century, has been far more isolated within the international economic system than has East Asia, which has complicated its adjustment to the forces of globalization. Even today, with marked changes in the thrust of economic policy in Latin America in support of export-oriented industrialization and strong demand for its natural resource–based exports, East Asia's participation in global trade still far surpasses that of Latin America, as reflected in its major presence within global value chains. Why these differences between the two regions have developed is one of the issues I attempt to explain in the remainder of this book.

In addition to my students at Johns Hopkins SAIS and DCID, I wish to thank a number of other people who have contributed to the production of this book or provided comments on an earlier draft. The following individuals were extremely generous in their time in reading and commenting on parts or all of the manuscript: Leonardo Cardemil, Rodrigo Cubero, Augusto de la Torre, Halliday Hart, Cory Krupp, Anaive Nadal, and Riordan Roett. None of these individuals should be held responsible for any errors of fact or analysis that are contained in the book. I also owe a special debt of gratitude to two students at Johns Hopkins SAIS who served at different times as research assistants for my work on this book, Robert Folley and Anaive Nadal. Both of these individuals provided valuable assistance in identifying source material for me and elaborating certain statistical information in tabular format. In addition, Ms. Nadal devoted considerable time to the preparation of a bibliography for the book, based on the disparate files that I had accumulated over time. Finally, I wish to thank Linda Carlson and her library staff at Johns Hopkins SAIS for many years of helpful advice and support in assembling reference material for my course and this related book project.

CHAPTER 1

Introduction—Globalization and Economic Divergence

In recent years, and in particular in the wake of the global financial crisis, there has been much commentary about the shifting balance of economic power in the global system from the advanced countries on both sides of the North Atlantic to the rising powers of East Asia centered around China in the Asia-Pacific region. This shift reflects one dramatic result of economic globalization that has allowed certain countries, in particular the new industrializing economies of East Asia, to enter into a process of convergence and catch-up with the advanced countries of North America and Western Europe. This pattern of development has been underway since the middle of the past century, but it has intensified since around 1980.

The rise of East Asia reflects the remarkable ability of this region to have taken advantage of the dramatic growth in global trade and financial flows, which have been supported by major improvements in transport and communications, as well as the transfer and mastery of technology from the advanced countries through imports, foreign direct investment, and licensing agreements. This pattern of globalization confirms one strong view about globalization advanced by leading economic academics, such as Robert Lucas, that points to an inevitable and gradual process of economic convergence in response to the integrating forces of trade, finance, and technological change.[1]

However, economic and financial globalization has also produced a broader pattern of economic divergence, which differs from the convergence scenario above, when one considers the performance of national economies across all the regions of the globe. Within this universe, one can find disparities in income per capita in the first decade of the twenty-first century of more than 100 to 1 between the richest and poorest economies, which have been growing over time. On the basis of the long-term historical data of Angus Maddison, which measure income per capita in constant dollars across countries on a purchasing power parity basis, economic divergence among countries has expanded sharply since the beginning of the nineteenth century.[2] At the dawn of the Industrial Revolution in the beginning of the nineteenth century, the disparity between the richest and poorest countries of the world was only around 5 to 1. By 1870, this ratio had increased to 8 to 1. At the dawn of the modern era in 1950, the disparity had reached around 30 to 1, which then rose to more than 100 to 1 in 2010, the last date for which national income estimates exist in the Maddison database. Within this long time span stretching from the beginning of the nineteenth century, one can also see a long U-shaped trajectory for the dominant position of China and India in global manufacturing output, which was eclipsed by the start of the Industrial Revolution in Western Europe in the early part of the nineteenth century, and is now in a phase of gradual resurgence with the dawn of the twenty-first century.[3]

The great divergence of income per capita that has emerged among countries, in particular during the second half of the twentieth century, has given rise to an enormous inequality of income that has been estimated in terms of Gini coefficients at around 65 percent toward the end of the past century, which is far greater than the measure of inequality in any particular country. According to the work of Branko Milanovic, around 85 percent of the measure of global income inequality at the beginning of the twenty-first century can be explained by differences in mean incomes across countries, with the remainder due to differences in meanincome within countries.[4] The reverse was true at the time of the Industrial Revolution in the early part of the nineteenth century.

The Big Reversal

Understanding the factors that can account for these patterns of economic convergence and divergence within the global economy is one of the major challenges of economics, and social science more generally. As a contribution to this inquiry, the present book attempts to explain the causes for this outcome of globalization by examining a particular example of economic convergence and divergence that is reflected in the comparative economic development of East Asia and Latin America since the middle of the past century.

Table 1.1 Real GDP per capita in relation to that of the United States[a]

	1950	1975	2000	2005	2010
East Asia[b]	0.127	0.199	0.380	0.419	0.510
East Asia (w/o China)	0.137	0.217	0.413	0.449	0.541
Latin America and Caribbean	0.266	0.271	0.188	0.196	0.240

[a] Measured in 1990 dollars (PPP basis).
[b] East Asia includes China, NIEs (Korea, Taiwan, Hong Kong, and Singapore), Indonesia, Malaysia, the Philippines, and Thailand.
Source: Maddison (2010).

Since 1950 these two regions have followed very different economic trajectories. At the beginning of the period, Latin America was the most important region in the developing world in terms of per capita income and the size of its manufacturing sector, while East Asia was relatively undeveloped. By the end of the past century, however, the relative positions of East Asia and Latin America (in terms of relative income per capita vis-à-vis the United States) had been reversed (Table 1.1). In fact, during a 30-year period (from 1975 to 2005), Latin America fell steadily behind the income level of the United States, while East Asia surged ahead.

This big reversal in the economic fortunes of the two regions is one of the most dramatic examples of "catching-up" and "falling behind" during the second half of the twentieth century.

Most of this reversal occurred after 1975, when Latin America went into a period of relative stagnation, while East Asia entered a period of sustained, rapid growth. In the case of Latin America, this outcome has been particularly troubling in view of the substantial economic reforms that have been implemented in the region since the mid-1980s, largely consistent with the precepts of the so-called Washington Consensus.[5] That framework, which was defined at the end of the 1980s, attempted to codify the lessons of economic policy among successful developing countries, in terms of advocating a less interventionist stance on the part of government policy while giving greater weight to the role of market forces and global integration in guiding economic activity. During the past two decades, there has been much debate on the appropriateness of the ten guiding principles of economic policy embodied in that consensus, which has tended to emphasize the factors or considerations that were missing from the original list.[6] In particular, there has been a reassessment of the role of government in the development process, which calls for a more balanced view of government policy and market forces as complements, rather than substitutes, in development policy. This evolution of thought about the conflicting or complementary roles of the state and the market in development policy will be examined in more detail in chapters 3 and 8.

Contrary to the Lucasian or neoclassical view of economic development referred to earlier, which argues that economic convergence is a relatively spontaneous process for countries once they adopt policies of economic and financial liberalization (consistent with the principles of the Washington Consensus) that make them responsive to the integrating forces of globalization, this book advances an alternative perspective based on the comparative experience of East Asia and Latin America. This alternative view of the development process identifies, on the one hand, the unique role that government economic policies can play in allowing countries to take advantage of global trends through a careful process of internal and external liberalization and, on the other hand, the forces of globalization as reflected in the operations of multinational corporations and global financial institutions that have benefitted from major improvements in transport and communication.

In this connection, it is important to recognize that, over the broad sweep of history, globalization has been driven by recurring waves of technological revolutions, which have facilitated international trade and investment and promoted a more interdependent international economic system. During the late nineteenth century and early twentieth century, global integration was driven by the combined forces of the telegraph, which made long-distance communication possible, and the steam engine that powered steam ships and locomotives, which made possible the separation of industry and commerce from the same location.[7] One can observe a strong inverse correlation between the growth of international trade and the pronounced decline in transportation costs during the second half of the nineteenth century, which sparked its expansion. Likewise, during the last quarter of the twentieth century, a second technological revolution associated with electronic information and communications technology or ICT has had a profound effect on business management and production, which has spurred the emergence of global production networks and the fragmenting of production and trade across different national boundaries.[8] In addition, global trade has been further propelled by the containerization of freight transport and the construction of large containerships.[9]

Over the past 30 years or so, a rising share of international trade and investment has been dominated by the activities of large multinational or transnational corporations, which at the turn of the past century accounted directly for around one-third of global trade in the form of intra-firm trade, and roughly two-thirds of global trade in transactions with other entities.[10] According to recent UNCTAD estimates, an even higher share of global trade in exports (around 80 percent) is linked to the global production networks managed by multinational corporations as either intra-firm or arms-length trade. The flows of global trade accelerated sharply during the second half of the twentieth century, and in particular since the 1970s. The value of exports and imports as a percent of global GDP has more than doubled from around 27 percent in 1970 to 57 percent in 2007 (Table 1.2). At the same time, financial globalization, as measured by the ratio of foreign assets and liabilities as a share of global GDP, has expanded by a factor of 4 between 1970 and 2007. Within these global trends, it is readily apparent that East

Table 1.2 Global trade and investment (in US$ billions or percent, as indicated)

	1970	1980	1990	2000	2007
World					
Total trade (exports plus imports)	793.7	4,340.1	8,509.3	16,011.5	32,046.7
Foreign assets + foreign liabilities (FA + FL)	253.0	1,450.0	3,866.5	7,643.1	20,201.8
Global GDP	2,896.8	11,020.8	21,976.8	32,329.4	55,796.1
Total trade/ global GDP	0.27	0.39	0.39	0.50	0.57
Foreign assets + foreign liabilities/ global GDP	0.09	0.13	0.18	0.24	0.36
East Asia + Latin America and the Caribbean					
East Asia (EA)					
Total trade	31.6	291.9	790.8	2,358.0	5,962.7
Foreign assets + foreign liabilities	7.9	84.4	410.1	901.5	2,637.1
Latin America & Caribbean (LAC)					
Total trade	34.7	215.0	315.5	848.1	1,694.7
Foreign assets + foreign liabilities	39.8	194.4	326.1	742.9	1,201.5
EA total trade/ world total trade	0.04	0.07	0.09	0.15	0.19
EA FA+FL/World FA+FL	0.03	0.06	0.11	0.12	0.13
LAC total trade/ world total trade	0.04	0.05	0.04	0.05	0.05
LAC FA+FL/World FA+FL	0.16	0.13	0.08	0.10	0.06

Source: World Bank, World Development Indicators and Lane and Milesi-Ferretti (2007).

Asia has achieved a much greater degree of integration into the global economy than Latin America.

Most of the expansion in economic and financial globalization has been managed through large private financial and nonfinancial multinational corporations operating among the advanced countries. However, since the mid-1980s, a growing share of global financial flows have been directed to low- and middle-income countries, driven largely by an increase in foreign direct investment, which in many cases has been linked to the development of export trade capacity in the recipient countries.[11] In the light of these developments, the achievement of successful economic development by low-income countries in the twenty-first century depends to a large extent on the degree to which a country is able to take advantage of these forces of globalization through an appropriate set of policies focused on its internal and external development. The comparative analysis of East Asian and Latin American economic development, especially during the last quarter of the twentieth century, can provide some insight into what policies might be appropriate for taking advantage of these new forces of globalization. In addition, this analysis should provide some insight into the problem of the "middle income trap" that has been identified with a number of countries, in particular in Latin America, that have experienced a marked slowdown in the pace of their economic growth on reaching a per capita income level in real purchasing power parity (PPP) terms of around US$7,000. By contrast, East Asia has emerged as one of the few regions in which countries such as Hong Kong, Korea, Singapore, and Taiwan have escaped that trap and have moved into advanced country status. Other countries in the region, in particular China, seem to be following the pattern of the four aforementioned countries.

In the light of the above observations and the complexity of the development process, this book attempts to understand the comparative economic development of East Asia and Latin America within an interdisciplinary framework that combines an analysis of economic issues relevant to the development process with historical, institutional, and political economy perspectives. In this connection, the study draws on a rich body of literature that has focused on one or more of these perspectives in a strictly regional context. However, few, if any, studies have tried to provide a unified framework for understanding the regional economic divergence between East Asia and Latin America from a multidimensional perspective.[12]

The Recent Experience of Economic Development in an Age of Globalization

In trying to understand the problems of economic divergence and convergence in an age of globalization, it is important to recognize that the process of economic growth outside the advanced countries since the middle of the past century has not been in conformity with the stylized results of standard models of economic growth. According to the neoclassical theory of economic growth, which guided the predictions associated with scholars such as Robert Lucas, economic development is a relatively steady, linear process of growth in real GDP per capita, which is roughly uniform over space and time, as countries expand their investment and take advantage of the diffusion of technological change. The US economy comes closest to exhibiting this long-run pattern of growth, through which sustained increases in income per capita were brought about by the steady accumulation of capital (both physical and human) and the continued application of new technology generated by innovation and research and development to foster improvements in productivity. Within this framework, poor countries with lower stocks of capital and a higher marginal productivity of capital than rich ones will achieve a convergence of income per capita with the advanced countries at a steady rate through high levels of investment and the absorption of foreign technology, as long as high rates of savings and low population growth are maintained. This vision of the growth process gave rise to the vision of a "steady state" as codified early on by Nicholas Kaldor in his six stylized facts of growth.[13]

What one observes in the pattern of economic growth of nations since the middle of the past century, however, is markedly different from the stylized results of the standard growth model described in the previous paragraph. As noted earlier, economic convergence is conditional, not absolute; and economic growth is not a steady, continuous linear process, which is spatially homogeneous within and across countries. Rather, it has tended to be lumpy in space and time, and concentrated in certain regions of the globe. Countries in the process of economic development experience spurts of economic growth, which are associated with a structural shift in employment and production away from primary activities based on natural resource endowments toward industrial activity that is linked to the export of manufactured goods. Sustained, high rates of economic growth have typically been experienced by countries that have been successful in achieving a dynamic structural transformation of their economies through a process of industrialization, in which manufacturing production is shifted over time toward more diversified and sophisticated goods that are competitive in export markets.[14] This pattern of structural change, which is critical to the experience of economic development, is largely ignored in the standard neoclassical model of economic growth referred to earlier, which focuses on the growth process at a much aggregated level. At its core, successful economic growth for developing countries involves a continuous process of structural change and industrial upgrading.[15]

The growth of manufacturing and its links to exports of increasing diversity and sophistication has been identified in much recent writing as a particular hallmark of successful development.[16] In this connection, rapid economic growth among developing countries has been associated with a diversification of production and exports, rather than specialization, as reflected in the standard theory of international trade based on comparative advantage and specialization according to a country's natural endowments. In addition, rapid economic growth has been accompanied by an expansion of the manufacturing sector in developing countries where the benefits of economies of scale, technological learning, and improvements in productivity can be more easily realized than in other sectors of the economy.[17]

This process of structural transformation in the advanced and leading emerging market economies has been driven predominantly by private entrepreneurship and innovation, but governments have been required to play a key role in overcoming key market failures in the development process, for example, related to the promotion of information flows, the coordination of complementary inputs and investment, the provision of adequate infrastructure and finance, and the promotion of externalities and technological spillovers.[18] Within this context, one can observe sharp differences in the process of structural change between the East Asia and Latin American regions that are closely associated with the pattern of their divergent economic development, which are examined in chapter 2.

This pattern of economic growth among developing countries as described above would not have taken place without a major expansion in global trade since the middle of the past century, which has been a key hallmark of the modern era of globalization. Since the formation of the GATT in 1947, which set in motion a process of tariff liberalization among the advanced countries, world trade has expanded at a compound annual growth rate of 10 percent and nearly three times faster than the growth of global output (Table 1.3).

Table 1.3 Global trade and GDP (in US$ billions)

World	1950	1970	1990	2010
Total trade (exports plus imports)	126.0	793.7	8,509.3	30,738.0
Global GDP	739.4	2,896.8	21,976.9	63,195.2
World trade/ global GDP (in percent)	17	27	39	49

Source: World Bank, World Development Indicators; WTO Statistics Database; Penn World Table.

Until the mid-1980s, this process of tariff liberalization was managed and concentrated among the advanced, industrial countries, which created significant export opportunities for developing economies. Then, beginning in the mid-1980s, there has been a substantial increase in the number of developing countries that have participated in the process of trade liberalization. In 1960, only 22 percent of all countries, representing 21 percent of the global population, were open to trade. By 2000, this share of countries had risen to 73 percent, with most of this increase occurring after 1985.[19] In this connection, it is also worth noting that the levels of real income per capita at the end of the past century across a broad cross section of countries were highly correlated with the level of manufacturing exports per capita, thus confirming some of the earlier discussion in this chapter about the key role of manufacturing development in successful growth outcomes.[20]

The participation of developing countries in the global trading system has given rise to an enormous literature and technical debate on the perceived benefits of openness to trade and economic growth. A consensus seems to have emerged that developing countries that are more open to trade over time have experienced higher rates of economic growth than those that are not.[21] This result can be explained by the impact of trade openness on knowledge spillovers and investment in innovation, improvements in productivity and growth arising from intra-industry resource reallocation, and the effect of export diversification on reducing the vulnerability of countries to terms of trade shocks and growth volatility.[22] The same conclusion about the positive effects of openness on economic growth, however, cannot be made for countries that have participated in the process of external financial liberalization.[23]

Notwithstanding the pattern of trade liberalization among advanced and developing countries described above, it is clear that the growth in trade has become more highly concentrated within the latter group, as certain emerging market economies have become more integrated in the global trading system than others and have developed a stronger capacity for the production of manufactured exports. Since 2000, more than 80 percent of manufactured exports from developing countries originated with only 10 countries, most of which were in the East Asian region. In the case of China alone, its share of developing countries' manufactured exports doubled during the past decade from just under 20 percent in 2000 to an estimated 40 percent in 2010.[24] In 1980, the top 10 developing country exporters accounted for 63 percent of total manufactured exports from this group.[25]

The growth in global trade since the middle of the past century has been accompanied by a sharp expansion in foreign direct investment, as noted earlier. However, as in the case of exports of developing countries, foreign direct investment has tended to be concentrated in specific locations, as certain countries have gained "first mover" advantages through the development of good infrastructure, a sound institutional and legal environment, and the promotion of a skilled labor force. More generally, the concentration of economic growth in certain locations within the developing world has been driven by economic "agglomeration effects" associated with the development of technological clusters, which allow for gains in value added associated with technological spillovers and synergies and increasing returns to scale in manufacturing production. It is also evident from the experience of developing countries in the second half of the twentieth century that technological gains are not absorbed automatically by countries, but rather they require the painstaking development of technological capability in the recipient countries in order for these benefits to be derived. In this respect, the development of technological capabilities in developing countries is a path-dependent process involving a mix of efforts to upgrade labor force skills, develop institutional capacity, and establish a favorable business environment. Since these objectives are beyond the capacity of individual entrepreneurs to provide, an active role of government is required.

The observed pattern of nonuniform growth among developing countries has also been driven by the emergence in recent decades of global production networks (GPNs) or Global Value Chains (GVCs) managed by multinational corporations.[26] As a result of this phenomenon, which is linked to the second large technological revolution noted earlier, the assembly of manufactured goods, in particular in the case of automobiles, garments, and electronic equipment, has been decentralized from a single location and separated into specific activities within the chain of production that are distributed across different countries depending on their labor cost advantages and technological capabilities. The growth of GPNs has been associated with a sharp rise in the trade of intermediate goods among certain countries as goods cross country borders more than once depending on the specific assembly operation undertaken by a given country.[27] As will be explained in more detail later on in this book, this process of intra-industry trade and production has operated in different ways in the East Asian and Latin American regions, with the former region a greater beneficiary than the latter.

The growth in intra-industry trade and, in particular, trade based on intermediate goods, has been a particular feature of the modern era of globalization. During the first era of globalization under the international gold standard (1870–1913), and throughout most of the twentieth century, international trade was based on inter-industry trade, as in the exchange of manufactured goods for primary commodities. During the current era of globalization, with the convergence of income among the advanced countries and a reduction in trade barriers, intra-industry trade began to develop with the exchange of differentiated goods within the same industry segment, the production of which benefitted from increasing returns to scale. Then, with the development of GPNs after the mid-1980s, intra-industry trade expanded further with the vertical specialization of production that has given rise to trade in similar goods at different stages of production. This phenomenon has been particularly evident in the production and trade of high-tech manufactured goods (such as electronics and computers) within the East Asian region and NAFTA and in trade between the EU and Eastern Europe.[28] As a result of the growth in the activities of GPNs, there has been a sharp rise in the share of foreign value added, as distinct from domestic value added, in global exports, which is estimated to have increased from 18 percent in 1970 to 33 percent in 2005.[29] Within East Asia, which is the largest region of the world in terms of GPN participation, the share of foreign value added in exports has risen to more than 40 percent in a number of countries, such as Singapore, Hong Kong, Korea, and Malaysia.

Main Themes of the Book

The remainder of this book expands on a number of the themes and issues raised in the preceding paragraphs. In broad terms, the conceptual framework used in this book for understanding the "Big Reversal" between East Asia and Latin America, which is explained more fully in chapter 3, is based on the so-called deep determinants of economic growth (i.e., geography, trade, and institutions), as distinct from the "proximate" determinants (factor accumulation and productivity growth) that are associated with the neoclassical growth model discussed earlier. Within the latter framework, differences in the economic growth of the two regions can readily be explained in terms of more rapid capital accumulation (both physical and human) and higher productivity growth in East Asia than in Latin America. However, from a development perspective, such a result is unsatisfactory or incomplete, as it leaves unexplained the policy, institutional and political economy factors that lie behind these proximate determinants. These more fundamental factors are the focus of this book, as defined by differences in the "initial conditions" of the two regions, economic policy choices, the role of institutions, and political economy factors. It is the main thesis of this book that these internal factors, rather than the spontaneous forces of economic and financial globalization, account for why some regions (e.g., East Asia) have prospered and moved toward convergence with the advanced countries, while others (e.g., Latin America) have not.

In keeping with this multidimensional approach, the study focuses first on the key differences in *the "initial conditions" of the two regions* in the immediate post–World War II era in terms of natural resource endowments, the impact of colonialism, the role of culture (Confucian vs. Iberian), social conditions (rural/urban division, inequality, ethnic composition), and the impact of ideology.

A large body of writing has shown that, notwithstanding differences in the timing of colonialism in the two regions, the colonial heritage of Latin America left a legacy of weak states, strong oligarchies, and marked economic and social inequality. By contrast, the colonial legacy in East Asia was far more diverse, including one case (the Philippines) that shares much in common with Latin America, and others (China and Thailand) that escaped colonialism. In general, though, strong states, weak oligarchies, and relative socioeconomic cohesion can be associated with the non-Iberian colonial heritage in East Asia.

Cultural factors have also played an important role in the divergent regional development of East Asia and Latin America, in terms of the degree of individual identification with a collective unit, paternalistic relationships in society, and the strength of social capital. In addition, ideology has played an important role in Latin American economic development, as reflected in the influence of "dependency theory" and the structuralist approach of the UN Economic Commission for Latin America (ECLA), which supported a highly interventionist role for the state in the development process. Then, in the wake of the regional debt crisis of the 1980s, governments in Latin America adopted a radically different development paradigm, largely in keeping with the principles of the Washington Consensus, in which the balance between government intervention and market forces was shifted strongly in favor of the latter. By contrast, in East Asia, the approach to economic development was more pragmatic and experimental, with important roles assigned to both market forces and government intervention.

In terms of *economic policy choices*, East Asia has been far more successful than Latin America in dealing with two fundamental constraints on economic development, namely, fiscal solvency and external sustainability. Sharp differences can be seen not only in the effectiveness of macroeconomic policy management in the two regions, but also in the degree to which the two regions have achieved integration into the global economy. East Asia has benefited greatly from the surge of globalization during the final decades of the twentieth century, as described earlier, whereas Latin America has not. These differences have been reinforced by the strength of regional trade and investment links within East Asia, and their relative absence in Latin America. One can also see important differences in the timing and pace of macroeconomic reform and liberalization in the two regions as part of the development process, with Latin America exhibiting more variability and abrupt change. Positive macroeconomic developments in East Asia were also accompanied by a persistent and marked shift in the structure of the regional economy toward the development of manufacturing, which reflected to a significant extent the impact of government policy intervention.

The differences in economic policy management just mentioned can be associated, to a large degree, with *differences in the strength of institutions* in the two regions and, in particular, the role of government and political leadership, which, in turn, can be linked to the colonial and cultural forces noted earlier. Both regions initially followed a strong state-led development path, but "developmental states" in East Asia were more effective than their counterparts in Latin America in terms of policy consistency and coherence and the effectiveness of the government bureaucracy in implementing policy programs. Governments in East Asia were also more effective in terms of promoting an environment conducive to long-term investment and industrialization, through the creation of effective government–business consultative mechanisms, and the development of human capital and technological capability. In addition, differences can be noted in the use of industrial policies, with notable success at early stages of the development process in East Asia for the government's role in overcoming certain kinds of market failure, for example, through the provision of key economic infrastructure, the promotion of labor training, support for the appropriation of rents from entrepreneurship and technological development, and the coordination of complementary investments.

The *role of political economy factors*, as reflected in differences in state–society relationships in the two regions, is critically important to an understanding of economic policy choices and the role of the government. The persistence, until recently, of macroeconomic instability in Latin America can be linked to distributional conflicts rooted in problems of economic and social inequality and the populist or patron–clientilistic orientation of political parties associated with that inequality. The relative autonomy of the state in East Asia vis-à-vis business and labor, especially in comparison with Latin America, is also important in determining the success of developmental states in the former region and the prevalence of rent seeking in the latter. In addition, political economy and cultural factors are important in understanding why authoritarian regimes, while present in both regions, tended to be more "developmental" in East Asia than in Latin America, in terms of their promotion of public goods, gains in social welfare, and rapid growth in per capita real income.

Outline of Chapters

The main topical content for the remaining chapters of the book is as follows.

Chapter 2 (The Economic Development of East Asia and Latin America in Comparative Perspective) provides a more detailed description of the divergent economic outcomes of the two regions during the period since the middle of the past century. Despite some natural heterogeneity within each region, strong differences can still be detected in the economic performance of the two regions in terms of the main macroeconomic aggregates, as well as key indicators for poverty, human development, and income inequality. The chapter also highlights an important variation in the pattern of structural change during the development process in each region.

Chapter 3 (Changing Paradigms in Development Economics) provides a summary review of the main changes in thinking about economic development that have taken place since the middle of the past century, that both have a bearing on, and have been influenced by, the experience of East Asia and Latin America. These changes are reflected in shifting debates about the role of the state versus the market in economic development, on the one hand, and the relative importance of market failure and government failure in the development process, on the other. The chapter also examines the shift in emphasis from the "proximate" to the "deep" determinants of development, and reviews the lessons learned from empirical studies of growth involving development accounting and growth regressions. In this connection, the debate over factor accumulation versus technological assimilation as a cause for the East Asian "miracle" is presented and assessed. Within the context of "deep" determinants, the chapter lays out the framework for comparing the development experience of the two regions in terms of the four factors mentioned earlier, namely, initial conditions, economic policy choices, institutions, and political economy factors.

Chapter 4 (Initial Conditions for the Postwar Development of East Asia and Latin America) compares the two regions in the middle of the twentieth century in terms of differences in geography and resource endowments, the legacy of colonialism, the impact of dominant cultural forces (e.g., Confucian versus Iberian), and the role of ideology in development strategies. The chapter also emphasizes the relatively advanced stage of import-substitution industrialization in Latin America, its higher degree of urbanization, and marked social and economic inequalities in comparison with East Asia. Finally, the chapter includes a brief discussion in Box 4.1 of how cultural factors and colonial legacy have made the Philippines more similar to Latin America than to other East Asian countries.

Chapters 5 (Economic Policy Choices—Macroeconomic and Financial Stability) and 6 (Economic Policy Choices—Savings, Investment, and Industrialization) examine the much different records of the two regions in dealing with the dual constraints of fiscal solvency and external viability that need to be addressed during the development process, and the reasons for these differences. Chapter 5 reviews the similarities and differences in the pace and timing of macroeconomic reforms in the two regions, and the reasons for the relatively weak growth response of the Latin American region to widespread economic reforms undertaken in the wake of the debt crisis of the early 1980s. The chapter also considers the role of finance in the development process in each region. Finally, the chapter includes a brief discussion in Box 5.1 of the key economic reforms undertaken by Chile to achieve macroeconomic stability that have set a pattern and model for the rest of the Latin American region. Chapter 6 then compares the two regions in terms of the relative importance given to import-substitution and export-oriented industrialization, and the degree to which they achieved integration into the global economy in terms of both trade and financial flows. In addition, the importance of strong regional trade and investment links in East Asia related to the development of GPNs and indigenous technological capability is explored as a key factor supporting dynamic growth in that region. The role of industrial policy in the development process of the two regions is also examined.

Chapter 7 (The Role of Institutions and Governance) discusses the role of institutions, in particular governmental institutions, in the development paths of East Asia and Latin America. According to a wide variety of governance indicators, East Asian governments have generally outperformed their counterparts in Latin America in terms of political stability, the rule of law, the protection of property rights, and bureaucratic effectiveness. In this connection, the chapter compares the role of developmental states in the two regions at an early stage of their development, and explains how East Asian governments were far more successful than their counterparts in Latin America in providing basic public goods, promoting technological capability, and sharing the benefits of economic growth. Finally, the chapter includes a brief essay in Box 7.1 on the role of institutional adaptations that China made to promote investment and growth in the nonstate sector that were critical for the success of the government's early economic reform efforts beginning in the late 1970s.

Chapter 8 (The Political Economy Factor in Comparative Economic Development) examines the role of state–society relationships in the development process and the nature of interactions among government, business, and labor groups that can promote or frustrate economic development. In addition, the possible links between authoritarian and democratic regimes, on the one hand, and economic development, on the other, are examined in the light of the experience in East Asia and Latin America. In particular, this chapter explores the cultural and political factors that may account for the fact that authoritarian regimes in East Asia have been more "enlightened" than those in Latin America in terms of their development focus. Insights from the literature on the political economy of reform are applied to the problems of macroeconomic volatility and external imbalances in Latin America. Finally, the chapter includes a brief analysis in Box 8.1 of the political economy factors that have accounted for the persistence of income inequality in Brazil, which has limited the potential for its successful economic development until the enactment of key social reforms in more recent years.

Chapter 9 (Three Cross-Regional Case Studies) illustrates the interplay of initial conditions, policy choices, institutions, and political economy factors for three pairs of countries from East Asia and Latin

America with divergent development outcomes: Jamaica and Singapore, Chile and Malaysia, and Indonesia and Venezuela. In the first comparison, the transition of Singapore to a high-growth scenario in the late 1960s and Jamaica's transition to a low-growth scenario in the early 1970s are examined, which have had enduring effects on the divergent development paths of these two societies. The comparison of Chile and Malaysia highlights the role of government policy in bridging ethnic and social differences and fostering technological capability and export diversification in the latter case, and their relative absence in the former case, which have significantly affected the development trajectories of these two countries. The final country comparison examines the interplay of forces that allowed Indonesia to escape the oil resource "curse" since the mid-1980s, and Venezuela not to do so during the same period.

Chapter 10 (Conclusions and Lessons for Development Policy) ties together the main conclusions of previous chapters in order to draw some key lessons for the design of development policy. It also attempts to evaluate the adequacy of the Washington Consensus and its derivatives as a framework for development policy and to define the appropriate role of the state in the development process.

Some discussion is warranted on the regional coverage chosen for this study. For the purposes of this study, Latin America is defined to cover South America, Central America, Mexico, and the Caribbean, which is a fairly standard presentation in international and cross-regional data comparisons. The impact of European colonial influence provides at one level a unifying feature of this region, notwithstanding cultural, linguistic, and historical differences among the colonial powers. As further explained in chapter 3, a common element among the colonizers was their focus on extracting natural resources, as distinct from forming settlements for future generations.

The definition of East Asia as a region requires a different explanation. From a geographical perspective, East Asia could be defined as a region stretching from Mongolia in the northeast down to the southern peninsula of Vietnam, Cambodia, and Laos and the archipelago of Indonesia and east to Myanmar, covering a total of some 16 countries. Culturally, the East Asian region could be defined more narrowly in terms of its dominant Confucian influence affecting eight countries: China, Japan, the two Koreas, Taiwan, Hong Kong, Singapore, and Vietnam. The 10 member countries of ASEAN offer another possible grouping. For purposes of this study, however, the East Asian region is defined to include a subset of all three of the groupings noted above, which have come to share strong economic ties among themselves: the four newly industrializing economies or NIEs (Hong Kong, Korea, Singapore, and Taiwan), or so-called tigers, the second-stage NIEs of Southeast Asia (Indonesia, Malaysia, the Philippines, and Thailand or the ASEAN-4), and China. Among these countries, the diversity of historical, cultural, and linguistic traditions is greater than in Latin America. This is particularly the case when one considers differences between Northeast Asia (China, Korea, Hong Kong, and Taiwan) and Southeast Asia (excluding Singapore). However, from an economic perspective, it makes sense to define a regional construct of East Asia including the nine countries listed above that can be identified in terms of a similar approach to economic policy choices, intra-regional dynamics, and the influence of hegemonic states, that is, Japan and the United States. These issues are explored in more detail in chapters 4, 5, and 6.

CHAPTER 2

The Economic Development of East Asia and Latin America in Comparative Perspective

This chapter outlines the key aspects of the economic development of East Asia and Latin America that can account for the "Big Reversal" in the economic fortunes of these two regions. The chapter also expands on the four factors that were identified in the previous chapter, which provide a framework for understanding how this Big Reversal came about. These four factors are examined in more detail in chapters 4 through 7.

The Economic Development of East Asia and Latin America in Historical Perspective

The long-term historical data developed by Angus Maddison provide a useful perspective on the post–World War II economic development of the two regions. The surge in the economic growth of East Asia since the 1950s can be understood as a process of restoring the economic importance that that region had prior to the Industrial Revolution, as noted earlier. By contrast, the recent stagnation of Latin America represents a change in a long trajectory of economic growth, which accelerated during the second half of the nineteenth century and was maintained during the first half of the twentieth century.

The "golden age" of economic growth in Latin America occurred during the so-called first era of globalization, at the height of the international gold standard (1870–1913), when large flows of foreign direct investment (FDI) from Europe (especially Great Britain), European

Table 2.1 Comparative regional growth, 1870–2008 (in percent)

	1870–1913	1913–1950	1950–1973	1973–2001	2001–2008
Global	1.3	0.9	2.9	1.4	4.1
W. Europe	1.3	0.8	4.1	1.9	1.6
USA	1.8	1.6	2.5	1.9	1.8
FSU	1.1	1.8	3.3	–1.0	6.2
LAC	1.8	1.4	2.6	0.9	3.1
Japan	1.5	0.9	8.1	2.1	1.1
Asia	0.4	–0.1	2.9	3.6	5.4
o/w China	(0.1)	(0.6)	(2.9)	(5.3)	(8.0)
o/w India	(0.5)	(0.2)	(1.4)	(3.0)	(6.5)
Africa	0.6	0.9	2.0	0.2	4.3

Note: FSU refers to countries of the former Soviet Union; LAC refers to countries of Latin America and the Caribbean.

Source: Maddison (2010).

migration, and demand in Europe for its large natural resource exports (grains and metals) supported high rates of economic expansion, similar to that of the United States and above that of the global economy (Table 2.1). By comparison, Asia was a relatively backward area economically, with the lowest growth rate of any region in the world.

Argentina was a major beneficiary of this pattern of global trade, migration, and investment and sustained the highest rate of growth in real income per capita of around 2½ percent per year among all countries of the world. By contrast, the "golden age" of economic growth for East Asia has coincided with the current (or second) globalization era since 1973, during which its exports of manufactured goods surged in response to a dramatic expansion in world trade, while the economic growth (and exports) of Latin America has stagnated.

While trade and investment flows expanded sharply during both Globalization Eras I and II, the nature of these flows has changed dramatically from one era to the other. During the first era of globalization and indeed up until the current era, most trade took the form of inter-industry trade, as noted earlier, reflecting the exchange of one form of commodity for another (e.g., raw materials for manufactures). FDI flowed mainly from developed to developing countries as new lands and natural resources in these countries were exploited, largely in conformity with the expectations of the neoclassical growth model.

During the current era of globalization, an increasing share of trade flows has taken the form of intra-industry trade reflecting a growing fragmentation of production processes across countries, managed by multinational corporations, and the specialization of countries within global production networks/global value chains (GPNs/GVCs). Most FDI flows have been increasingly concentrated among developed countries and those developing countries, in particular, which have been most successful in being integrated within international production networks. During 1990–2010, for example, only 10 countries (including 4 in East Asia) accounted for around 70 percent of the increase in the stock of FDI in developing countries.[1]

As will be further explored in later chapters, East Asia's recent success as an exporting region reflects an important advantage it has gained with respect to Latin America in terms of the development of its technological capabilities and its capacity to adapt to rapid changes in the pattern of globalized production and trade that have been key drivers of recent economic and financial globalization. In this connection, a key question to be answered by this study is why East Asia has been able to take greater advantage of these changes in the global trading and investment system than Latin America.

East Asia and Latin America during the Current Era of Globalization

Notwithstanding certain differences in the level of income per capita and industrial development of the two regions at mid-century, other dimensions of macroeconomic performance for the two regions were not that different during the decade of the 1960s. As noted in Table 2.2, while the extent of trade openness (as measured by the ratio of exports and imports of goods and services to GDP) was higher in East Asia, the two regions were fairly similar in terms of the growth in real GDP per capita, savings and investment ratios, and the size of financial intermediation in the early years of the postwar period. Over the following three decades, however, significant differences in these aspects of macroeconomic performance emerged, which widened over time. In particular, gross domestic investment as a ratio to GDP has expanded much more sharply in East Asia than in Latin America, with a higher share of it being financed by domestic savings. In fact, during only one of the past four decades of the twentieth century was domestic savings in East Asia, on average, less than domestic investment. By contrast, the ratio of domestic investment to GDP for Latin America during this same period was consistently higher than that for domestic savings. As a result, the trade balance for East Asia has tended to be in surplus during the period under review, even though the shares of total trade (both exports and imports) to GDP for East Asia

Table 2.2 Comparative macroeconomic data for East Asia (EA) and Latin America and the Caribbean (LAC)

	1961–1970		1971–1980		1981–1990		1991–2000		2001–2008	
	EA	LAC	EA	LAC	EA	LAC	EA	LAC	EA	LAC
	(percentage change)									
Real GDP per capita	2.7	2.5	4.8	3.6	6.1	−0.6	7.0	1.8	7.4	2.4
Consumer prices	35.4	3.4	10.3	30.9	6.3	337.7	5.9	45.4	3.2	8.5
Terms of trade (std. dev.)	...	...	4.3	6.6	6.7	4.9	1.3	4.4	4.2	9.7
	(in percent of GDP)									
Gross Domestic Investment	19.5	21.0	28.8	23.4	31.4	21.3	34.2	21.1	32.7	20.0
Gross National Savings	20.3	20.0	30.1	20.0	30.9	19.5	35.6	18.2	39.9	20.4
Broad money	22.0	18.4	29.5	17.7	58.6	27.6	100.0	36.1	125.3	35.3
Overall government deficit	...	...	−0.3	−2.2	−1.5	−3.7	−1.5	−1.6	−0.9	−2.2
Exports and imports (G&S)	30.6	20.0	41.2	21.2	57.4	27.3	62.4	35.8	89.4	45.6
Trade balance	...	...	1.0	−2.2	1.1	2.2	1.8	−1.5	5.5	2.0
Foreign Direct Investment	...	...	0.8	0.2	1.9	0.7	3.3	3.2	5.2	3.9
Priv. cap. flows (std. dev.)	...	...	...	...	4.3	5.2	4.9	5.8	4.1	2.3

Note: Data are averages for each region based on PPP country weights, except those for consumer prices, terms of trade, private capital flows, and foreign direct investment, which are based on equal country weights. For 1961–1970, only selected EA countries included for inflation, broad money, and foreign trade data; also gross domestic savings is calculated instead of gross national savings.

Source: World Bank World Development Indicators Database for 1961–1970 and IMF WEO Database for later years.

have expanded much more sharply than for Latin America. The converse is true for Latin America, as that region has tended to exhibit a chronic trade (and current account) deficit during the latter part of the past century. Historically, the persistence of a relatively low level of domestic savings for Latin America, together with a negative trade balance, has made that region much more dependent on foreign borrowing than East Asia, and thus more vulnerable to external shocks.

One can also detect in Table 2.2 a relatively low and unsteady trajectory of real GDP per capita in Latin America since the 1960s, whereas real GDP growth rates have been significantly higher and more persistent in the case of East Asia. Studies by the Economic Commission for Latin America (ECLA) have shown that the growth of real GDP per capita in Latin America has been more volatile than in most other regions of the globe and that this cyclical component has been the major determinant of the region's weak growth trend.[2] In addition, the rate of inflation in Latin America has been significantly higher than in East Asia and far more volatile.[3] These conditions of macroeconomic instability in Latin America, involving high and variable inflation and an uneven pace of economic growth, coupled with the external instability noted earlier, have created a weak environment for sustained investment and technological innovation. The factors that can account for these conditions in Latin America, and their relative absence in East Asia, are explored in subsequent chapters of this book.

East Asia's macroeconomic performance during the second half of the twentieth century was superior to that of Latin America not only in terms of the growth in income per capita, but also in terms of income distribution and poverty reduction. Throughout the post–World War II period, median Gini coefficients for East Asian countries have been significantly lower than those for Latin America, and in six out of the nine cases for which fairly reliable, historical measures of income distribution are available, income distribution improved during the region's period of high growth.[4] One country where this is not observed is China, as rapid economic growth in certain urban areas and coastal provinces has worsened income inequality, especially in the period since 1990. For Latin America during most of the postwar period, no discernible trend is observed among the 15 countries for which historical Gini coefficients are available: In seven cases a worsening was observed, while in seven others an improvement was recorded; in two others, income distribution remained roughly unchanged. However, what is clear is that at the end of the twentieth-century Latin America remained the region with the largest inequality of incomes in the world, with a difference of more around 15 percentage points in the average regional Gini coefficient with respect to that of East Asia (55 vs. 40).[5]

It is significant to note, however, that since the early years of the past decade, a number of countries in Latin America, in particular, Argentina, Brazil, Mexico, and Uruguay, have begun to reverse the historical pattern of income inequality, in part through effective programs of government intervention.[6] These programs have focused on improving the accessibility of tertiary education in public universities among those below the privileged upper class and on tying income support for the poor to participation in education and basic health maintenance. These policy initiatives can be seen as having more enduring effects on income distribution than the large redistribution schemes of countries such as Bolivia, Ecuador, and Venezuela, which are not sustainable from a fiscal perspective and do not equip the poor with the tools they need to become more productive members of society.

Conversely, since the final decade of the past century, one can identify a worsening of income inequality in a number of countries in East Asia. This has been particularly pronounced in the case of China, which may be displaying the classic pattern of income redistribution associated with the inverse-U curve that was identified by Simon Kuznets. With the massive shift of workers from rural areas to new urban industrialized zones and limitations on the rate of labor transfers under the "hukou" system, there has been a sharp redistribution of income to urban workers and certain regions of the country.[7] However, another likely cause of the rise in income inequality in China is the pervasive effect of corruption within the upper ranks of the Communist Party, which has enriched certain families and groups associated with key party officials.[8]

Headcount measures of poverty in East Asia were reduced sharply during the second half of the twentieth century, especially as regards the incidence of extreme poverty (i.e., those living on an income basket of less than $1.25 a day). This progress was particularly pronounced in the case of China, but it applies generally in the region, as well. As a result, East Asia is well on its way to meeting the Millennium Development Goals in this area. Latin America, by contrast, has shown no significant change until recently in its poverty indicators. During the first half of the period under review, there was some reduction in the poverty headcount, but this trend was reversed during the second half. As in the case of income inequality, however, macroeconomic stabilization and higher economic growth during the past decade (2001–2010) have been accompanied by an improvement in Latin America's poverty indicators (Table 2.3).

On a broader measure of development, as measured by the UNDP's human development index, East Asia has also been more successful than Latin America. East Asian countries have performed better than those of Latin America, not only in the component of the index related to income per capita, but also in terms of educational attainment and life expectancy.

Other key differences between the two regions can be seen in the degree of their structural economic change since the middle of the past century. In East Asia, one can see a classic example of sectoral shifts within the overall structure of the regional economies consistent with

Table 2.3 Poverty headcount table

A. Share of Population living below US $1 a day

(1981–2008 per day in 2005 PPP)

	1981	1990	2002	2008
East Asia (EA)	66.1	40.6	17.8	7.8
o/w China	(73.5)	(44.0)	(19.1)	(7.4)
Latin America & Caribbean (LAC)	7.9	8.8	8.9	5.0

B. Human Development Index

	1975	1985	2000	2005	2008
East Asia	0.63	0.70	0.80	0.72	0.74
Latin America & Caribbean	0.65	0.69	0.74	0.70	0.72
EA/ LAC	0.98	1.03	1.08	1.03	1.03

Sources: Part A: Chen and Ravallion (2012); Part B: UNDP.

a pattern of strong economic growth and development, as discussed in the previous chapter. On the basis of average shares of production for the nine economies that comprise East Asia for purposes of this study, the share of agriculture was reduced from around 34 percent in 1960 to 20 percent in 1980, and then to a little under 8 percent in 2005. By contrast, the share of manufacturing nearly doubled over the same time period, along with a significant growth in the share of the service sector (Table 2.4). The sectoral shifts in employment over the same time period show a similar, but even more pronounced pattern of structural change in East Asia.

By contrast, there have been much more modest changes in the structure of the Latin America economies, as reflected in average shares of the primary, secondary, and tertiary sectors for the region. Agriculture has undergone a relatively small reduction in its share of the Latin America economy, while that of industry has tended to stay unchanged, with a slight increase during the period from 1960 to 1980 being reversed during the next 20-year period. More dramatically, the share of manufacturing in Latin America has shown a steady, relative decline throughout the period under review, suggesting a pattern of deindustrialization.

Another feature of the economic structure of the Latin American economy that sharply distinguishes it from that of East Asia is the size of the informal sector, that is, the share of economic and labor

Table 2.4 Structural economic change: East Asia and Latin America and the Caribbean (as a percent of GDP)

	1960	1970	1980	1990	2000	2005	2010
East Asia							
Agriculture	34.3	32.4	20.4	15.1	8.4	7.5	7.9
Industry	25.8	28.3	38.7	38.3	37.6	37.5	35.7
o/w Manufacturing	13.6	19.2	24.8	26.0	25.9	25.6	23.8
Services	39.9	39.3	40.9	46.7	54.0	55.0	56.4
Latin America & Caribbean							
Agriculture	20.0	17.3	14.0	12.0	9.1	8.9	10.1
Industry	31.3	33.6	33.8	33.3	30.9	33.1	32.3
o/w Manufacturing	20.0	20.9	19.7	18.6	17.0	16.4	15.2
Services	48.7	49.1	52.2	54.7	60.0	58.0	57.6

Source: World Bank, World Development Indicators.

force activity that takes place outside the framework of the regulated and legal scope of taxation, social protection, and labor market codes. Estimates of the size of the informal economy in Latin America vary greatly by indicator and by country, but according to one World Bank study, a typical country in Latin America at the turn of the past century was producing 40 percent of GDP and employing 70 percent of the labor force in the informal sector.[9] These estimates are truly dramatic in terms of the scope of the dual economy structure they suggest for Latin America and their implications for the ineffectiveness of state institutions and the low level of social trust, which are examined in chapter 7. To a significant extent, the phenomenon of informality in Latin America is rooted in problems of persistent poverty and inequality, which have been a problem especially for large segments of the population working in rural areas or those engaged in self-employment or household enterprises in large urban areas.[10]

The patterns in the evolution of the domestic economic structure of the two regional economies described above are broadly reflected, as well, in the structure of their exports. In the case of Latin America, from the first half of the 1960s to the second half of the 1990s, primary products represented the largest component of its trade, and as a share of total exports increased slightly from 34 percent to 36 percent.[11] Over the same period, there was a marked shift in the structure of manufactured exports out of medium- and high-tech goods toward low- and medium-tech goods. By contrast, in the case of East Asia, there was a significant shift downward in the share of primary product exports in total exports from 15 percent to 10 percent, while the share of medium- and high-tech manufactured export goods rose from 36 percent to 51 percent. Among developing regions, East Asia accounted for around 85 percent of total exports of high-tech manufactures, reflecting the region's growing specialization in the manufacture of electronic and telecommunication hardware, consistent with its designation as "factory Asia."[12] Since the late 1990s, all 9 of the East Asian countries included in this study have been among the top 15 exporters of manufactured goods among developing countries, whereas only Brazil and Mexico can be included in this grouping from the Latin American region.[13]

The transformation of East Asia's export structure is also consistent with a greater degree of export diversification than in the case of Latin America. As noted in chapter 1, such diversification has been identified as a hallmark of successful economic development during the second half of the twentieth century. For example, in comparing the composition of exports of the two regions for the year 2000, one can detect that the top 10 categories of export products accounted for 40 percent of total exports, on average, for East Asia, whereas a similar grouping for Latin America accounted for 57 percent of that region's exports, on average.[14]

It is also interesting to note that the growth of manufactured exports from East Asia has been accompanied by a sharp expansion in its intra-industry trade, as reflected in the exchange of parts and components for manufacturing production. This phenomenon is consistent with the growing participation of East Asian economies in GPNs, as noted earlier, which is largely absent in Latin America, except for the case of Mexico and its participation in GPNs within NAFTA, and certain parts of Central America. East Asia (including Japan) has become the largest source of this kind of intra-industry trade in the global economy, with its share of global trade in parts and components rising from 27 percent in 1992–1993 to nearly 40 percent in 2005–2007.[15] By contrast, the comparable share for such trade within NAFTA in the latter time period was only 19 percent.

As a result of East Asia's large degree of participation in GVCs, 7 of the 9 East Asian economies (all except Indonesia and the Philippines) have taken their place among the top 25 largest global exporters as of 2010, whereas only Mexico and Brazil were among that group (UNCTAD 2013). Another interesting perspective on this regional difference in trade patterns is provided by the recent UNCTAD study just cited on the impact of GVCs in global trade. According to UNCTAD estimates, the share of foreign value added in total exports, which is one measure of a country's participation in GVCs, had risen to close to 40 percent, on average, for all nine countries of the East Asian region, compared with less than 20 percent for the six largest exporters of Latin America (Mexico, Brazil, Chile, Argentina, Colombia, and Peru).

The pattern of structural change observed in East Asia can be shown to have followed closely that exhibited by Japan during its transition from an agrarian to an industrial nation. In many ways, Japan's experience of structural change and development has served as a model for the rest of East Asia, and has been promoted by a pattern of regional investment and trade during the postwar period. In the writings of many East Asian development thinkers, this pattern has been characterized as the "flying geese" model of economic development, in which successive states in East Asia, beginning with Japan, have taken the lead in the development of certain industries, beginning with labor intensive manufacturing, and have then transferred that lead to another country, as the first leader of that industry moved to higher value-added production with the development of technological capability and a skilled labor force.[16] This phenomenon will be examined in more detail in chapter 6 in the context of the development of GPNs within the East Asian region. To an important extent, the successful pattern of structural change and economic growth in East Asia has to be attributed to its development of technological capability in terms of labor force skills and the mastery of sophisticated production processes by domestic industries. Natural resource endowments in terms of a low ratio of arable land per person also played a role in orienting the region's comparative advantage toward industry and manufacturing. In addition, the role of government in nurturing a process of "dynamic" comparative advantage toward more technology-intensive areas of industrial activity in East Asia is explored in chapter 6.

No similar pattern of economic development based on rapid industrialization can be observed in Latin America. While many governments in Latin America started to promote industrialization in response to the upheaval of the Great Depression and the associated collapse of the terms of trade for its natural resource-based exports, this pattern of development was gradually reversed during the postwar decades, as the region entered into a phase of deindustrialization. In the early post–World War II decades, Latin America pursued an inward development strategy that was a reaction against certain features of the global economic system engendered in part by its northern regional partner, the United States, in contrast with East Asia, which, as noted above, pursued an economic strategy emulating that of its dominant regional partner (Japan).

After 1980, however, Latin America's approach to economic development shifted. In part, this transition was a response to the new thinking at the global level about development paradigms noted earlier. As a result of the more liberalized economic environment encouraged under the precepts of the Washington Consensus, many of the industries that thrived during the structuralist phase of Latin America's early postwar development prior to 1980 proved to be unviable because of their uncompetitive price structure and dependence on government subsidies or tariff protection. This phenomenon coincided with what a number of development analysts have referred to as the problem of the "middle-income trap."[17] In recent years, this pattern has been reinforced by growing demand for natural resources on the part of China, India, and other countries in East Asia. In view of the sharp differences in the pattern of structural change in the two regional economies, some researchers have established that a significant share of the difference in regional economic growth rates can be attributed to the contribution of structural change to the overall labor productivity in East Asia, which is discussed in the next section of this chapter.

During the past couple of decades, the Latin American region has made major progress in establishing conditions of macroeconomic stability, following the example set by Chile since the late 1970s. Nevertheless, growth in real income per capita during the first decade of the new century remained still below that of East Asia, while an expansion in trade was significantly dependent on favorable terms of trade and a strong demand for primary commodities, emanating in part from China and India.[18] In the light of these developments, it is interesting to see that China in the current century, through its trade and investment activity in Latin America, is playing a role reminiscent of that played by Great Britain in South America during the nineteenth century. While this might be true for countries such as Argentina, Brazil, Chile, and Peru in terms of the development and export of their large natural resource-based exports, such as soybeans, wheat, copper, and iron ore, China is playing a very competitive role with other countries in the Latin American region, which has been one factor that has contributed to the phase of deindustrialization noted earlier.

Accounting for the Divergent Pattern of Regional Economic Development

Most studies of economic growth and development attempt to "explain" observed patterns of aggregate economic behavior through the prism of the neoclassical growth model and the technique of growth or development accounting.[19] Because of a number of limitations in the reliability and explanatory power of this accounting, which is examined in the next chapter, this study relies mainly on a broader framework of analysis, as noted in chapter 1. However, it is useful nonetheless to take account of the results of growth accounting exercises, as a prelude to the development of that broader frame of reference.

One of the simplest economic accounting frameworks that one can use to explain differences in the growth experience of East Asia and Latin America is the Harrod–Domar (H-D) model, which preceded the neoclassical growth model. Based on the early post–World War II dominance of the Keynesian approach to macroeconomic analysis, the H-D model essentially explained economic growth as resulting from the interaction of the savings-income and incremental capital-output ratios. In one recent study, a team led by Jeffrey Sachs performed a simple simulation exercise, based on the H-D framework, using a commonly assumed incremental capital-output ratio of 3 and actual data for savings and depreciation (as a share of national income) and population growth averaged across the two regions for the period 1980–2001. Remarkably, this relatively simple accounting framework could account for the 6-percentage point difference in the observed growth of per capita income, which was 6.4 percent in the case of East Asia and 0.4 percent for Latin America.[20] The basic reason this calculation worked so well is that the national savings ratio for East Asia during this period (and as a result the rate of capital accumulation) was nearly double that of Latin America. As noted earlier, throughout the second half of the past century, the rate of investment as a share of gross domestic product was also significantly higher in East Asia than in Latin America. Given the importance of capital accumulation as a basis for changes in labor productivity and growth in per capital income, one cannot deny that this factor has played a key role in accounting for the difference in economic growth across the two regions that we observe during the post–World War II era. This basic result is also derived from growth accounting exercises based on the neoclassical growth model, as noted below.

In the light of this kind of quantitative result, one is left with the basic question of what more fundamental factors can account for the substantial difference in the rate of capital accumulation between the two regions that has occurred since the middle of the past century, which plays such a key role in determining the divergent pattern of economic growth between East Asia and Latin America. This question is one of the reasons why this study is rooted in the so-called deep determinants of growth, as distinct from the "proximate" determinants of growth that are rooted in the Keynesian (i.e., the H-D model) and the neoclassical growth models, as explained in more detail in the next chapter.

As distinct from the H-D model, the neoclassical approach to growth accounting decomposes the measure of capital accumulation into a specific factor for physical capital formation (corresponding to the notion of investment in national income accounting) and one for human capital accumulation (h). It also changes the nature of the relationship between Y (output) and K (physical capital) in the H-D model by including a measure of total factor productivity (TFP), which is usually labeled "A."[21] Since TFP cannot be measured directly, it is derived as a residual in growth accounting exercises, given specific estimates that are derived for income per capita, investment or physical capital accumulation, and human capital formation. However, since A is a residual calculation in these exercises, it also captures any errors in the estimation of the other factors used in such exercises, which means that it can vary significantly from one study to another.[22]

One of the most often cited studies of cross-regional economic growth based on the neoclassical growth accounting framework is that done by Barry Bosworth and Susan Collins (2003). For the period 1960–2000, they calculated the growth of real income per worker in terms of the contribution of the growth in capital per worker, human capital per worker, and, by residual, the contribution of technological change (or TFP), as reported in Table 2.5.

During the period of the study, the growth rate in real income per worker for East Asia was three and a half times higher than in the case of Latin America. Notwithstanding this significant difference, somewhat more than half of the growth in real income per worker in the two regions could be explained by the contribution of capital per worker, which is qualitatively consistent with the results of the H-D exercise for a different time period described earlier. The contribution of the growth in human capital per worker is fairly similar in both regions, whereas that of TFP growth in significantly higher in East Asia, which may be related to the stronger attributes of technological capability that can be attributed to that region, as noted earlier. The lower rate of TFP

Table 2.5 Growth decomposition

East Asia vs. Latin America & Caribbean (1960–2000) (percentage change)

	Output per worker	Capital per worker	Schooling per worker	Total Factor Productivity (TFP)
East Asia	3.9	2.1	0.5	1.0
Latin America & Caribbean	1.1	0.0	0.4	0.2

Source: Collins and Bosworth (2003).

growth also reflects a relatively long history in Latin America of higher tariff barriers than in East Asia and higher barriers to domestic competition arising from high entry costs for business, poorly functioning financial markets, and low labor market flexibility.[23]

A more recent study by Margaret McMillan and Dani Rodrik (2011), utilizing a relatively new cross-regional database developed by the Groningen Growth and Development Center (see Timmer and DeVries 2007), provides additional insight into the divergent growth experience of East Asia and Latin America on the basis of production and employment data disaggregated by major sector of the regional economies. These analysts attempt to quantify differences in labor productivity growth, which is the principal source of economic growth in the two regions given the marked differences in capital per worker discussed earlier. Based on the observed structural change among the primary, secondary, and tertiary sectors of the two regional economies, these economists calculated for the period 1990–2005 the growth of labor productivity as the sum of two components: one is the growth of productivity in a given sector (a so-called within component), and the other is the growth of productivity that can be attributed to shifts in labor to other sectors of higher or lower productivity than in a worker's sector of origin (a so-called structural component). As displayed in Table 2.6, the growth in labor productivity was nearly three times higher in East Asia than in Latin America for the time period of the study, which is broadly consistent with differences in the growth of real GDP per capita quantified in the two sets of studies discussed above. In the case of East Asia, most of this productivity growth can be explained by productivity growth in each of the three sectors (i.e., agriculture, industry, and services); however, a significant share is also due to the structural shifts of labor that occurred during 1990–2005, which was a period of marked structural change consistent with observations made earlier in this chapter. By contrast, the contribution of the "structural" component in the

Table 2.6   Decomposition of productivity growth, 1990–2005 (percentage change)

	Labor Productivity Growth	Components due to	
		Sectoral productivity change	Productivity growth due to structural change
East Asia	3.87	3.31	0.57
Latin America	1.35	2.24	−0.88

Note: East Asia includes India; Latin America includes Argentina, Bolivia, Brazil, Chile, Costa Rica, Colombia, Mexico, Peru, and Venezuela.

Source: McMillan and Rodrik (2011).

case of Latin America was significantly negative, giving rise to a total absolute difference in the contribution of structural change to regional growth in labor productivity of around 1½ percentage points.

These results for the period in question are broadly consistent with other studies conducted by the Inter-American Development Bank (IADB) for Latin America that cover the second half of the twentieth century. In a recent study by Pages (2010), one can clearly see a marked difference in overall labor productivity growth in the periods before and after 1975. During 1950–1975, which marked the period of inward development noted earlier, overall productivity growth in Latin America was high, at close to 4 percent per year, with roughly equal contributions from the sectoral growth and the structural change components. However, during the period after 1975, which coincides with Latin America's shift to a more outward-oriented approach to development, total productivity growth drops substantially, especially during 1975–1990 when Latin America suffered the brunt of the debt crisis following the two oil shocks of the 1970s. During 1990–2005, the IADB team calculated a negative contribution of the "structural" component to overall productivity growth, similar to the results of McMillan and Rodrik summarized above, although the quantitative magnitude of the result is somewhat less than in the latter study.

In addition to these studies of the IADB, it is interesting to consider some of the more recent insights of the official development community that have a bearing on the comparative development of East Asia and Latin America, as reflected, for example, in the report of the World Bank Growth Commission, which was published in 2008. The Growth Commission comprised a group of leading practitioners and officials from developing countries and academic experts under the chairmanship of Nobel Laureate Michael Spence. The Commission's Report was the result of an elaborate series of consultations and workshops on four continents with other leading academics and policy makers that reviewed and discussed some 40 thematic and country case studies during a period of two years. These studies covered many different aspects of the development process, such as equity and income distribution, health, technology transfer, and macroeconomic policy, as well as 15 country studies drawn from Africa, East Asia, the Middle East, and Latin America. These studies, as well as the full report of the Commission, are available on the Commission website (www.growthcommission.org).

The specific sample of high-growth cases on which the Commission based its report was determined by selecting those countries that had experienced a growth rate in real GDP of 7 percent for a period of at least 25 years since 1950. While the Commission's report claims that this group is "remarkably diverse," it turns out that 9 of the 13 selected countries are from East Asia: China, Hong Kong, Indonesia, Japan, Korea, Malaysia, Singapore, Taiwan, and Thailand. (This sample includes eight of the nine members of the East Asian region chosen for this study, excluding Japan and the Philippines.) The other four cases include Botswana, Brazil, Malta, and Oman. Brazil is a somewhat anomalous case in that its period of "miracle growth" occurred during 1950–1980, according to the selection criterion of the Growth Commission, after which it entered into a period of relative decline. Except for a brief (half-page) box on p. 21 of the report, this case does not feature in any of the analysis of the Commission, as it does not share any of the lessons drawn from the other 12 cases. In this respect, the sample of the Commission appears heavily skewed toward East Asia, as very little is said about, nor is there any case material, for Botswana, Malta, and Oman, in addition to Brazil. It remains a question why the Commission did not set its selection criterion somewhat lower than it did in order to generate a more diverse set of countries.

The Commission concludes that the 12 cases of sustained high growth (excluding Brazil) shared five common elements: "a) they fully exploited the world economy; b) they maintained macroeconomic stability; c) they mustered high rates of saving and investment; d) they let markets allocate resources; and e) they had committed, credible, and capable governments (page 21)." Much of the report elaborates on the various policy dimensions of each of these elements. The report also includes a chapter on the development challenge for sub-Saharan Africa, small states, middle-income countries, and resource-rich countries. The concluding chapter includes reflections on a number of current global challenges including climate change, income distribution, migration and demographic change, and global governance.

The background studies for the Commission, which presumably represented the inputs for the Commission's deliberations, cover a range of interesting development topics and case study material. However, they are uneven in quality and presentation, with some topics covered in papers of only a few pages, while others are only in PowerPoint format. Some studies have not yet been made publicly available.

Given that East Asian countries dominate the sample of countries chosen by the Growth Commission, it is interesting to note that this sample (with the exception of China) is the same group of countries chosen for the World Bank's East Asia Miracle study of 1993.[24] Such a comparison raises the obvious question as to what, if anything, is new in the Bank's interpretation of these countries' development experience, given that it was one of the sponsors of the Growth Commission? How has the Bank's understanding of the East Asian development record changed in the past 15 years?

At one level, as reflected in the five common elements noted above, not much has changed. Each of the five characteristics of successful development cited earlier was already emphasized in the earlier East Asia Miracle study and is clearly part of mainstream development thinking. The importance of openness as an underpinning of successful growth and of growth as an essential aspect of poverty alleviation have long been stressed by the Bank in connection with the notion that "openness is good for growth, and growth is good for poverty alleviation."[25] Similarly, most development economists accept the proposition that macroeconomic stability is a necessary, if not sufficient, condition for growth. In addition, the promotion of high savings and investment and the presence of sound public administration have long been emphasized as striking features of the East Asian development experience.

At another level, it is clear that the Commission did not wish to adopt a prescriptive stance on development policy consistent with its view that each country must find its own way to development. It also advanced a relatively agnostic view about industrial policy, which has been extensively debated within the East Asian context and is reviewed later in chapter 6.

On this basis, one is led to conclude that the Growth Commission did not provide any new insight into the development process based on its examination of the East Asian experience. As a result, the Growth Commission report does not have any direct relevance for this study, which is grounded in certain concepts related to the fundamental or "deep" determinants of economic growth that are reviewed in the next chapter.

CHAPTER 3

Changing Paradigms in Development Economics

This chapter reviews the major changes that have taken place in the theoretical approaches that economists have used to understand the process of economic growth and development, and sets out a broad conceptual framework for understanding the multidimensional aspects of comparative economic development in East Asia and Latin America that is used to organize the discussion in the remainder of the book.

During the post–World War II era, there have been profound changes in the conceptual framework of development economics. These can be summarized, first, in terms of a shift in thinking from the "proximate" to the "deep" determinants of economic growth, and, secondly, in terms of a changing view about the role of the state in economic development. As noted in the previous two chapters, both of these changes are relevant to the comparative study of economic development in East Asia and Latin America. Each of these changes is examined below.

The Search for the Fundamental Determinants of Economic Growth

Since the late 1950s, economists' thinking about economic growth and development has been commonly organized within the framework of the neoclassical growth model associated with Robert Solow and Robert Lucas, as noted in chapters 1 and 2.[1] This framework focused on the role of factor accumulation and productivity growth, the so-called proximate determinants of economic growth. Out of this framework developed the approaches of growth accounting (to explain changes in economic growth rates across countries over time), as illustrated by the study of Collins and Bosworth (2003) referred to in chapter 2, and development accounting (to explain changes in the level of per capita real income over time).[2] Emphasis on knowledge acquisition, or human capital, led to the incorporation of human capital as an explicit factor in accounting for economic growth along with physical capital, labor force growth, and technological change. Later on, with the emergence of the so-called endogenous growth literature since the late 1980s, the neoclassical framework has been extended to explain changes in technology or total factor productivity (TFP) as an (endogenous) element determined within the growth model rather than an exogenous change outside the model.[3] This extension led to an emphasis on the role of externalities or spillovers from R&D efforts of firms or advances in technological innovation that allowed firms in an industry to achieve scale economies and competitive advantage. In this connection, the focus on endogenous growth models envisaged a role for government in encouraging technological development and in fostering an environment that was conducive to innovation and entrepreneurship. As a result, there has been a surge in the development of cross-country growth studies since the early 1990s that have focused on the critical policy changes or the enabling environment (sometimes called the "social infrastructure") created by governments that could account for changes in technological growth, or growth in TFP, as a key component of the economic growth process. These are reviewed later on in this section.

As already discussed in chapter 2, the results of growth accounting for the two regions under examination in this study do not provide strong insights into their different growth experiences. Differences in the rate of economic growth between the two regions can be largely explained by differences in factor accumulation (in particular, physical capital), which is consistent with the larger rates of gross domestic investment that one can observe over an extended period of time for East Asia. The contribution of TFP growth in these growth accounting exercises, contrary to the results for larger cross-country and historical studies, is much less important, although it is still higher in East Asia than in Latin America.[4]

Notwithstanding the widespread use of growth accounting in development studies, it is important to understand the assumptions that are implicit in the underlying theoretical model for this framework that limit its relevance and applicability to the experience of developing countries. One is that the aggregate production function of the neoclassical growth model exhibits constant returns to scale; a second is that factor and product markets are perfectly competitive, which implies that returns to capital and labor are determined by their marginal productivities, and that there are no externalities in production so that private and social returns to production are equivalent; a third is that technology is freely available and relatively costless for countries to obtain and apply in production; and finally the model assumes that changes in each factor are small. This last assumption is important, as large changes in factors of production would alter the stability of factor shares in the production function and the reliability of the growth accounting results.[5]

None of the four assumptions of growth accounting just listed is applicable to developing countries undergoing rapid structural transformation, and thus the results of growth accounting must be seen as biased and unreliable, apart from the significant statistical problems that may arise in the measurement of the basic inputs for such accounting exercises.

Another important limitation of the neoclassical growth model, as noted earlier, is that the four assumptions discussed above imply that the predicted pattern of economic growth is a smooth and continuous process that is evenly spread over space and time. However, these implications are clearly inconsistent with the observed pattern of economic growth discussed in chapter 1, which is one that is lumpy over time and concentrated in space. In addition, it is important to realize that the neoclassical model obscures, if not ignores, the essential feature of structural change during the process of economic development, which further limits its usefulness.[6] In this context, it should be noted that some theoretical attempts have been made to accommodate elements of structural change within the balanced growth path of the neoclassical growth model, but these efforts have not as of yet led to a revision of the traditional focus on aggregate production functions and the standard approaches to growth accounting described above.[7]

In the light of these considerations, it should be recognized that growth accounting is most relevant or applicable to advanced countries, such as the United States or the United Kingdom, which come closest to being in conformity with the assumptions of the neoclassical model. In fact, Solow's original studies for the neoclassical growth model were restricted to advanced countries.

In the context of the above discussion, it is interesting to note that the results of growth accounting have given rise to an important debate between the so-called accumulationists and evolutionists in understanding the growth process in East Asia. Within the former group, some economists such as Paul Krugman have argued on the basis of studies elaborated by Alwyn Young that, since East Asia's strong economic growth can be easily explained by large rates of capital accumulation within the framework of growth accounting, it was not fundamentally different from the high rates of economic growth observed in the early period of Soviet Russia, which were propelled by high rates of forced savings and investment.[8] In this sense, Krugman has characterized the growth process of East Asia as all "perspiration" and no "inspiration."

By contrast, the Evolutionist School of development thinkers, exemplified by economists such as Richard Nelson and Howard Pack, has countered this argument by claiming that the sustained, high rates of capital accumulation observed in East Asia would not have been possible without massive technological learning and the development of technological capability.[9] The evolutionist critique is based on the idea that technology is not freely available and easily adapted by developing countries, in the sense that full knowledge of the techniques for its use is available to all firms and can be readily absorbed with minimum cost and learning, as implied by the neoclassical model. Rather, the "evolutionists" argue that the absorption of foreign technology requires a strong degree of "tacit" knowledge that can only be obtained by costly effort in the form of technical training and "learning by doing" if developing countries wish to master and adapt it to local firm circumstances and conditions. In this sense, critics of growth accounting argue that the conventional measurement of technological change or TFP growth inevitably understates the true extent of technological learning or capability that is required for successful investment to promote industrialization.

Nelson and Pack also raise an important methodological problem in growth accounting, consistent with the limitations noted earlier, which is not often recognized by economic researchers in this field. The problem they identify is that it is impossible in growth accounting exercises to distinguish unambiguously between movements along the production function (reflecting capital accumulation) and upward shifts in the production function (reflecting technological improvements) without making certain assumptions about the nature of the production function and the implicit elasticity of substitution between capital and labor. Most studies of growth accounting assume a certain kind of production function (i.e., the so-called Cobb–Douglas form, which exhibits constant returns to scale) in which the elasticity of factor substitution is 1.

This restrictive assumption, along with the others noted earlier, creates a certain bias in measuring the contribution of technological change to the growth of aggregate output or income per capita. Thus, there is what economists call an "identification problem" inherent in these accounting exercises that makes it impossible to differentiate unambiguously between the "accumulationist" and the "evolutionist" theory of economic growth in East Asia. This important consideration has largely been ignored in empirical growth studies of developing countries. More broadly, the evolutionists have made an important contribution in pointing to the critical role that technological capability, which requires joint efforts by business and government to acquire and maintain, plays in the development process.

A further concern with growth accounting, as noted already in chapter 2, is that the measure of technological progress (or TFP) is inherently indirect and is captured statistically by a residual term that reflects whatever errors and omissions are associated with the estimated contribution of capital and labor inputs and the assumed shares of capital and labor income in production. More specifically, any measurement errors related to changes in the quality of capital and labor stocks, or in the level of capital utilization, or in the use of land (a factor excluded from growth accounting exercises) are automatically imputed to TFP. Thus, measures of technological change, or growth in TFP, are inherently imprecise and are subject to wide margins of error. One example of this kind of problem can be seen in the application of growth accounting to the case of China since the beginning of its reform experience in the late 1970s. Recent studies for China's post-reform period since 1978 offer estimates of annual growth in TFP anywhere in the range of 2.2 to 7.7 percent. This is an enormous range of variation, and undoubtedly reflects problems in the underlying national accounts for China used to measure factor accumulation, even apart from the dubious validity of the restrictive assumptions of the growth accounting model noted above.[10]

Apart from the problem of direct measurement, another shortcoming in the application of the neoclassical growth model to developing countries is that the concept of TFP is something of a "black box," in that it encompasses a host of factors that affect the degree to which countries are able to absorb technological change made available by advanced countries. One factor is the notion of technological capability already discussed, which is related in part to the development of human capital and local technical skills. In addition, the level of TFP in developing countries depends on the quality of entrepreneurial and managerial skills that exist for building effective business organizations, the possibilities for networking in the communication of ideas, and the institutional arrangements that provide appropriate incentives for entrepreneurship, competition, and sound resource allocation.[11] The consideration of these factors associated with the absorption of TFP gives some hint of the positive contribution that technological clusters and R&D promotion can provide as sources of economic growth in developing countries, which are discussed later on in this chapter.

Since the late 1980s, endogenous growth theory has been developed as an extension of the neoclassical growth model in an effort to explain the factors behind, and the causes of, growth in TFP. The simplest formulation of this approach (the so-called AK model) in effect mimics the results of the early Harrod–Domar (H-D) framework (as discussed in chapter 2) and its vision of continuous growth linked to capital accumulation and the capital-output ratio. Instead of defining "A" as the inverse of the capital-output ratio and K as simply physical capital accumulation, the AK model defines A as technological change (as in the neoclassical model) and K more broadly to include not only physical capital, but also human capital and R&D activities, more generally. The basic idea in the endogenous growth model is that consideration of this broader definition of K allows for the effect of synergies between physical and human capital and technological innovation that can account for increases in TFP or A. The development of clusters of hi-tech industries with R&D labs linked to research institutes and universities (as exemplified by Silicon Valley) provides one example of how synergies and spillover effects in the linkage of entrepreneurial activity and innovation can arise. This so-called agglomeration effect of clusters, just described, means that diminishing returns to capital at the individual plant level are offset by knowledge externalities among firms engaged in R&D, leading to constant returns to capital at the aggregate level and, thus, re-creating the notion of perpetual growth embodied in the H-D model. In this way, the impact of diminishing returns to physical and human capital (which are ignored in the H-D model, but are central to the neoclassical framework) are offset by increases in technological progress to create a process of steady, persistent growth.[12]

In a second wave of endogenous growth models, the focus on innovation and technological progress as a source of TFP growth was further refined through a closer examination of the role of externalities and spillovers involved in clusters and networked behavior, on the one hand, and the role of the policy environment, on the other. In the latter category, importance was placed on the role of strong property rights protection, the elimination of credit restraints, labor force skills, and macroeconomic stability, which required effective government support, in order to create an environment that would allow entrepreneurs to innovate and upgrade the technological level of their business activities. These models also pointed to the important strategic role of government in the design and implementation of public expenditure programs and focused support for a limited number of economic activities and sectors where innovation and entrepreneurship were developing.

Since the early 1990s, following the development of endogenous growth theory, there has been a flood of studies employing cross-country growth regressions, pioneered by Robert Barro and Xavier Sala-i-Martin,[13] which have attempted to identify the main macroeconomic and structural determinants of differences in economic growth rates across countries and the key elements of an infrastructure that would support technological progress. Notwithstanding the use of sophisticated econometric techniques, these studies are burdened with problems of endogeneity or simultaneity bias arising from the two-way interactive effects of changes in the policy or institutional environment and the pace of economic growth. There is also little scope for discriminating among the more than 100 purportedly independent variables that have been identified in these studies as primary, causal factors in the economic growth process. Accordingly, in a recent study, Robert Barro has admitted that it is impossible to pinpoint exactly which of the numerous so-called exogenous variables used in these studies is critical for the growth process.[14]

Nor can one determine from these studies the proper sequencing or mix of policy interventions that should be adopted to influence favorably the growth process. A study by Bill Easterly has shown that many of the putatively robust findings of cross-country growth studies are, in fact, highly influenced by the presence of statistical outliers, and that, once these observations are removed, the findings are much less significant statistically.[15] Clearly, these problems point to the fact that the neoclassical growth model is not able to identify the range of variables that are relevant to the development process, beyond certain basic factors such as factor accumulation, population growth, schooling, and innovation, which limits its suitability for the elaboration of growth regressions.

The kinds of technical issues summarized above have led research away from a focus on the proximate determinants of growth to one on the deep determinants, namely, geography, trade, and institutions.[16] These deep determinants can be seen as the fundamental factors that influence factor accumulation and improvements in TFP. The emphasis on institutions began with the work of Douglas North, who argued that legal and political regimes that protected contract and property rights were fundamental determinants of economic development in Western Europe and the United States.[17] Geography is commonly understood in terms of a country's physical endowment, for example, the presence or absence of natural resources, its exposure to tropical or temperate climates, and its distance from major markets, all of which have been shown to have an influence on economic development. Such factors are truly exogenous in the development process. Trade (which can be understood as a proxy for the policies that support openness) and institutions are less clearly exogenous factors in development, and are themselves influenced by geography.

In the past few years, intensive econometric work has been carried out to try to disentangle the effects of these three factors, and a consensus seems to be forming that institutions represent the most important of the three "deep" determinants of economic growth and development, and that geography's influence is mainly through its impact on the other two.[18] Institutions can be understood as both formal and informal, and either private or public. They can also be identified with the ingredients of the "black box" containing TFP absorption discussed earlier. However, most often, they are seen as manifested in the workings of the government, in terms of bureaucratic capacity, the rule of law, and the promotion of a sound business environment. This notion leads naturally to the consideration of the role of the state in economic development. For the purposes of this study, both trade and institutions play a key role in the explanation of the divergent development trajectories of East Asia and Latin America, along with initial conditions and political economy factors.

The Role of the State in Economic Development

The second key strain of empirical and theoretical debate on the causes of economic development during the second half of the twentieth century relates to the role of the state and state–society relations. Prior to the Keynesian revolution, government was assumed to play a limited, social guardian or "night watchman" role in the economy, based on the classical tenets of welfare economics. The role of government was to provide essential public goods in the form of infrastructure and education, and to use tax policy to deal with negative externalities (e.g., pollution) and its regulatory authority to deal with natural monopolies.

Early writing in the post–World War II era, under the influence of the Keynesian revolution and Russia's experience with industrialization, greatly augmented the potential scope for government intervention in the economy and emphasized the importance of central planning and public investment for promoting economic growth. Market failures were seen as pervasive in developing countries, and government action was considered necessary to overcome defects of the price system and coordination failures in private investment. This approach to development policy led to an emphasis on extensive government intervention in key sectors and markets in order to promote inward development through the application of controls on credit allocation and interest rates to influence certain kinds of state-directed investment, as well as widespread restrictions on exchange and trade transactions to allow for essential imports for priority investments and industries. Such an approach was associated with the concept of import-substitution industrialization that was widely adopted by developing countries, and by Latin America in particular, in the 1950s and 1960s, as discussed in chapter 2.

During the 1970s, a reaction began to develop against this approach to development policy as a result of some pioneering cross-country studies that assessed the negative impact on economic growth of extensive trade and exchange restrictions in developing countries and the growth-enhancing effects of trade and exchange liberalization.[19] These studies also pointed to the growth-retarding effect of "rent-seeking" behavior on the part of private business operations that enjoyed privileged access to government decision makers and received open-ended protection or subsidies for inefficient industries.[20]

This line of research was reinforced by advocates of Public Choice theory, who emphasized the motivation of politicians and bureaucrats to perpetuate office holding through patronage, bribes, and corruption, which supported unproductive activities and a diversion of resources away from wealth creation.[21] Within the framework of rent-seeking and public choice, government failures were seen as much more pervasive than market failures in economic development. These developments in economic thinking led to a reaction against activist or so-called developmental states (see further text) and an appeal for a much more limited role for government in the development process. Such a vision of government was enshrined in the "Washington Consensus" of the late 1980s.

The Washington Consensus, a term coined by John Williamson in 1990, represented an attempt to capture the key lessons for development

policy arising from East Asia's experience with export-oriented industrialization and Latin America's attempt to deal with the effects of the
debt crisis of the early 1980s.[22] The ten precepts that are laid out in the
Consensus have been summarized as "stabilize, liberalize, and priva-
tize," and pointed to the perverse effects of government intervention in
Latin America and the allegedly beneficial effects of market forces in the
development experience of East Asia. The framework of the Washington
Consensus held much credence in a number of Washington-based international institutions (in particular, the IMF and World Bank), and was
very influential in the design of policies associated with the resolution
of international debt crises beginning in the late 1980s in a number of
Latin America governments.[23] As suggested above, primary attention
in the design of economic policies was to be given to the establishment
of a sound macroeconomic framework involving low inflation, fiscal
consolidation, trade opening, and a more market-oriented approach to
monetary and exchange rate policies. Such a framework was seen as
an essential precondition for sound economic growth, which was particularly relevant for the case of Latin America given its history since
the Great Depression of macroeconomic instability. Essentially, the
Washington Consensus encapsulated a notion of spontaneous development, once certain preconditions were in place to spur private sector
activity. However, while macroeconomic stability may be considered a
necessary condition for sound economic growth, there has been a growing recognition among development experts and practitioners that it is
not a sufficient condition.[24] In this regard, both experience and further
theoretical considerations have led to a refocusing of the development
agenda on some of the factors that need to be present beyond macroeconomic stability to support economic growth and development. Some of
these factors are related to the role of government in helping to provide
some of the ingredients of the "black box" of TFP absorption discussed
earlier.

Certain theoretical developments since the 1980s have refocused
attention on the problem of market failures in the development process,
through an examination of the limitations of the neoclassical paradigm,
for example, in the writings of Joseph Stiglitz. His work has demonstrated the importance of imperfect or asymmetric information and
incomplete markets in understanding the functioning of financial and
labor markets, and the potential role that government can play in overcoming the effects of these departures from a model of perfect competition.[25] At the same time, mainstream economic thinking has given new
emphasis to problems of coordination failures, collective action, and

externalities in the development process, as well as latent comparative advantage and increasing returns to scale in export-oriented activities, which give rise to an argument in favor of government intervention, for example, for the support of new firms that demonstrate the ability to master or adapt current technologies for commercial application, for the development of technological clusters and R&D activity, and through various forms of export promotion. As Paul Krugman has shown, some of the insights of early post–World War II "high development" theorists, such as Albert Hirschman and Paul Rosenstein-Rodan, on the role of government in overcoming coordination problems in the development process have been given new validity through the application of rigorous analytical modeling.[26]

These developments in the literature have led to a more nuanced appreciation of the role of government in economic development, which falls somewhere between the extremes of post–World War II development planning and the limited state of the dominant neoliberal approach to economic reform (Washington Consensus). In the past decade, writers such as Ricardo Hausmann, Dani Rodrik, and Sanjaya Lall have been particularly prominent in refocusing attention on the appropriate role of government in supporting the development of technological capability and industrial upgrading in the development process.[27] In this regard, these authors have helped to refocus attention on the important role of structural change in the process of development, which is largely ignored in the neoclassical model discussed earlier, and the key contribution of industrialization in promoting high rates of economic growth.

The writers cited above have also refocused attention on the role of integration or trade in the development process by showing that it is not just openness to trade that is important for technological learning and industrial development, but that it is also the nature of what a country exports and the technological upgrading involved in export-oriented industrialization that accounts for successful economic growth and development ("What You Export Matters" is the title of a recent influential study in this field of study).[28] This feature of the "new structuralist" view of the development process points to a particularly important differentiating characteristic of the development process in East Asia and Latin America that can help to explain their divergent growth experience. As already discussed in chapter 2, East Asia has been far more successful than Latin America in developing a comparative advantage in the export of medium- and high-technology manufactured goods.[29] In line with these results, recent studies have shown that cases of rapid economic growth among developing countries have been associated with a process of diversification in production, employment, and exports up to a certain level of income per capita, which is consistent with the "new structuralist" view of the development process.[30] More specifically, scholars at the Harvard Kennedy School of Government (Ricardo Hausmann and Dani Rodrik) have developed a model and empirical results demonstrating that the overall sophistication of a developing or emerging market economy's exports, in terms of their similarity with exports produced by countries with higher levels of income, is strongly associated with rapid economic growth.[31]

The emphasis on the development of manufacturing in cases of successful developing countries points to an important pattern of structural change that occurred during the nineteenth century in the experience of the current advanced countries. But in the context of the current emphasis on structural change in the development process, it points to the important gains in labor productivity and income growth that accrue from the mastery and application of technological improvements in manufacturing activities, which can be a spur to rapid economic growth. Does this mean that countries, which have significant natural resource endowment reflected in their exports, cannot experience economic development? No, it does not; however, it does mean that over time, such countries, for which there are many examples in Latin America, need to follow the pattern of advanced countries with significant natural resource endowments, such as the Nordics, Canada, and Australia, which have fostered derivative manufacturing activities related to the processing of by-products from those natural endowments that have commercial applications. Of particular interest in this regard is the case of Malaysia that has followed this approach through the processing of commercial products related to its primary production of palm oil, which have benefitted from various forms of government incentives. Chile has also followed this model on a smaller scale with the processing of various forms of prepared salmon products related to the abundance of natural fish habitats in that country, which only began to be exploited by private entrepreneurs on a significant commercial scale with the support of a special government-sponsored innovation fund (Fundacion Chile).

The New Structuralist framework is also highly relevant to an understanding of the fundamental changes in the global trading system since the 1970s related to the growth of intra-industry trade and the fragmentation of the production process through the development of global production networks (GPNs) or global value chains (GVCs), as discussed in chapter 1. Participation in GVCs has become an increasingly important feature of the major exporting economies. Moreover, according to recent UNCTAD estimates, GVCs managed by transnational corporations account for around 80 percent of global export trade of goods and services.[32] As noted earlier, these changes in the trading system help to explain how some regions or subregions have been able to take advantage of the "agglomeration effects" associated with linkages among closely related clusters of industrial and R&D activities, supported by government policy and close ties between private business and university research outlets, as a means of capturing the benefits of specialization within these networks and value chains. Once established, these clusters of industrial activity for export tend to develop "first mover" advantages for the countries involved, which, with a supportive environment for business investment, can begin the process of technological and industrial upgrading within GPNs and GVCs. In these conditions, the potential gains from increasing returns to scale can take hold. This process also helps to explain how the development process can become lumpy with respect to location and time, and can allow for growth spurts that create significant differences in economic growth between regions.[33]

By contrast, within the confines of the neoclassical growth model, which assumes constant returns to scale, the costless acquisition of information, and the absence of externalities, the role of agglomeration forces in jump-starting economic growth within a cluster of local industries linked to GPNs cannot be explained, and production is expected to be spatially dispersed and evenly spread among countries that share a certain set of similar endowments. More specifically, it will be shown in chapter 6 that East Asia has been far more successful than Latin America in taking advantage of these structural changes in the global trading environment during the past few decades. Why some countries have been able to enter into a process of industrial upgrading within the GPNs, while others have not, is an important issue that needs to be addressed in understanding some of the factors associated with the divergent development paths of East Asia and Latin America.

The Conceptual Framework for This Book

The rise of the "new structuralist" school of development thinking with its focus on the "deep determinants" of growth and development and the reassessment of the government's potential role in overcoming market failures in the development process has been paralleled by new thinking in the comparative political economy of economic development.[34] This field of research has focused on the nature of the policy-making process in government and the role of state–society relations in its formulation and implementation.

While the proponents of "deep" determinants" and the role of institutions in the development process have emphasized the important role of government in protecting property rights and securing contracts as a spur to investment and growth, the political economy school has pointed to the role of bureaucratic effectiveness and its insulation from political influence as a basis for rational decision making. Scholars in the latter group have also highlighted the importance of state capacity and the balance of power in state–society relationships in explaining the effectiveness of government decision making. Where state capacity is weak, and business interests predominate in government decision making, the result is rent seeking, or worse, neo-patrimonialism. Within a neo-patrimonial state, there is no distinction between public and private interests, and political leaders use government power to favor special or favored interests for personal or group enrichment. Conversely, where state capacity is strong, and government decision making is insulated from political influence, a sound, consistent, and stable policy framework can result, which is essential for supporting the protection of property rights and long-term investment.[35]

One offshoot of the comparative political economy school has focused on the successful cases of so-called developmental states at an early stage in East Asia's development process and their relative absence in Latin America. This issue is taken up in chapter 8 of this study. While there is a fairly strong unanimity of views among political economists on the nature and role of developmental states, there is much less unanimity among economists on their economic impact.

Another branch of comparative political economy has looked at the ways in which political forces have impeded or promoted economic policy reform, which has particular relevance for understanding the role of "vested interests" in maintaining a status quo policy regime and frustrating reform efforts, as well as the interplay of factors of production (i.e., labor, capital, and land) as political forces in determining certain policy outcomes. This perspective also needs to be taken into account in trying to understand the different development outcomes one observes in East Asia and Latin America.

The triad of deep determinants (i.e., geography, trade, and institutions) provides the conceptual framework for this study with an emphasis on the interplay of trade (or policies) and institutions. Geography does not seem to be a key discriminating factor in looking at the comparative development of East Asia and Latin America, as both regions fall predominantly in the tropical zone, and include countries that are both resource-rich and resource-poor. Studies by the IADB have shown that East Asia and Latin America are fairly similar according to various measures of geography, and that geographic characteristics do not account statistically for any of the difference in their economic growth performance.[36] Within the realm of policies, it will be argued that East Asia has been far more successful than Latin America in its ability to maintain macroeconomic stability, which, as noted earlier, can be considered to be a necessary condition for successful development, and in its pursuit of structural policies that supported the development process through an expansion of export trade and the region's integration with the global economy. East Asia can also be shown generally to have had better institutions than Latin America, primarily in regard to the effectiveness of government bureaucracies and the consistency and stability of the region's policy framework.

One cannot understand the interplay of policy choices and institutions in the development process, however, without consideration of certain initial conditions in terms of historical and sociocultural factors that are unique to a given region. These factors, in turn, can help to explain the nature of state–society relationships in each region and the political economy factors that affect the interplay of policies and institutions in a given national or regional setting. This complex of forces can be understood as following a certain simple, causal trajectory with positive or negative feedback effects that reinforce certain patterns of development over time. Initial conditions, for example, can be seen as having a fundamental effect on political economy forces and institutions, which, in turn, influence policy choices. The positive or negative development outcome of those policy choices can have positive or negative reinforcing effects on political economy forces and institutions, thus perpetuating a country or region's positive or negative development track. Alternatively, a crisis induced by poor policy choices can be seen as having a corrective impact on the political economy and/or institutional factor, thus bringing about a positive change in a country's development trajectory. As noted earlier, it is the interplay of these four dimensions (initial conditions, policy choices, institutions, and political economy factors) in determining the divergent development experience of East Asia and Latin America that is the focus of the remainder of this book.

CHAPTER 4

Initial Conditions for the Postwar Development of East Asia and Latin America

This chapter identifies some of the critical differences in the historical background of the two regions that are relevant for understanding their economic development since the middle of the twentieth century. In particular, the chapter examines differences in the impact of colonialism, the role of cultural factors, and the influence of ideology or development thinking in each region.

The divergence in the paths of economic development of East Asia and Latin America cannot be understood without some attention to "initial conditions" of the two regions at the beginning of the post–World War II era. A clear difference between the two regions can be seen in the fact that most of the countries of East Asia (except China and Thailand) at the close of World War II were still under, or had been recently freed from, foreign colonial administration or Japanese military occupation, whereas Latin American countries (except for islands in the English-speaking Caribbean) had been independent nations since the early nineteenth century. More generally, it is important to identify the key differences in the "initial conditions" of the two regions that are relevant to understanding their different development trajectories since the middle of the past century.

The Impact of Colonialism

The historical record shows that British, Dutch, and Japanese colonial administration, by and large, left the newly independent states of

Malaysia, Singapore, Indonesia, Korea, and Taiwan with strong bureaucracies and important infrastructural and physical investment for industrial production and commodity exports. The case of the Philippines is atypical, as many legacies of the Spanish colonial regime remained unchanged under US administration in the first half of the twentieth century, while education, democratic electoral procedures, and foreign direct investment were promoted. Strong rural elites associated with large landholdings that were fostered under Spanish rule continued in place under US administration, alongside a relatively weak central administrative structure. In this respect, the Philippines share an important historical characteristic with Latin America, along with the dominance of a strong Catholic religious tradition. As evidence of this fact, it is interesting to note that the Spanish colonial administration of the Philippines was subordinated to the Vice-Royalty of the Spanish Crown located in Mexico City, thus establishing a direct link of the Philippines with Latin America (see Box 4.1 on how the Philippines is more similar to Latin America than other East Asian countries).

Box 4.1 Are the Philippines More Similar to Latin America than East Asia?

The Philippines have been somewhat of an outlier within the East Asian grouping, in that its record of economic development has been less dynamic than that of its regional neighbors, even while it has benefitted from the favorable neighborhood effects of being in a high-growth region. For example, its level of real income per capita in relation to that of the United States since 1950 has declined somewhat, similar to the experience of Latin America, while that of the rest of East Asia has shown a steady convergence. The Philippines also have registered a much higher rate of income inequality than the rest of East Asia, similar to that of Latin America, along with a significant degree of macroeconomic instability.

This relative stagnation of the Philippine economy has been considered something of an economic development puzzle among many analysts in the region (e.g., Hill and Balisacan (2002) and Nelson (2007)). However, in many respects the Philippines are more similar to Latin America than they are to East Asia, especially in terms of both its historical and cultural traits and record of economic and political instability during the second half of the twentieth century. The colonial origins of the Philippines, which it shares with Latin America, can account for much of its anomalous, economic experience in comparison with the rest of East Asia.

The Philippines were a colony of Spain for longer than Latin America, that is, from 1565 to 1898, and its name derives from the Spanish (Las Islas Filipinas), which was given in homage to the reigning monarch of the Spanish Empire at the time of its discovery (King Phillip II). For much of its colonial experience, the Philippines were administered under the Vice-Royalty of Mexico until the latter territory's independence in 1821, after which it was administered directly from Spain. The Philippines were also linked directly by trade with Mexico by means of the famous Manila Galleons, which carried silver and precious metals from New

Spain in the Americas in exchange for spices from the Far East. In this respect, the Philippines share the same legacy of colonization as Latin America with regard to its extractive character and the burden of inequality associated with institutions such as the "encomienda." Through the pervasive missionary influence of the Catholic Church, the Philippines, like the Americas, were also imbued with the same influence of the counter-reformation as regards its rigid belief systems and its absolutist, corporatist, feudal, and hierarchical social and institutional structures. In this respect, the Philippines conform very well to the "extractive," as distinct from "settler," model within the "colonial origins" framework of Acemoglu, Johnson, and Robinson (2001) and their institutionalist approach to economic development.

Following its independence from Spain in 1898 as a result of the Spanish-American War, the Philippines became in effect a colony of the United States until 1947 (except for a period of military rule by Japan during the Second World War). Under the administration of the United States, basic education, economic infrastructure, and foreign investment were introduced, along with political reform to establish the procedural basis for electoral politics. However, in the opinion of many scholars (e.g., Anderson (1988) and Hutchcroft and Rocamora (2003)), these political reforms marginalized the great mass of the local population and reinforced the power and influence of rural, landed oligarchs who had held privileged positions under Spanish colonial rule. Since independence, political life in the Philippines has been characterized by what has been called "cacique" democracy, which has involved the rotation in power of political parties linked to oligarchic groups of large, elite extended families that have overwhelmed a weak central government with patronage demands and rent-seeking, followed by strong-man military rule (under Ferdinand Marcos) and subsequent political regimes with deep pockets of corruption that have faced the recurring threat of military coups. Given the traditional importance of nepotism and patron-clientilism in political life, the Philippines again have much in common with Latin America.

The history of political instability in the Philippines, together with a weak administrative apparatus of the central government, has created an environment that has made it difficult to sustain macroeconomic stability and attract foreign direct investment on a sustained basis. This problem was particularly apparent during the period prior to 1980 when the country was pursuing a strategy of import-substitution industrialization similar to that of Latin America. Because of the heavy import-dependency of this process and the lax fiscal and monetary policies that accompanied it, the Philippines were the only country in East Asia to experience a debt crisis in the early 1980s, as did most of the Latin American region for similar reasons.

In general, the colonial heritage of Latin America, as in the case of the Philippines, created a legacy of weak central administration, strong regional identifications, and marked social and economic inequalities, which have remained in evidence up to the present day. This tradition created a fragmented political culture and social instability that have been deterrents to sustained economic development in the post–World War II period. Most Latin American societies have lacked the social cohesion of states in East Asia. Moreover, the dominant position of Europeans in Latin American states where there were heavy concentrations of native ethnic groups and African slaves fostered severe social and economic inequalities that have persisted to the present day in

Brazil, Mexico, Central America (except Costa Rica), and the Andean nations.

The role of colonial forces in economic development has been given prominence in a seminal study by Acemoglu, Johnson, and Robinson (AJR 2001), which strongly reinforces the institutionalist approach to economic development discussed in chapter 3. These authors argue, and demonstrate empirically, that differences in the current level of economic development of many countries (as measured by real income per capita) can be attributed to differences in the quality of colonial institutions associated with whether, as former colonies of European powers, they were viewed primarily as destinations for settlement or for resource extraction. Within this framework, AJR posit that "settler" and "extractive" colonies can be distinguished by the incidence of tropical diseases as reflected in data on settler mortality. Settler colonies are best exemplified by Australia, Canada, New Zealand, and the United States, which were more habitable to European settlers because of local health conditions, whereas extractive colonies were typically found in Latin America, the Caribbean, and Africa, and some parts of Asia where tropical diseases such as malaria and yellow fever were common. These differences in the nature and quality of colonial institutions, in turn, can be shown to be significantly related to the quality of economic institutions at subsequent stages of a country's development.

These two different colonial characteristics (i.e., whether as destinations for natural resource extraction or settlement) has been shown to be strongly identified empirically with a divergence in their trajectories of real income per capita, with a clear advantage in favor of former settler colonies. As such, the AJR thesis is a good example of the role of path dependence in economic development, in that early institutional arrangements can be found to have had long-term effects on the course of economic development, as the elements of modern institutions take form over the course of many years, even centuries, with clear roots in the past.

The example of Latin America conforms very closely with the AJR conceptual framework, as the quality of its modern governmental institutions (as reflected in attributes such as the risk of expropriation, the strength of rule of law, the incidence of corruption, and bureaucratic effectiveness) has been significantly weaker than in East Asia. This thesis will be examined in more detail in chapter 7. In no small way, this reality is a legacy of the region's colonial history and culture, and can be seen as a significant factor in explaining its relative economic decline during the second half of the twentieth century, as the Latin American region has tried to adapt to the forces of globalization.

The Spanish and Portuguese colonization of Latin America occurred under monarchical regimes in the fifteenth and sixteenth centuries, which embraced the counter-reformation in Europe and rejected many of the liberalizing influences of the Reformation in Northern Europe that ultimately developed into a tradition of individual rights and liberties. Thus, the Iberian regimes imposed a highly centralized administrative control of their colonies within a political culture that was strongly authoritarian, corporatist, feudal, and mercantilist, and one that was infused with a very dogmatic form of Catholicism. Settlement by Portuguese and Spanish subjects was not encouraged on a large scale by the crown, but was rather a privilege granted by royal prerogative to certain members of the noble classes.[1] One of the benefits of colonial privileges was the control of large tracts of property in the New World, from which any discoveries of gold and silver were surrendered to the crown.

An inherent feature of Spanish colonialism in Latin America was a highly stratified social order and very inequitable distribution of wealth and land holding. In addition to the practice of African slavery, which was widespread in the Americas, large groups of indigenous populations in Latin America were effectively enslaved under the colonial system of "encomienda," under which rights of control over property and local indigenous groups were conveyed by the Spanish crown to military explorers ("conquistadores").[2] In this regard, it is important to recognize that during the period of more than three and half centuries of the existence of slavery, arrivals of African slaves to the European colonies in Latin America and the Caribbean outnumbered those who were brought to the United States, a prime example of colonial settlement (or "settler" case) in the AJR framework, by a factor of nearly 35 to 1. Moreover, in 1820, the ratio of nonwhites to whites in Latin America and the Caribbean was around 5 to 1, whereas in the United States it was just the reverse.[3] These comparisons serve to highlight the marked difference that existed between North America as a destination of settlement and the rest of the hemisphere as a destination for resource extraction.

With the independence movement in Latin America in the early part of the nineteenth century led by patriots such as Simon Bolivar of the Grancolombian region, a host of new governments in the region aspired to the establishment of representative government based on republican principles that had been adopted by new governments in the Northern

Hemisphere. However, the liberal statesmen of the newly independent states in Latin America invariably found themselves in conflict with powerful interests residing in the church, the military, and a wealthy class of landowners and merchants that had enjoyed special, corporate rights and privileges under the colonial regime. In the absence of a political culture rooted in self-government, such as the one that developed in the United States, Latin America entered into a period of political struggles between the interests of the old and new regimes, interrupted by intervals of "strong man" (or "caudillo") rule to maintain a semblance of political order.

In conformity with the AJR thesis, the impact and legacy of this historical experience on the economic, political, and social development of Latin America has been very deep and burdensome in many respects. Inequality in income, wealth, and land holdings became deeply ingrained in the economic and social order of Latin America, and oligarchic forces associated with powerful agrarian and mining interests fostered a tradition of military or "strong man" rule well into the second half of the twentieth century as a means of resisting economic and political reforms more favorable to the majority of the population.[4] As will be explained in more detail in chapter 8, the colonial legacy of Latin America can also be associated with a fragmented political culture that has been overly focused on short-term distributional concerns to the detriment of long-term economic development. In addition, the political culture of Latin America has been dominated by a variety of historical conflicts rooted in colonial experience between rural oligarchic and urban industrial/worker interests and between regional and central governmental administrations, as well as in struggles over direct taxation of income and wealth and indirect taxation of domestic sales and foreign trade.

By contrast with Latin America, East Asia does not fit neatly into one or the other colonial regimes laid out in the AJR study. In fact, two countries (China and Thailand) largely escaped colonial influence altogether. Indonesia (under Dutch rule) and the Philippines (under Spanish rule) can be labeled as extractive colonies, even though data on settler mortality is only provided for the former case in the AJR study. However, unlike the Philippines, the legacy of colonial influence in Indonesia is somewhat mixed, as during the first half of the twentieth century, the commercialization of agricultural pursuits and an incipient industrialization process began with Dutch investment in basic infrastructure and factory sites.[5]

Curiously, Hong Kong, Malaysia, and Singapore fall into the "settler" category in the AJR study, ostensibly because of a low measure of settler mortality, which is somewhat anomalous, as none of these sites was the destination for large settlements of Europeans as in the case of Australia, Canada, and the United States.[6] What has perhaps been more determinative of their successful economic development is the fact that each of these states was the locus of direct British rule that left a legacy of sound property rights under a common law tradition and effective governmental administration. The common law tradition, as distinct from the civil law tradition that flowed from France through Spain and Portugal to their colonies, has been associated with the strong protection of property rights, which is a basic pillar of the institutionalist school of development.[7] The common law tradition, with its respect for private arrangements for contract rights and rules for arbitration and strong protection for property rights and rules of enforcement, has been an essential underpinning for capitalist development. By contrast, the tradition of positive law and civil codes associated with the Napoleonic legal tradition, which was transferred directly to Latin America via its colonial heritage, has given rise to a very top-down arrangement of executive order and decrees covering all aspects of economic and social life. Among other things, this legacy can be associated with the widespread development of illegal or underground economic activities and a large parallel economy in many Latin American countries, as discussed at the end of chapter 2.

The AJR study does not cover the experience of Korea and Taiwan, even though each of these countries were colonies of Japan, a non-European power, for half a century up to the end of World War II. Most recent studies of this colonial experience have shown that Japan's influence on Korea and Taiwan, while repressive and harsh, had a strong developmental impact in terms of fostering institutions of effective public administration and a sound infrastructure for agricultural and industrial development.[8]

In light of the differences highlighted above between the colonial experience of the two regions, a prominent development writer of Chilean origin (Kay 2001) has offered the following characterization of the legacy of the colonial traditions in each region: the colonial legacy in Latin America established a tradition of weak states, strong rural oligarchies and poorly developed physical and human capital, whereas for much of East Asia (i.e., excluding the Philippines, for example) strong states, weak rural oligarchies and relatively well-developed human and physical capital resulted from colonial influence. These differences in the colonial legacy of the two regions are critically important for understanding the role of political economy factors in their development, as will be discussed in chapter 8.

Cultural Influences in Regional Development

Cultural influences are also important in tracing differences in the development trajectories of the East Asian and Latin American regions. Latin America's cultural heritage from Spain and Portugal transplanted values in Latin American society of the Catholic counter-reformation that were directly contrary to those modernizing elements of Protestant culture, which, along with the Enlightenment values of liberty, individual rights, and due process of law, underpinned the development of Western capitalism and popular sovereignty. As noted earlier, Iberian political culture was rigid, hierarchical, corporatist, militaristic, and orthodox; and these were the values that were transplanted during Latin America's colonial experience.[9] Iberian culture valued individual dignity, based on a religious concept of the worth of the soul, but this concept did not translate into a political culture of liberty and individual rights, in view of the centralized, corporatist, and hierarchical structure of Iberian rule. Family ties were paramount, which fostered a culture of nepotism and personal loyalties to those with economic and political power. At the same time, Iberian culture fostered relatively weak administrative states in Latin America, because of the strong centralist tendency of the monarchy. Office-holding was considered a reward for personal ties with the monarch, while state power was viewed as a source of benefits and favors for individuals with close personal ties to a leader, as in the case of licenses to carry out certain economic activities. Iberian culture also was fatalistic, given its religious emphasis on the after-life, and fostered the pursuit of humanistic (as distinct from scientific or material) endeavors.[10]

As already noted in the previous section of this chapter, Latin America has a long history of absolutist rule and military or "strong man" dictatorships since its independence movement in the early nineteenth century, consistent with its Iberian political culture. Even in today's world, in the wake of the second wave of democratization in Latin America since the mid-1980s, such rule is still clearly a force in political life, as exemplified by Evo Morales in Bolivia, the Castro brothers in Cuba, and the late Hugo Chavez of Venezuela. The survival of these (and other similar) regimes in Latin America can only be understood in terms of the lingering effects of deep social and economic inequities in these societies and the appeal of populist rule in the absence of a strong political culture based on a broad-based participatory democracy and enduring and inclusive political institutions.

The Iberian cultural traditions identified above for Latin America can be associated with a number of problematic tendencies for the development of an effective economic and political order. One is the inherent weakness of the central government because of its mercantilistic roots, its strong links to favored interests in society, and the absence of any notion of an independent, professional bureaucracy. The absence of a clear separation between the public and private spheres in Iberian culture can be linked to rent-seeking, clientilistic politics and, in the extreme, neo-patrimonial behavior on the part of governmental leaders. The long history of strong-man rule, either in the guise of democratic politics or military dictatorships, which exemplify this tradition, is personified in the twentieth-century experience by the rule of Ferdinand Marcos in the Philippines, Juan Peron in Argentina, Rafael Trujillo of the Dominican Republic, Manuel Noriega of Panama, and Fernando Ortega of Nicaragua, in addition to those authoritarian leaders mentioned in the previous paragraph. In this regard, it is important to note that in 1975 only four republics, involving less than 15 percent of the population of Latin America, were representative democracies. (One can exclude the Philippines, as well, from this short list.) The region's major transition to democracy during the last quarter of the twentieth century represents the fulfillment of a long struggle to overcome the legacy of its antidemocratic Iberian heritage and establish the bases of a reasonably stable political order grounded in popular sovereignty.

The cultural legacy of East Asia differs significantly from that of Latin America. A Confucian culture has been dominant in many states of East Asia, including Hong Kong, Korea, Taiwan, and Singapore in addition to China and Japan, which can be associated with, among other things, the emergence of strong bureaucracies in those states. Confucian thinking placed a strong value on learning and intellectual pursuits, as exemplified by the prestige given to a well-educated mandarin or administrative class in Chinese society, which has carried over to the present day. In addition, these societies have tended to be fairly homogeneous, or at least reflect a dominant Chinese culture as in case of Singapore. Buddhist or Islamic cultures have been dominant in some parts of Southeast Asia such as Indonesia, Malaysia, and Thailand, but nevertheless within each of these countries, there were important groups of expatriate Chinese who played an important role in the business life of these countries. With the exception of the Philippines, all of the states of East Asia have tended historically to foster strong paternalistic political regimes, with individual citizens strongly attached to collective identities.

In many cases, Confucian culture manifested itself in autocratic political structures during the twentieth century, in that within that tradition there was no recognition of the rights of citizens against the state, whereas maintenance of order and respect for a political hierarchy were central values. However, the experience of Japan, Korea, and Taiwan has shown that Confucian culture is not incompatible with democracy or the functioning of a civil society.[11] Generally, it can be said that many states in East Asia (with the key exception of China), in a somewhat parallel pattern to that of Latin America, began to make an important transition from autocratic regimes to more democratic republics during the last quarter of the twentieth century.

Confucian culture also was hierarchical and family-centered, but ties outside the family and loyalty to political leaders were highly valued, as well, which were rooted in the idea of the family as a model for social and political life. In addition, achievement and self-improvement through hard work, study, and personal discipline were fostered, and Confucian culture placed a high value in the social hierarchy on the administrative or mandarin class, which served as the state's administrators, as noted above. More generally, in traditional Confucian societies, the group was emphasized over the individual, authority over liberty, and responsibilities over rights, while harmony and cooperation were preferred over disagreement and competition. The Confucian concept of "min-ben" created an expectation that leaders should pursue policies that would promote the general welfare, in exchange for the loyalty of the people.[12] Thus, in Confucian culture, a ruler was legitimized, not so much by the process through which he was selected, but rather by the policies he pursued on behalf of the general welfare.[13]

Confucian humanism fostered certain cultural values that have been supportive of modernization in East Asia: delayed gratification and saving, self-improvement, group loyalties and strong social networks, and distributive justice. Confucian culture also emphasized the role of good fortune in personal affairs, and opportunities associated with markets. Strong social networks ("guan-xi") have been particularly important in the influence of the Chinese business communities throughout East Asia noted earlier, which embodied norms that supported the fulfillment of contract obligations and the protection of property rights in the absence of a formal legal code. In more recent times, ties of "guan-xi" among expatriate business leaders and investors living in Hong Kong and Taiwan with family roots in Guandong Province in Mainland China have fostered strong flows of foreign investment to China following the economic reforms that started in 1978. The existence of these strong business networks is a good example of an indigenous form of "social capital" or interpersonal trust that many analysts have pointed to as a significant force in the economic development of other regions.[14]

On the basis of the above discussion, it seems fair to conclude that the traditions and principles of Confucian culture were principally oriented to the establishment of a framework for a stable political order, even though it was up to each leader to decide whether or not to follow those principles. This culture could be seen as a stabilizing influence on the region in the wake of the important economic and political changes that occurred during the second half of the twentieth century. By contrast, the political order that developed out of Iberian culture within Latin America was far more conflictive and anarchic. In the light of history, one implication of this heritage has been that the challenges of economic development for Latin America during the second half of the twentieth century were made more difficult by the political instability that accompanied the region's efforts to establish the basis of an enduring political order associated with participatory democracy, which continues to the present day.

The role of culture in economic development has been subject to strong debate, with strong proponents for its positive role in East Asia and negative role in Latin America, as suggested by some of the commentary provided above. Nevertheless, one has to recognize that there is at least one significant problem with the cultural determinism of economic development, in that it cannot explain the turning points of economic development or the different development outcomes among countries of a similar cultural background. The case of China prior to, and since, the economic reforms of 1978 is one case in point, as is the contrasting experience of North and South Koreas since the end of the Korean War. Clearly, in both cases, it was a change in policies and institutions, and not culture, which accounted for the different development outcomes. Accordingly, one can argue that once an enabling environment was created that provided incentives for profitable economic behavior, cultural attributes supportive of such behavior could be revealed. In this sense, institutions trump culture, as in the extreme, predatory, or totalitarian dictatorships preclude normal human behavior based on individual preferences and personal interrelationships rooted in cultural traditions. As will be explained in chapter 8, one can also observe in East Asia and Latin America the role that culture has played in shaping the style and behavior of political leaders and institutions, which have been a significant factor in the divergent development trajectories of the two regions.

Other Initial Conditions

In addition to the impact of colonialism and culture on regional development, one should consider the possible influence of other "initial conditions" such as geography, experience with industrialization, and ideology on the divergent paths of development of East Asia and Latin America.

Geography

The influence of geography on development has been an important focus of debate among scholars, with Jeffrey Sachs as a leading proponent of its role in constraining development outcomes.[15] Geography naturally makes up one of the three components of the "deep determinants" of economic development, as explained in chapter 3. It also lies at the root of the institutionalist approach to development, as exemplified in the studies of AJR discussed earlier in this chapter. While Latin America falls uniformly within the "extractive" category of states because of the dominantly tropical nature of its environment, East Asia is somewhat more a mixed case, as noted earlier, with some states in the "extractive category," but some others (such as Hong Kong and Malaysia) in the "settler" category (for purposes of the AJR study), and still others (China and Thailand) outside altogether because of their lack of direct colonial experience. Thus, it is important to consider in somewhat more detail to what extent there are important geographic differences in the two regions that could play a role in their development outcomes.

In the recent literature on economic development, analysts have shown that certain national geographic characteristics, such as the share of land in the tropical zone, as distinct from temperate zone, distance from major markets, and access to the sea, can account for some of the differences in real income per capita observed among developing countries.[16] By these measures, it turns out that the two regions are fairly similar, as suggested already in chapter 3. Both regions are predominantly in the tropical zone, as measured by distance from the equator, but they both also extend partially into the temperate zone, pushing North in the case of East Asia and South in the case of Latin America. In addition, both regions are somewhat similarly placed with respect to major markets. As a result, it has been estimated that transportation costs as a share of the total value of imports during a sample period of the last quarter of the twentieth century were roughly similar in the case of East Asia and Latin America and considerably less than those for sub-Saharan Africa, which is more centrally located in the tropical zone and not well situated with respect to major trade routes.[17]

The extent of a country's natural endowments in terms of mineral or agricultural resources has been considered as another important geographic determinant of development. In this regard, Latin America is well known for its rich agricultural and mining resources, and has traditionally depended on them for a significant share of its export earnings. East Asia is more mixed in this regard. Northeast Asia is not well endowed with natural resources, whereas Southeast Asia is. In this regard, countries of the latter subregion share a common trait with Latin America in that exports of natural resource-based commodities formed a significant share of their foreign exchange earnings in the middle of the twentieth century at the time of their independence. What is significant, however, is that countries in Southeast Asia have tended to reduce their relative dependence on natural resource-based exports significantly, as industrialization has taken hold, whereas Latin America has not. Why this has been the case will be examined in the next three chapters.

On the basis of the above considerations, it would appear that geography should not be seen as a major differentiating factor in the "initial conditions" of the two regions. Indeed, in one study by the Inter-American Development Bank (IADB 2000), cited in chapter 3, it was demonstrated empirically that geographic factors were not a statistically significant factor in explaining differences in the real income per capita of the two regions.

Prior Industrialization

Another important difference in the "initial conditions" between the two regions is that Latin America began its industrialization effort much earlier than East Asia, first under the influence of European investment and migration in the decades prior to World War I, and later in response to the impact of the Great Depression. As noted earlier, the colonial experience in East Asia created some of the basic infrastructure and investment for industrialization in East Asian economies, which were nationalized with independence, but this stock of capital was generally of a much-reduced scale in comparison with that of Latin America. Thus, at mid-century, East Asian economies were generally much less urbanized and industrialized than many of their counterparts in Latin America, which is consistent with the fact that real incomes per capita, on average, were higher in Latin America than in East Asia in the middle of the past century.

In 1960, around 70 percent of the labor force in East Asian economies was employed in agriculture, compared with 51 percent in Latin America (Table 4.1). At the same time, only 22 percent of the population in East Asian countries (excluding the city-states of Hong Kong and Singapore) lived in urban areas, compared with 42 percent in Latin America. Notwithstanding these differences, indicators for adult literacy and school enrollment were somewhat higher in East Asia than in Latin America.

The Role of Hegemonic States

Global political forces have also played a role in the different paths of the two regions in their economic development. Throughout East Asia, newly independent states in the early post–World War II era faced a struggle to find an alternative development path to communism. The sense of competition with communism was particularly strong in the Korean peninsula, as a result of the partition between North and South Korea in 1950, and in the separation of Taiwan political administration from that of Mainland China after the Communist take-over there in 1949. In addition, the appeal of the Communist party ideology was notably strong in Singapore, Malaysia, and Indonesia. In view of these conditions in East Asia, the United States remained actively involved in the region after World War II. Clearly, the East Asian region (including Japan) benefited from the role of the US navy in maintaining open shipping lanes for international trade and a strong security umbrella that minimized the need for regional defense expenditures against any potential Communist aggression in the region. In addition, the role

Table 4.1 Initial social conditions in East Asia and Latin America (1960) (in percent)

	East Asia	Latin America
Share of labor force in agriculture	69.8	50.6
Share of urban population	22.2	42.3
Primary school enrollment	92.4	85.1
Secondary school enrollment	20.4	16.1
Adult literacy	62.2	57.2

Notes: East Asia excludes Taiwan; shares for agricultural labor force and urban population exclude Hong Kong and Singapore.

Source: World Bank, World Development Indicators.

of US economic assistance was especially important in the early post-war development of South Korea and Taiwan, and later in the case of Indonesia, the Philippines, and Thailand, in fostering policy implementation and institutional development that would counter the appeal of Communism as a social and political force. In addition to the influence of the United States, Japan has consistently adopted a strong client interest in the development of the rest of East Asia; first by promoting itself as a model for economic development, and second by fostering strong trade and investment linkages with the rest of the region, as explained further below.

Latin America was much more insulated from extra-regional threats in the early post–World War II era than East Asia and maintained very strong trade and investment links to the United States. However, official aid flows from the United States only became an important element in inter-American relations in the wake of the Cuban revolution in 1959 and the growing concern over indigenous revolutionary movements. This concern on the part of the United States with leftist insurgent movements in the hemisphere also led to a record of frequent interventions, both overt and covert, in the political affairs of the region. The Philippines, with the large security umbrella afforded by US military bases on its soil, and a growing domestic insurgency, was again more similar to Latin America than it was to the rest of East Asia.

Ideology

Ideology also has played an important differentiating role in the economic development of each region. For much of the early postwar period, dependency and structuralist theory rooted in the historical experience of Latin America was a dominant influence in the thinking of its economic and political leaders. This thinking, which was indigenous to the region, was given particular currency and popularity by the UN Economic Commission of Latin America (ECLA), especially under the leadership of Raul Prebisch, its first Executive Director. The "dependency school," which originated in Latin America, emphasized the adverse effects of the international system on Latin America arising from the unequal terms of exchange between primary commodity producers in the developing world (the periphery) and exporters of manufactures in the industrialized world (the center) and from the unfavorable terms of trade for the region's main commodity exports. Development thinkers associated with ECLA emphasized profound pessimism about the prospects for export growth and a deep suspicion of the role of market forces in economic development. Thus, they espoused a strong role for the state in economic development and an autarchic style of industrialization through import-substitution and government planning.[18] This approach to economic development was strongly promulgated by ECLA throughout the region during the 1950s and 1960s by means of its active program of publications, conferences and seminars, as well as direct advisory functions with member governments.[19]

In many respects, this ideological approach to development reinforced an already strong tendency toward inward development that had begun in Latin America prior to the Great Depression, which was accelerated by the collapse of trade and investment during the 1930s. Studies by John Coatsworth and Jeffrey Williamson have shown that Latin America historically has been a region of relatively high protection going back into the nineteenth century, in contrast to East Asia, where average tariffs were very low until the Great Depression.[20] During 1865–1930, average tariff levels were in the range of 5 to 10 percent in East Asia, whereas they were around 30 percent in Latin America.

By contrast, the approach to economic policy making in East Asia tended to be nonideological: a pragmatic and experimental approach to policy making was pursued. East Asian governments adopted a more balanced view of the role of the market and government in promoting economic development, and recognized that the government had certain responsibilities for supporting the public welfare, consistent with a dominant Confucian culture in the region.

Economic development became a key strategic objective for East Asian governments in the early post–World War II period. In part, this was a response to the experience and influence of Japan in its drive for industrialization, which began prior to World War II, and in part it was a response to the competition with communism, which took hold in China and North Korea and represented an active force in the political life of many countries of Southeast Asia. In this sense, East Asian states displayed a strong "will to develop," in the words of Ronald Dore, for which Japan could serve as a successful model of late development.[21] Japan, in turn, during its formative period of development beginning in the late nineteenth century looked to the experience of Prussia or Germany in its rise to great power status through accelerated economic development as a model for "late" development.

As noted already in chapter 2, one concrete expression of Japan's influence on the rest of East Asia as a model of "catch-up" development was embodied in the so-called "flying geese" model of economic development that was first formulated in Japanese writings by Kaname

Akamatsu in the mid-1930s and later in English in the early 1960s.[22] Akamatsu was a Japanese economist who was not trained in the West, and sought to give expression to a pattern of development that he had observed in Japan and was being replicated in certain parts of Northeast Asia. The figure of "flying geese" was chosen to suggest a pattern of regional economic development in which Japan as "lead goose" in its industrialization effort would be followed in an inverted-V formation (that flying geese tend to follow in their migratory activity) by successive groups of other countries (or "geese") in the rest of East Asia. These groups in historical order are first, the four newly industrializing economies or so-called tiger economies (Hong Kong, Korea, Singapore,. and Taiwan); second, the ASEAN-4 (Indonesia, Malaysia, the Philippines, and Thailand); third, mainland China; and finally, the Asian Transition Economies (ATE3), Cambodia, Laos, and Vietnam).

The "flying geese" model can be seen as an early version of the "trade cycle" model developed in the West by Raymond Vernon that shows a natural progression of industrialization, which many countries have followed, from labor-intensive to more capital-intensive forms of production that is driven by technological absorption and the rise of incomes and wages. The transition from one stage of industrialization to another is driven by the rise and fall of a nation's competitiveness, as measured by profit margins or the unit cost of labor. At each stage in which one industry begins to lose competitiveness, the leaders of that industry actively seek overseas sites, which offer easy access for transport and a more competitive wage structure, where production can be transferred by foreign direct investment. The "flying geese" model can be applied to a progression of four or five industries, such as textiles, chemicals, iron and steel, automobiles, and electronics, each of which could be understood to emerge in sequence over time, as technological capability and skills improved, in Japan, as well as in each of the four other country tiers noted earlier.

One study by UNIDO, which appeared in its World Investment Report for 1995, showed how the sequence of industrialization by Japan since the 1950s has broadly conformed to the idealized sequence just described. In the case of Japan, as shown in Table 4.2, its industrialization effort during the second half of the twentieth century has gradually shifted over the course of three to four decades from labor-intensive to more capital-intensive manufacturing as the technological capabilities of its business operations and labor force skills have improved. Given the significant outward orientation of Japan's industry, this progression can also be seen in its export performance, as well as in successive

Table 4.2 Flying geese pattern: Structural economic shifts for Japan (percentage of manufacturing total)

Year	Labor-intensive light industries				Capital-, assembly-, and knowledge-intensive industries			
	Food, beverages and tobacco	Textiles, apparel, and leather	Other manufac- turing [a]	Total	Chemicals, petroleum, and coal products	Basic and fabricated metal products	Machinery, transport equipment, and electronics	Total
A. Manufacturing output [b]								
1955	42.5	11.9	20.3	74.7	7.2	10.7	7.3	25.2
1970	17.4	7.6	21.4	46.4	14.0	16.6	22.8	53.4
1980	14.4	6.1	18.4	38.9	13.8	16.3	31.1	61.2
1990	9.1	3.5	15.6	28.2	13.7	12.4	45.7	71.8
B. Manufacturing exports								
1955	6.2	37.3	...	43.5	5.1	19.2	...	24.3
1970	3.4	12.5	11.8	27.7	6.4	19.7	46.3	72.4
1980	1.2	4.8	9.5	15.5	5.3	16.5	62.7	84.5
1990	0.6	2.5	9.6	12.7	5.5	6.8	74.9	87.2
C. Manufacturing FDI outflows								
First wave 1696–1973	5.0	23.8	14.7	43.5	18.9	14.7	22.9	56.5
Second Wave 1978–1985	4.3	5.2	10.5	20.0	16.6	25.2	38.2	80
Third Wave 1986–1990	5.2	3.3	17.9	26.4	12.2	8.9	52.5	73.6

Notes: [a] Including mostly labor-intensive industries such as toys, table and kitchenware, sporting equipment, and travel luggage.
[b] Measured by GDP at constant 1985 market prices.

Source: UNCTAD World Investment Report 1995: Transnational Corporations and Competitiveness, Table V.2, p. 242 (reprinted with permission).

waves of foreign direct investment through which it has transplanted production for these industries in other parts of East Asia, largely in conformity with the "flying geese" model.[23]

A broadly similar form of industrial development, reflecting a pronounced structural shift in the economy from rural sector to secondary sector activities, can be seen in each of the other tiers of the East Asian economic region noted earlier, roughly in conformity with the predictive pattern of the "flying geese" model. One adaptation that needs to be made to this model, which will be examined in chapter 6, is the shift from a pattern of inter-industry trade implicit in the preceding discussion to one of intra-industry trade, which has become predominant in the region with the development of global production networks (GPNs) and global value chains (GVCs), in particular since the mid-1980s.

The "flying geese" model is of interest not only because of its origins within the East Asian region and marked difference with respect to the inward development model of ECLA for Latin America, but also because it represents an early vision of the new structuralist approach to economic development that has become a central focus of current analytical research, as discussed in chapter 3.

What role then do "initial conditions," as described above, play in the post–World War II economic development of East Asia and Latin America? Latin America, at mid-century, certainly carried a negative historical burden, as the legacy of its colonial experience and subsequent history perpetuated patterns of social exclusion and income inequality, which created the conditions for social conflict and political instability during the twentieth century that were inimical to sustained economic development. In addition, because of its large natural resources and domestic markets, Latin American was well established on a path of inward-oriented development. This tendency was reinforced after World War II by an economic ideology, rooted in dependency theory, which promoted isolation from international markets, a suspicion of the market mechanism, and a heavy reliance on government intervention as a basis for promoting economic development.

By contrast, East Asia, reflecting in many cases the conditions of newly independent states, started its early post–World War II development path at a lower level of national income with more freedom of choice in its policy orientation. Generally, these states were more cohesive socially, although the threat of communist insurgency was strong among rural, poor indigenous groups. While more ethnically diverse than Latin America, a number of states in East Asia shared a common Confucian culture, which provided a framework for social and political order. As in the case of Japan, East Asian governments saw economic development as their most important strategic objective, in part to provide an antidote to the appeal of Communist ideology. In this endeavor, they were thus less burdened by ideology and prior development experience than their counterparts in Latin America.

CHAPTER 5

Economic Policy Choices— Macroeconomic and Financial Stability

This chapter and the next examine the second of the four dimensions that were identified earlier in the book as relevant for understanding the different development paths of East Asia and Latin America, namely, the role of economic policy choices. As noted earlier, governments in East Asia and Latin America have dealt very differently with the two basic macroeconomic constraints that have a bearing on development outcomes. One is fiscal solvency and the management of a generally sound path for the public finances that avoids the excesses of both chronic inflation and public debt problems; the degree to which countries manage this first constraint will determine to a great extent whether they are able to maintain approximate macroeconomic stability, which is a necessary condition for sustained growth and development. The other constraint is external sustainability. This constraint involves the management of a viable balance of payments position over time through export promotion and the encouragement of non-debt–creating capital inflows consistent with a sound public and private debt position. Obviously, these twin macroeconomic constraints or objectives of fiscal solvency and external viability are interrelated, as it is difficult for a country to sustain one without the other. In dealing with these constraints, it is clear that East Asia has been far more successful than Latin America, which is an important reason why the former region has been able to sustain more rapid economic growth and structural change than the latter.

The first constraint noted above is examined in this chapter, while the second is discussed in chapter 6. In addition, this chapter considers the role of the financial sector in the economic development of the two regions, where once again one can identify very different experiences and outcomes in the two regions. Latin America, for example, has been plagued by financial crises of various kinds, which have had negative feedback effects on its development outcomes, as well as on its macroeconomic stability.

Within the topic of policy choices, chapter 6 also explores the different ways in which the two regions approached the issue of industrial policy and the development of a viable industrial sector, which is key to the process of structural change that drives sustained economic development and external sustainability. This is one of the most contentious issues in the study of economic development, and very different lessons can be drawn from the experience of East Asia and Latin America, with the former region generally more successful than the latter.

Economic Policy Choices and the Twin Macroeconomic Constraints

As suggested earlier in chapter 2, the record of macroeconomic management in the two regions has been substantially different, with Latin America characterized during most of the post–World War II era by chronic high inflation and considerable volatility in the growth of real GDP, on a scale that was unmatched by any other region in the world. During 1960–2000, the average annual rate of inflation for the region as a whole amounted to a little over 100 percent, while the growth in output per capita was only around 1½ percent, on average, per year. In addition, the volatility of output growth was extremely high, as reflected in Chart 5.1. (By contrast, during the same period the growth in output per capita in East Asia was three times higher than that for Latin America, while the average rate of inflation was less than one-seventh that of Latin America.) A significant negative relationship has been established between the volatility of output growth and the average growth in real income per capita over time. In the case of Latin America, for example, it has been estimated that the average growth in real income per capita was reduced by ½ percent for every 1 percent increase in the standard deviation of output growth over 1970–2004.[1] As a result, IMF economists have calculated that less than half of the growth spells initiated in the post–World War II era in Latin America continued after 5 years, whereas this proportion was close to 100 percent in the case of East Asia.[2] Other economists have also shown that the typical business cycle in Latin America differed significantly from that of East Asia, in that the expansion phase has usually been weaker, while the contraction phases have been similar.[3]

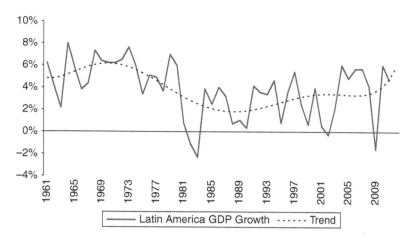

Chart 5.1 Latin America and the Caribbean: Rate of GDP growth 1961–2011.

Notwithstanding this record, it is important to note that since the turn of the new century, the incidence of high inflation and volatile growth has been substantially reduced in the Latin American region as a result of improvements in the conduct of macroeconomic policy, which is one important reason why its growth and inflation performance in the past decade was better than in any previous decade since the 1960s. These results reflect, on the one hand, sustained efforts to improve macroeconomic policy management in the region from an institutional and policy perspective, and, on the other, favorable terms and trade and external conditions, which have allowed the region to accommodate more easily the second (external) constraint on its development prospects, noted earlier.

The macroeconomic behavior of East Asia during the second half of the twentieth century was substantially different from that of Latin America, with high, sustained growth over many years in an environment of relatively low inflation. Notably, there were two significant bouts of hyperinflation in the region, in Taiwan and Indonesia in the early days of their independence, which have not been repeated elsewhere. The Philippines, however, has generally sustained more macroeconomic instability than other countries in the region, which is another way in which that country has been more like Latin America than East Asia. The political economy and institutional factors behind these regional differences will be noted later in the chapter and explored in more depth in chapters 7 and 8.

Macroeconomic Policy Management

Throughout most of the second half of the twentieth century, Latin America has struggled with the maintenance of macroeconomic stability more broadly defined, again in marked contrast with East Asia. Macroeconomic stability needs to be understood in a broader sense than just the low variability of economic growth and the absence of rapid or high inflation, to include the following elements: a relatively low and predictable rate of inflation; a level of interest rates that is generally positive in real terms; a stable and sustainable fiscal policy; the maintenance of a real exchange rate that is competitive and relatively stable; and a viable external payments situation. Through a variety of studies, it has now become reasonably well established that the absence of macroeconomic stability in the broad terms just noted can be a powerful constraint on sustained economic growth.[4] Among a number of channels of this influence, the following can be noted: A sustained and variable rate of inflation can substantially weaken the allocative efficiency of the price system and reduce the level of productivity in the economy, while lowering the level of private investment; sustained fiscal imbalances can lead to a crowding out of private investment and severe inflation and/or balance of payments problems and possibly exchange rate crises; overvalued exchange rates are likely to lead to external payments difficulties through a dampening of exports and rapid growth in imports; and interest rates that are negative in real terms can dampen incentives for saving (especially in the form of bank deposits) and promote inefficient investment. In addition to these channels of adverse policy influence on growth, the instability of policy administration itself can be a powerful influence on the volatility of economic growth, which in turn can also be a significant deterrent to sustained economic growth. In this connection, it is not surprising that Latin America has exhibited a high degree of policy variability in the macroeconomic sphere, which can be linked to its chronic problems with macroeconomic instability, as discussed earlier.[5]

For purposes of understanding the history of economic policy in Latin America, it is useful to break the period between 1950 and 2010 into two equal periods, before and after 1980. The early 1980s marked the beginning of the region's major external debt crisis, reflecting a series of economic problems that had emerged during the decade of the 1970s because of the prevailing approach to economic development and macroeconomic policy management. The watershed of 1980 also marked the beginning of a transition to a more liberal and market-oriented approach to economic policy within the region, which culminated in the conquest of macroeconomic instability in the first decade of the current century, as noted earlier, and its successful response to the global financial crisis that began in the latter part of 2008.

During the first half of the period under review, Latin America remained heavily influenced by the inward-oriented development strategy of the UN Economic Commission for Latin America (ECLA), which, as noted in the previous chapter, grew out of the region's experience in coping with the effects of the Great Depression and ECLA's profound pessimism about Latin America's dependence on primary commodities and the region's international division of labor with the advanced industrialized countries. An inward development strategy based on import-substitution industrialization (ISI) and indicative planning, as espoused by ECLA, led to heavy government intervention in the management of macroeconomic, trade, and exchange rate policies. The development framework of ECLA also did not place a high weight on the control of inflationary pressures, as it tended to view a rise in inflation as an inevitable component of the growth process. This structural view of inflation on the part of ECLA led to sharp policy conflicts with other institutions such as the IMF that also was active in the region through its surveillance and lending activities in which it advanced a more conservative stance on the merits of relative price stability.[6]

While the period 1950–1980 was one of a relatively high rate of economic growth within the region, the ISI strategy gradually became unsustainable because of its heavy dependence on imported inputs and intermediate goods, which led to recurring balance of payments problems and an accumulation of domestic and external public debt, especially in the wake of the two oil shocks of the 1970s. A further complication for the management of macroeconomic policy during this period was Latin America's historic neglect of its agricultural sector, with its highly unequal system of landholdings and underinvestment in the production of foodstuffs to support the industrialization process through the development of a vibrant rural economy, which was reinforced by policies that promoted a "closed" economy. This experience stands in sharp contrast with that of East Asia, where governments (with the exception of the Philippines) tended to deal early on with the requirements of the rural sector, where large masses of the population lived, through land reform and critical infrastructural investment in order to generate an economic surplus that could be used to finance an important part of the industrialization process.[7]

During the 1970s, there were some notable early attempts in Latin America to shift to a more liberal, trade-oriented approach to economic stabilization and growth following the military takeover in Chile in the early 1970s, and subsequent military coups in Argentina and Uruguay in the mid-1970s. Among these early experiments in the adoption of a neoliberal approach to economic policy making, it was only the Chilean experience that had an enduring impact on the region because of the persistence of the government's policy approach and the lessons it provided for other countries in the wake of the regional debt crisis. These are discussed further in Box 5.1.

Box 5.1   Chile's Struggle to Achieve Macroeconomic Stability

During the last quarter of the twentieth century, Chile went through a long and difficult process of adjustment to establish the institutional foundations of macroeconomic stability. Today these institutions represent the "gold standard" for emerging market economies, especially in the light of the sound policy track record that the Chilean government has achieved since the mid-1980s, and the strong political commitment that underpins the objective of macroeconomic stability.

Prior to the mid-1970s, Chile had pursued an economic program that was typical of Latin America as regards its inward-oriented development. The government was committed to a strong policy of import-substitution industrialization with reliance on copper exports for 70 percent of its export proceeds. With a very closed economy and weak fiscal management, the country was subject to chronic inflation and periodic balance of payments crises. Following a very tumultuous period of a radically socialist government under Salvador Allende during 1970–1973, a military government led by Augusto Pinochet took over by coup d'etat in September 1973, which continued in control through March 1990.

During the period of military rule, government policy makers embarked on a radical agenda of economic reforms in the fiscal, monetary, external, financial, and pension areas that were designed to achieve a private sector-driven, price-deregulated, and outward-oriented market economy. Because many of the economic policy leaders chosen by the military government were trained at the University of Chicago, they became widely known as the "Chicago Boys." In view of the size and suddenness of many of the economic adjustments that were introduced by the economic team, the term "shock treatment" has been applied to their scope and impact. However, issues of sequencing and timing of the economic policy adjustments were often ignored, which created problems in implementation. In the financial area, in particular, a program of rapid liberalization of the banking system was introduced, with very generous deposit insurance and lender of last resort facilities in the central bank, but without adequate safeguards in terms of prudential requirements and the establishment of a strong supervisory authority. Notwithstanding the elements of moral hazard that the authorities had introduced, they believed that market forces and reputational integrity on the part of bank managers would induce prudent behavior in the support of sound investment and productive activity. In the event, a large credit "bubble" ensued that resulted in a major financial crisis in 1983 when external lenders decided to withdraw foreign lines of credit and a large commercial bank declared insolvency because of losses on nonperforming loans (NPLs). In order to stem depositor panic and further bank closures, the government guaranteed all bank debt and covered all the banks' NPLs with government bonds. These actions stabilized the financial system but, together with the cost of bank restructuring and recapitalization, resulted in an increase of government debt on the order of 40 percent of GDP. This crisis, which was followed by many other similar ones in Latin America, was memorialized in an article titled "Good-bye Financial Repression, Hello Financial Crash" (Diaz-Alejandro 1985).

This crisis was followed by a restoration of macroeconomic stability during 1985–1989, although the average annual rate of inflation remained around 20 percent. This period closed with the creation of a new central bank law that established its institutional and policy independence and the control of inflation as its primary mandate. In addition, the first free elections since 1971 occurred in December 1989, which established a coalition arrangement among the three major political parties known as "concertacion" that began in March 1990. During the next ten years, the central bank followed an informal inflation-targeting regime with annual price targets that resulted in a gradual reduction in the rate of inflation from around 30 percent in 1990 to 3 percent in 1999 (Ffrench-Davis 2002).

In September 1999, the central bank announced that it would begin a formal regime of full-fledged inflation targeting beginning in 2001, the first such experiment in Latin America, which has continued in place to the present day. Under this program, a target band of 2 to 4 percent has been set for "headline" inflation, with a policy horizon of 1 to 2 years in order to anchor price expectations. As an essential complement to this regime, the government has committed itself to a formal "fiscal rule" involving a target for the "structural" government balance (initially a surplus of 1 percent of GDP), which would allow the actual government balance consistent with that target only to be adjusted on a cyclical basis for the impact on government receipts arising from the output gap and any variation in the long-term export or "reference" price of copper. This initiative, which was also unprecedented in Latin America, eliminated the problem of pro-cyclical fiscal policy and established automatic stabilizers for central government receipts. At the same time, the government created a Copper Stabilization Fund, which was converted into a sovereign wealth fund (The Economic and Social Stabilization Fund—ESSF) in 2006, to manage the sterilization or withdrawal of copper export tax receipts with respect to a certain "reference" price established for budgetary purposes. In 2002, an expert panel was installed to determine that "reference" price, which was followed in 2003 by the installation of an expert panel to determine the size of the output gap, which is conventionally defined as the difference between actual and potential GDP (Kalter et al. 2004).

The inflation-targeting regime, along with a flexible exchange rate policy and the structural balance rule, has served Chile extremely well, and has set a model for other emerging market economies to follow. The rate of inflation has remained within the band initially established in 2001, whereas the structural balance rule has allowed the government to shift its net asset position from a negative 3 ¼ percent of GDP to 19 ½ percent of GDP in 2008; during the same time period, the net foreign asset position of its main sovereign wealth fund (ESSF) rose to US$ 20 billion. The structural balance target was maintained at a constant surplus of 1 percent of GDP from 2001 to 2007, and since then has been adjusted flexibly, in particular during the global financial crisis of 2008–2009; for the current budget period of 2010–2014, a target deficit equivalent to 1 percent of GDP has been set to be achieved by the end of the period (IMF 2012).

As a sign of its economic maturity, Chile began the process for its accession to the OECD in 2007, which was approved in May 2010; thus, it became only the second country from Latin America to be granted membership in the OECD along with Mexico, which joined in 1994.

Throughout the periods before and after 1980, the persistence of rapid inflation in many countries of Latin America (especially South America) could generally be explained by chronic imbalances in the government's fiscal operations and the subordination of monetary policy to fiscal policy requirements (i.e., so-called fiscal dominance). In many cases, the management of fiscal policy typically followed a cyclical pattern, in which periods of expansion were accompanied by growing external imbalances associated with the maintenance of a fixed exchange rate that resulted in an excessive accumulation of private and/or public external debt. These cases of coincident fiscal and external cycles usually ended in an exchange rate crisis, as an overvalued currency was devalued sharply by official intervention or by means of a sudden liberalization of the foreign exchange market in a moment of crisis as foreign financing was withdrawn or a terms of trade shock occurred. These events would also inevitably lead to a sudden decline in the growth or level of aggregate economic activity, as private investment and government spending, which were critically reliant on external financing, were curtailed. Such cycles are one common cause for the volatility of economic growth in Latin America noted earlier, but the region also experienced similar cycles that have been triggered by a collapse of the domestic financial system or a suspension of public debt payments, either as isolated or as coincident events (i.e., single, double, or triple crises). In this regard, it is important to realize that during 1970–2004, Latin America experienced more financial crises than any other region of the world (involving a currency, banking, or public debt collapse).[8] Indeed, it has been estimated that during the aforementioned period 17 countries accounting for most of the Latin American region were experiencing one form of financial crisis or another roughly half the time. While Latin America has been vulnerable to external shocks associated with a sudden change in its terms of trade or capital flow availability, most of the volatility (nearly 75 percent) in its growth in real GDP during 1970–2004 can be attributed to country-specific or domestically generated shocks, according to studies of the IMF.[9]

As suggested above, one of the principal domestic factors that have been a source of the volatility of economic growth has been fiscal policy. A number of studies since the late 1990s have pointed to the fact that traditionally in Latin America the behavior of fiscal policy has been strongly pro-cyclical, that is, it has varied in sync with the upswings and downswings of aggregate economic activity, and in fact has exacerbated the amplitude of economic cycles in the region.[10] Accordingly, the overall government deficit has tended to increase during periods of economic expansion, and to contract during periods of recession, contrary to the normal prescription for sound fiscal management as explained below. In this connection, it should be noted that monetary policy has generally been very passive, as central bank policy rates have also tended to be pro-cyclical, that is, with a lowering of these rates during economic upswings and an increase during periods of negative shocks to output.[11]

According to the principles of sound public finance, the behavior of fiscal policy should be countercyclical, rather than pro-cyclical, in order to dampen the volatility of economic activity and smoothen the business cycle. In line with this approach, the government finances should tend to move toward an overall surplus position during an expansionary phase of economic activity as tax revenues improve with the buoyancy of the economy, and expenditures are restrained to temper the growth aggregate demand. Conversely, during an economic downturn as government revenues tend to weaken, government spending should be increased in order to restrain the compression of aggregate demand, if not sustain it based on the impact of positive multiplier effects. In most advanced countries, these countercyclical features of fiscal policy have been institutionalized through so-called automatic stabilizers, in particular on the expenditure side of government budgets through the payment of unemployment insurance and other forms of public support in the wake of a recession, as hiring is reduced and temporary workers are laid off by firms. In serious downturns, such as the one of 2008–2009, major discretionary increases in government outlays may be called for, in addition to the triggering of "automatic stabilizers," to stabilize economic activity.

In Latin America, governments have only recently been able to implement countercyclical fiscal policy, as a result of a long struggle to reduce public debt burdens, strengthen revenue administration, and improve budgetary discipline. However, through most of the second half of the twentieth century, the mismanagement of fiscal policy was a leading cause of output volatility, inflationary pressures, external instability, and public debt problems. By contrast, fiscal policy has tended to be neutral or somewhat countercyclical in the case of East Asia, for reasons that will be discussed below.

The causes of pro-cyclical fiscal policy in Latin America have a number of technical, policy, and political economy dimensions. At an institutional level, it is important to recognize that traditionally budgetary discipline and tax administration have tended to be weak in Latin America, which has led to basic problems in fiscal policy management for a number of years until recently. The management of government expenditure has been particularly erratic, as discretionary spending has been very high and unpredictable. On the other side of the ledger, tax revenues have in many countries tended to rely heavily on indirect taxes and commodity-based tax proceeds, which are more volatile than income taxes. In addition, the earmarking of taxes for certain expenditures has been common, whereas significant components of government expenditure have been mandated by legislative decree, which has limited the scope for fiscal discipline or rational management over the business cycle.

Another problem in the management of fiscal policy is that traditionally there have been large segments of public sector operations outside the control of the budgetary authority in the form of state enterprise activities and decentralized governmental operations in countries with a strong federal structure of fiscal operations, such as Argentina and Brazil, where state governments have considerable autonomy in their budgetary functions. It has also been the case that many so-called quasi-fiscal operations have been undertaken by central banks through exchange and interest rate subsidies or selective credit operations for activities favored by the government, which have given rise to central bank losses that require periodic transfers from the government budget for their elimination. These "disguised" fiscal activities also should be included in any proper accounting of public sector operations in order to measure the "true" economic impact of the government sector.

Political economy factors have also played a role in the problem of fiscal mismanagement and pro-cyclicality that Latin America has traditionally confronted. To a large extent, these factors can be associated with the endemic problem of high inequality in Latin America and the conflicts this issue has created in terms of political fragmentation and social class divisions. In general, it can be said that Latin America's long-term inflation and fiscal problems throughout most of the second half of the twentieth century reflected political conflicts arising from its historic mal-distribution of income and conflicts among different economic, social, and ethnic groups. In this context, many analysts have pointed to the phenomenon of a "voracity effect" or "commons problem" that can exist in systems of weak public administration, where the presence of a fiscal surplus or windfall tax gain from high exports, for example, will lead to competition for new spending among political groups in the legislature, rather than any effort to reduce indebtedness or to build up fiscal assets to deal with any future revenue shortfall. These pressures will be stronger in political systems that are highly fragmented along class, income, ethnic, or regional groups. More generally, in a system of high inequality with a weak middle class, strong tensions are likely to exist between high-income groups that will resist direct taxation and low-income groups that will exert strong public pressure for social spending, which can give rise to serious problems of fiscal management and control.[12]

Another political economy model that has been helpful in understanding the problem of macroeconomic volatility in Latin America from a broader perspective than that of fiscal operations is referred to as the "populist business cycle."[13] This type of economic cycle was strongly identified in the behavior of countries in the Southern Cone, where there were important cleavages between the interests of an urban working class and those of rural oligarchs who controlled most of the traditional exports of beef and grains. In these countries, during a period of favorable export prices, populist governments favoring the interests of the urban industrial workers would favor expansionary fiscal and monetary policies to promote economic expansion and the maintenance of a fixed exchange rate regime to restrain inflationary pressures and ensure the supply of imported inputs for the industrial sector and essential foodstuffs for workers. An upswing in economic activity would persist for a time, but gradually wage rates would be allowed to increase, and pressures would begin to build on the prices of nontradable goods, thus eroding the competitiveness of the exchange rate and nontraditional exports, while growing imports would lead to an imbalance on the external current account and downward pressure on official reserves. Ultimately, these expansionary forces would lead to growing pressures for a significant downward adjustment of the exchange rate, which would be accompanied by a sharp increase in inflation and fiscal retrenchment. In these conditions, the expansionary impulse of fiscal and monetary policies would be reversed, and the economy would swing into recession.

In countries such as Argentina, economic cycles like the one just described have played out many times, often accompanied by a shift in government with elected leaders favored by the urban working class replaced by military autocrats protective of the interests of the landed elite. More generally, the exchange rate itself has often been the focus of political struggle, with urban groups in favor of fixed exchange rates along with high taxes on traditional exports, which would be opposed by landed elites more favorable to flexible exchange rates and low taxes on traditional exports. This tension between opposing urban and rural interests in exchange rate policy has been particularly evident in Argentina since 2003 during the governments led by Nestor and Cristina Fernandez de Kirchner.

It should be noted that in more recent times populism has reemerged as a factor in the political economy dynamics of several South American countries, given the favorable prices for many of the region's primary commodity exports and continuing concerns over high income inequality and poverty rates in countries such as Argentina, Bolivia, Ecuador, Nicaragua, and Venezuela. Recent economic developments in the last-mentioned country illustrate in bold relief the typical pattern of pro-cyclical fiscal policy supporting a populist business cycle, which ultimately will become unsustainable, notwithstanding the strength of global prices for oil, Venezuela's major export. In this regard, it is striking to see in the region that, notwithstanding general improvements that have been made since the late 1980s in public financial management, the maintenance of fiscal sustainability remains an important challenge in many countries due to unresolved issues of poverty and income inequality and the political economy dynamics associated with these problems.

The problem of pro-cyclical fiscal policy and weak fiscal management has been a major factor in Latin America's persistent debt problems. During the post–World War II era, Latin America experienced more debt defaults than any other region of the world.[14] As a result, it developed the problem of what has been called "debt intolerance," by which is meant the tendency of governments to enter into default at lower levels of debt burden than other countries given the perceived high risk of government borrowing and weak fiscal administration.[15] The region's low level of debt tolerance also reflected its burden of so-called original sin, by which is meant that there has not been any scope until recently for the placement abroad of public debt denominated in local currency, given the region's poor track record of fiscal policy management and the relatively small size of its export sector.[16] As a result of the latter problem, Latin America tended to have one of the largest burdens of (dollar-denominated) external debt in relation to export earnings. In Table 5.1, a sample of countries from East Asia and Latin America are compared according to various measures of "debt intolerance," which show marked differences between the two regions, in particular, in regard to the period of time during the nineteenth and twentieth centuries when countries in the two regions were in default or debt restructuring. Specifically, during the period 1824 to 1999, Latin America, on average, was around one-third of the time in a state of default or restructuring on its debt. (In East Asia, the Philippines

Table 5.1 Indicators for "debt intolerance"

	% of 12-month periods with inflation ≥ 40% (1958–2001)	Number of defaults or restructuring episodes (1824–1999)	Percentage of years in default or restructuring (1824–1999)	External debt–GDP ratio (1970–2000)	External debt–export ratio (1970–2000)	Institutional investors ratings (Sept 2002)
Latin America & the Caribbean						
Argentina	47.2	4.0	25.6	37.1	368.8	15.8
Brazil	59.0	7.0	25.6	30.5	330.7	39.9
Chile	18.6	3.0	23.3	58.4	220.7	66.4
Colombia	0.8	7.0	38.6	33.6	193.5	38.7
Mexico	16.7	8.0	46.9	38.2	200.2	59.0
Venezuela	11.6	9.0	38.6	41.3	145.9	30.6
Average	25.7	6.3	33.1	40.0	243.3	41.7
East Asia						
Korea	...	...	...	31.9	85.7	65.6
Malaysia	...	...	...	40.1	60.6	57.7
Singapore	...	...	...	7.7	4.5	86.1
Thailand	...	...	...	36.3	110.5	51.9
Philippines	2.1	1.0	18.5	55.2	200.3	44.9
Average	...	...	...	34.2	92.3	61.2

Source: Reinhart, Rogoff, and Savastano (2003).

was the only country that exhibited behavior similar to that of Latin America.) In addition, it is noteworthy that, while the overall debt to GDP ratio has not been significantly different across the two regions, the ratio of external debt to export earnings in Latin America has been more than twice as high as in East Asia, signaling an important vulnerability for the former region.

As noted earlier, the macroeconomic policy management of East Asia stands in sharp contrast with that of Latin America during the second half of the twentieth century. With the exception of the regional financial crisis of 1997–1998, the East Asian region has been able to maintain relatively low inflation and a sustained, a rapid increase in the growth of real GDP per capita within a framework of relatively sound public finances and an environment of competitive exchange rates and remunerative interest rates. Some of the reasons related to bureaucratic strength that can account for this behavior in East Asia point, as well, to important institutional deficiencies in the Latin American case. For example, most of the governments in East Asia have recognized that the conduct of fiscal and monetary policy, in particular, should be relatively insulated from political interference. Thus, central banks and ministries of finance have been given an important degree of independence from the political process. By contrast, in the case of Latin America, the adoption of such a model for institutional behavior has only emerged as a result of a long struggle to deal with the problems of macroeconomic mismanagement, which has yielded significant improvements in macroeconomic stabilization in a number of countries since the late 1990s.

This traditional point of difference between the two regions ties in with a broader consideration relating to the relative strength of bureaucratic effectiveness in a number of East Asian governments, especially in comparison with that of Latin America, which is explored in more detail in chapter 7. The importance given to practices of sound public administration is certainly consistent with the Confucian tradition of an elite mandarin or administrative corps in states such as Hong Kong, Korea, Singapore, and Taiwan, as well as with the legacy of direct British rule, which placed a high value on sound public administration in states such as Malaysia, Hong Kong, and Singapore. By contrast, there has been no similar tradition in Latin America, or in its colonial heritage, favoring the development of an elite professional bureaucracy. This ideal has only begun to be developed, as a number of governments in the region, such as Chile, Brazil, and Mexico, have recognized the importance of technocratic management of fiscal and monetary policies as a result of long struggles with fiscal instability and problems of inflation.

Another factor that should be considered in explaining East Asia's more dedicated attention to macroeconomic stability is the long-term strategic orientation of governments in that region to issues of economic and development policy. Whether it was in imitation of Japan's experience with "catch-up" development or out of a sense of competition with the alternative development path of communism offered by China and North Korea, governments in East Asia early on in the second half of the twentieth century established economic development as an important long-term strategic goal of state policy. This orientation stands in sharp contrast with the focus of governments in Latin America, which, because of the instability in the region associated with political fragmentation and sharp class and social tensions, were inevitably focused to a great extent on short-term goals and objectives.

The Financial Sector

Until recently, the role of the financial sector has not been given major importance in development studies, in part because it was difficult to determine what were the causal links between financial sector development and economic growth, given their likely two-way interactive effects on each other. However, within the past decade it has now been fairly well established in empirical studies that a sound financial sector does play an important leading role in supporting economic development and that countries with more developed financial sectors tend to experience higher rates of economic growth.[17]

For the comparative analysis of East Asia and Latin America, this causal relationship is particularly striking, as the financial sector has been highly repressed in Latin America, whereas, by contrast, there has been strong evidence of financial deepening in East Asia. It is also the case that the financial sector in Latin America has been highly unstable, as the region has suffered more banking crises, in particular during the last quarter of the twentieth century, than any other region in the global economy. During 1976–2003, for example, the Latin American region experienced 30 systemic banking crises (apart from debt or currency crises), compared with 8 in the East Asian region, most of which occurred in the context of the regional financial crisis of 1997–1998.[18] These crises typically resulted in substantial increases in public debt, along with sharp declines in the level of economic activity and bank lending operations, as governments were required to contribute to the cost of bank restructuring and the recapitalization of the banking sector. Thus, the frequency of boom and bust cycles in the financial sector can be viewed as another factor contributing to Latin America's extreme degree of macroeconomic volatility and "debt intolerance." During the third quarter of the past century, it should be noted, banking crises were a far more rare phenomenon because of the extensive controls that were placed on bank activity and interest rate movements.

The concept of financial depth, which is a commonly used gauge to the development of the financial sector, is usually measured by the ratio of broad money to GDP. Such a measure can also be viewed as the relative share of private savings that is reflected in financial assets. Broad cross-country comparisons have confirmed the relationship that an increase of 10 percentage points in this measure of financial depth is associated with an increase in the growth rate of real GDP per capita of 0.6–1.0 percent.[19] Such a relationship is consistent with the differences in financial depth and real income growth that one can observe between East Asia and Latin America in the latter part of the twentieth century. As shown in Table 5.2, the growth in financial depth in East Asia parallels its strong growth in total savings, and is mirrored in a significant expansion in total bank credit and credit to the private sector, which was essential for that region's successful industrialization drive.

In this context, it is interesting to note that in the neoclassical growth model, there is no role for the financial sector, as with full information and the absence of frictions, investors can transact directly with savers in perfect markets without the need for financial intermediation. But in the real world, the financial sector plays an indispensable role, if it is operating effectively, in bringing savers and investors together by providing convenient financial instruments for individuals or businesses to use in allocating their savings, and by selecting among various investment proposals seeking finance those that offer the best prospects for a sound rate of return. Ideally, it also provides a number of ancillary benefits for a growing economy by supporting the exchange of goods and services through the operations of a sound payments system; by facilitating the trading, diversification, and management of risk; and through the monitoring of investment and the promotion of sound corporate governance that are essential for productive business activity.

It is important to realize that some of the "deep" determinants of finance are similar to those that were examined in chapter 3 in relation to aggregate economic growth. The nature of "colonial origins," as reflected in the distinction between "settler" and "extractive" states, common law and civil law traditions, and protestant and catholic religious orientation, has been found to have a significant influence on financial development, with Latin America sharing each of the three

Table 5.2 Financial savings, bank credit, and real lending rates

	1981–1985	1986–1990	1991–1995	1996–2000	2001–2005	2006–2010
	Money and Quasi-money (as a percent of GDP)					
East Asia	42.5	48.2	47.5	50.8	62.2	72.8
Latin America & the Caribbean	34.3	38.4	34.8	37.9	43.4	46.0
	Bank Credit (as a percent of GDP)					
Total						
East Asia	58	68	81	104	101	100
Latin America & the Caribbean	51	52	45	42	45	44
Private Sector						
East Asia	48	57	79	101	92	90
Latin America & the Caribbean	34	31	29	33	32	35
	Real lending rate (in percent per annum)					
East Asia	13.4	12.5	11.8	11.6	7.8	7.4
Latin America & the Caribbean	31.6	30.1	34.3	29.1	23.1	16.1
	Real exchange rate (2005=100)					
East Asia	180.0	123.8	116.0	117.7	104.2	110.7
Latin America & the Caribbean	162.4	99.7	98.1	108.1	102.6	112.5

Source: World Bank, World Development Indicators.

characteristics listed above that have been shown to act as a deterrent to financial deepening (its extractive, civil law, and catholic origins). In addition, societies that have been subject to strong ethnic, social, or class tensions, again characteristic of Latin America, have typically not experienced strong financial development, as dominant groups seek to expropriate resources and limit access to finance in an effort to maintain effective control of economic resources.[20]

It is also well established that economic and political instability, widespread corruption, and problems of fiscal management can significantly inhibit the growth of the financial sector. Fiscal instability can lead to financial repression because of the government's effective control of the central bank, which leads to a manipulation of the banking system in order to provide a captive market for government debt through high reserve and/or liquid asset requirements, interest rate controls, and the contamination of public banks' balance sheets. In view of Latin America's long history of fiscal instability, as chronicled earlier, the examples of financial abuse just noted have been frequent occurrences. As an exceptional case within East Asia, it is interesting to note that the Philippines, again in similarity with many countries in Latin America, has suffered until recently from a problem of widespread corruption in the public sector along with a long tradition of fiscal dominance of its public financial institutions. After years of political abuse of the central bank, for example, it became technically insolvent, and had to be reorganized with new capital in 1993 as a result of a debt burden that could not be absorbed directly by the central government budget.[21] The new central bank was also given a charter of institutional independence from the central government.

In addition to many of the features of financial disorder noted above, which has been a chronic problem for Latin America, it must be recognized that the frequency of systemic banking crises contributed significantly to the region's public debt burden. Typically, a systemic banking crisis would result in claims on the central government associated with bank restructuring or the recapitalization of public banks, as noted earlier, that were covered by public debt issuance often in the range of 10 to 50 percent of GDP. In this regard, banking crises, along with currency crises, could frequently be the precursor of a public debt crisis, which over time would contribute significantly to the problem of "debt intolerance" that was discussed earlier.

The experience of Latin America has also shown that one of the common antecedents of a systemic banking crisis was an episode of financial liberalization, which was a common occurrence during the last quarter of the twentieth century with the extensive economic reform efforts that governments initiated, consistent with the principles of the "Washington Consensus." One of the most serious examples of this linkage occurred in Chile in the early 1980s as part of the Pinochet government's bold attempts to liberalize economic and financial markets, as recounted in Box 5.1. The liberalization of the financial sector in Chile, which began in the late 1970s, was intended to allow market discipline, as manifested through the free exchange of information and the sound assessment of risk by private bank owners and managers, to replace direct intervention by the government in the operations of the banking sector. Unfortunately, in such an environment, along with lax bank supervision, the government maintained a fixed exchange rate, which created the false expectation on the part of a number of banks of an implicit guarantee on foreign borrowing to finance domestic credit operations. In the context of a strong private sector boom in the early 1980s, a bubble phenomenon developed in real estate activity, in which the banks were heavily involved. Once a change in expectations set in, and foreign creditors began to withdraw short-term lines of credit to domestic banks, there was a sudden drop in the value of the Chilean peso and a sharp contraction in bank credit activity. The major downward adjustment of mortgage values that ensued resulted in substantial losses for banks and the closure of 14 banks and finance institutions. In addition, the ultimate cost of the bank restructuring process for the central government that stretched over 1982–1989 amounted to around 40 percent of GDP.[22]

As a general matter, governments in East Asia tended to monitor the operations of the banking system carefully, consistent with their commitment to macroeconomic stability. As suggested earlier, government oversight of bank activity was maintained for purposes of limiting consumer or mortgage finance and for enforcing prudential requirements to preserve the solvency of banks. Also, public development banks tended to be operated on a commercial basis, with much less political interference than was common in the case of Latin America. Selective credit mechanisms or directed credit were often used as a tool of industrial policy, but consistent with the principles of sound industrial policy as discussed in chapter 6, these operations were subject to close monitoring and suspension in the event that agreed performance targets were not satisfied.[23]

The one exception to this record of sound financial activity was the regional financial crisis of 1997–1998, which, as was often the case in Latin America, was preceded by a period of financial liberalization. In an environment of weak supervision, banks entered into increasingly risky behavior associated with either a bubble phenomenon in real estate or "insider" lending tied to business–bank relationships that were not grounded in sound commercial operations. The preconditions for the crisis were also complicated by the fact that many governments in the region had actively encouraged banks to increase their recourse to short-term funding from abroad in the context of a general move toward external capital account liberalization.[24] This policy had the result of creating a problem of so-called double mismatches in the balance sheets of regional banks whereby risky medium- or long-term loans in local currency were matched by short-term liabilities in foreign currency, creating risks of a maturity mismatch as well as a currency mismatch. Moreover, most banks participating in these kinds of operations came to expect that governments were effectively guaranteeing the exchange risk on their foreign obligations in connection with the maintenance of fixed exchange rates, in a somewhat similar fashion to the experience of banks in Chile in the early 1980s. Because of the extensive nature of foreign financial involvement in the operations of banks (and businesses) in the region, once a panic developed in the case of Thailand in 1997, there were quick repercussions in the form of "sudden stops" and reversals in foreign capital flows that created extensive market turmoil throughout the region. The financial crises in Thailand, Indonesia, and Korea resulted in massive financial assistance from the IMF, major bank and corporate restructuring, and substantial increases in public debt to cover the cost of bailouts and recapitalization efforts.[25]

Latin America has struggled in more recent times with a number of difficult legacies from its history of financial turmoil, which have acted as a constraint on private investment and economic development at least through the end of the past century. One important problem has been the growth of dollarization in the banking and financial systems of the region, which reflected a pervasive lack of confidence within the private sector regarding the risks of maintaining financial assets in local currency and the fragility of domestic banks. In certain cases, such as Ecuador and El Salvador, these concerns led to the abandonment of a local currency at the turn of the new century, and the adoption of the US dollar as the official medium of exchange. In many other cases, banks have had to offer foreign exchange-denominated (usually the US dollar) deposits in order to attract loanable funds from the public. As a result, by 2001, for example, the share of dollar-denominated deposits in total banking system deposits had peaked at around 80 percent for 10 countries in Latin America, with a somewhat lower share for the dollarized share of credit operations.[26] (By contrast, the only country in East Asia that has experienced dollarization is Cambodia, which is not surprising given its recent history of political and economic turmoil.) One consequence of dollarization is that it institutionalizes, in effect, the problem of "double mismatches" within the banking system, noted earlier, because of the imbalance in the impact of dollarization on the asset and liability side of banks' balance sheets. Once in place, dollarization becomes difficult to eradicate, although it should be noted that the incidence of dollarization in Latin America was reduced significantly in the past decade with the region-wide improvement in fiscal and monetary management, discussed earlier, and in macroeconomic conditions more generally.

The problem of financial repression and crises in Latin America has also been reflected in a tendency for interest rate spreads and lending rates to be very high as a result of the perception of high risk in the banking system. This perception of risk was usually associated with a history of high and volatile inflation and inefficiencies in banking operations arising from the heavy burden of legal reserve requirements and bank transactions taxes, weak collateral requirements for lending, and high bank administrative costs. On the one hand, private businesses and individuals have demanded a high risk premium for the placement of financial savings in local currency bank deposits, while, on the other hand, bank managers have only been willing to grant loans to their customers at shorter maturities and with a high risk premium in the rates they charge for their loans. In Brazil, for example, the problem of high lending rates and spreads has been particularly acute, as at the beginning of the past decade deposit rates averaged in the range of 20–30 percent, whereas lending rates tended to be in the range of 60–70 percent, even though the annual rate of inflation was less than 10 percent, on average. Only in the past few years have the central bank and private banks in that country been able to lower these rates gradually, through a downward adjustment of policy rates, lower inflation, and improved administrative practices on the part of the banks. Notwithstanding this progress, Brazil continues to have the highest level of real lending rates among the emerging market economies, with rates for consumer credit ranging from 20 to 35 percent for loans that are typically available only on a short-term basis, in an environment in which the rate of inflation continues to be in the single digits.

The World Bank has recently developed a set of comprehensive criteria and quantitative measures for judging the access, depth, efficiency, and stability of financial systems in countries around the world for the period 2008–2010 in its first Global Financial Development Report.[27] The regional averages for the four quantitative measures just mentioned for countries in East Asia and Latin America strongly confirm the more robust features of financial institutions and financial markets in the former region, as well as their more positive contribution to macroeconomic stability and economic growth that was portrayed in this chapter.

CHAPTER 6

Economic Policy Choices—Savings, Investment, and Industrialization

This chapter examines the role of economic policy choices in determining the very divergent patterns of industrialization and export performance that can be observed between East Asia and Latin America since the middle of the past century. Obviously, these patterns were significantly affected by differences in the macroeconomic policy framework of the two regions, which had important implications for savings and investment as a basis for promoting industrialization. However, in addition, industrial policy played an important role in determining East Asia's earlier orientation toward export-oriented industrialization and Latin America's strong attachment to import-substitution industrialization.

Savings, Investment, and Industrialization

In the light of the contrasts in the macroeconomic policy management between East Asia and Latin America discussed in the previous chapter, it should not be surprising to learn that there has been a marked divergence since the 1960s in the behavior of savings and investment in the two regions. While the value of national savings and investment as a ratio to GDP has remained relatively unchanged or has declined somewhat in Latin America during the past four and half decades, these ratios have nearly doubled in the case of East Asia over the same time period. Moreover, national savings has typically exceeded domestic investment in the case of East Asia implying less reliance on foreign borrowing, whereas the opposite has been true for Latin America, which has exhibited a heavy reliance on foreign capital inflows. This latter pattern is consistent with the problem of "debt intolerance" in Latin America that was discussed in the previous chapter.

One can point to a number of problematic concerns about the macroeconomic policy framework in Latin America discussed earlier that would have been a deterrent to a more robust behavior of savings and investment. The variability of output growth and inflation, as well as the volatility of the real rate of interest and limits on access to foreign exchange, would have created a climate of uncertainty for investment and unclear signals for efficient resource allocation. These factors also would have discouraged the mobilization of savings in the financial system and encouraged the transfer of savings abroad, including by way of disguised capital flight if exchange controls prevented foreign financial investment through the official exchange market.

In the case of East Asia, national savings was generated not only at the personal level, but also within the corporate and government sectors. Saving by individuals seems to have been responsive to a number of government interventions. In addition to an environment in which deposit rates of interest were generally positive in real terms, saving was encouraged through easy access to national postal savings systems in some countries, as well as by high contribution requirements for participation in pension fund schemes such as the Central Provident Funds of Malaysia and Singapore. Generally, retirement benefit programs, where available, were based on a defined-contribution basis, rather than a defined-benefit basis that was more common in Latin America where the presence of trade unions was stronger. Another way in which government policy interventions could have played a role in fostering high savings in East Asia is through the application of high taxes on consumer goods and restrictions on domestic bank credit for the purchase of consumer durables. Throughout most of the second half of the twentieth century, strict limitations were in place on the transfer of savings abroad via the exchange system. In the case of China today, which still lags the rest of East Asia in the level of its per capita real income, all of the factors described above have been at work in driving a high rate of personal savings, in addition to an apparent, strong cultural trait to save in the absence of government funding for education, health care, and retirement. All of these factors promoting a high rate of savings were geared toward the financing of investment in an environment where rapid industrialization was being encouraged.

Another important factor influencing the growth in savings in the early post–World War II decades in East Asia was the "demographic transition" that was associated with a sequential decline in the rate of mortality and the rate of fertility. This "double decline" would not have been possible without the availability of new medicines to control the onset of disease and modern techniques of family planning. China's "one child" policy could be seen as a blunt form of government intervention to achieve a demographic transition at a more accelerated pace than occurred more naturally in the rest of East Asia. The medium-term effect of the demographic transition was to bring about a drop in the dependency ratio and a rise in the available labor force during 1965–1990, when governments in the region were launching a major drive toward industrialization, thus giving rise to a "demographic dividend." In a seminal study by Bloom and Williamson (1998), it was estimated that roughly one-third to one-half of East Asia's exceptional growth in real output per capita during the period just noted (of around 6%) could be attributed to the savings and labor force growth associated with this demographic dividend.

In Latin America, a demographic transition has been much slower and more muted in its manifestation, in part because a strong Catholic tradition in the region would have discouraged the use of family planning techniques, whereas lower fertility rates have traditionally not been encouraged, as opportunities for female education and labor force participation have been limited. More generally, the buoyancy of personal savings has been dampened by high levels of income inequality in the LAC region.

In regard to investment, as noted earlier, it is clear from the discussion in chapter 5 that the general macroeconomic environment was far more favorable in East Asia than in Latin America. Sustained investment and industrial development can only take place if certain economic and political conditions are present. The absence of macroeconomic stability in Latin America for much of the second half of the twentieth century was obviously a serious deterrent to private sector investment planning and business development, other than for short-term profits and speculative activity. In addition to macroeconomic stability, clarity and predictability in the policy environment must be viewed as an essential prerequisite for productive capital accumulation and capacity building in the private sector, along with clear safeguards for the protection of property rights. Generally, governments in East Asia were much more successful in meeting these conditions than were their counterparts in Latin America.

More specifically, governments in East Asia have taken a number of specific actions to encourage investment through the development of sound infrastructure and the promotion of technological capability by means of labor skills development, factory-based training programs, and the encouragement of business clusters actively engaged in applied R&D and medium- and high-tech manufacturing. One innovation in the development of new manufacturing activity, which was pioneered in East Asia and has become ubiquitous within developing countries in more recent times, was the creation of special economic or export processing zones (SEZs/EPZs). These zones were developed to accelerate the process of creating high-class conditions for new business development in a targeted area, for example, in terms of basic infrastructure, regulatory frameworks, and trade logistics, by countries where these conditions might not have been more generally available. More recently, China has relied extensively on these institutional arrangements to foster foreign direct investment in the creation of assembly operations for high-tech manufacturing equipment.

Another important ingredient in the investment promotion campaigns of successful East Asian governments was the establishment of high-level "deliberation councils" to facilitate the exchange of information between business representatives and government policy makers on the possibilities for new business development and the policy requirements to support such activity.[1] (These councils are discussed in more detail in chapter 7.) Often these councils, or public–private alliances, included a representative of labor groups, as well. By contrast, business, labor, and government in Latin America have traditionally operated in a more conflictive environment, depending on the nature of the government in power, whereas business–government relations have been characterized more by rent-seeking behavior than arms-length consultation on business needs and the direction of government policy.

In recent years, a number of efforts at the international level have been launched to try to provide a more quantitative evaluation of the business and investment environment in emerging market economies (in particular, in East Asia and Latin America), which have tended to validate the general comments presented above regarding the more favorable investment climate sustained in East Asia than in Latin America. One of these is the World Bank's *Ease of Doing Business* indicators (DBI), which score countries across the globe on a range of measures affecting the promotion of investment, such as the time involved in starting a business or enforcing contracts, access to credit, the protection of property rights, and ease of cross-border trade.[2] In each of the eight categories monitored by the Bank, in recent years, East Asia has shown a clear advantage over Latin America (Table 6.1). As a result of these

Table 6.1 World Bank doing business indicators

Overall	2006	2008	2010	2012
East Asia (EA)	48	51	51	47
Latin America and the Caribbean (LAC)	76	85	93	94
Starting a Business				
EA	...	88	80	71
LAC	...	89	105	103
Getting Credit				
EA	...	41	52	53
LAC	...	68	67	69
Enforcing Contracts				
EA	...	52	53	50
LAC	...	98	103	104
Trading Across Borders				
EA	...	29	28	25
LAC	...	87	87	83
Protecting Investors				
EA	...	49	55	51
LAC	...	77	82	91

Note: Data are for average country rankings.
Source: World Bank, Doing Business indicators.

scores, six of the nine countries in East Asia have usually clustered in the top third of the 178 countries surveyed by the Bank, with Singapore and Hong Kong commonly ranked among the top five. Indonesia and the Philippines have tended to be outliers for the East Asia region, with marked deficiencies in some areas. By contrast, only three countries in Latin America (Chile, Mexico, and Peru) have been placed within the top third of the country rankings, with the average rank for Latin America somewhat below the mid-point of the full country rankings and that of East Asia in the top third.

While these indicators are only available from the middle of the past decade, it would seem that the significant differences in the current readings for the two regions can be extrapolated back in time based on what we know about the marked divergence in their pattern of investment and industrialization over time. The degree to which Latin America today generally shows such a marked deficiency in the quality of its investment climate in comparison with that of East Asia reveals how the history of economic and political instability in the former region has placed a burden on its growth prospects and potential.

Another survey that dates from about the same time as that of the World Bank, which has received much attention in country evaluations by international agencies and financial market institutions, is the *Global Competitiveness Index* (GCI) of the World Economic Forum.[3] This survey covers a very broad array of country economic characteristics, which have a bearing not only on the investment climate, but also on a country's ability to operate competitively in a globalized economy. Accordingly, the GCI ranks countries across a range of 12 characteristics, including the quality of their infrastructure and educational and training facilities; the efficiency of goods, labor, and financial markets; and the extent of technological readiness and capacity for innovation. Again, over the past decade, there has been a persistent difference in the results of this survey in favor of East Asia, with its average score gradually increasing to around 5 (out of a maximum of 7), and that for Latin America relatively stable at around 4. By country rankings, East Asia, on average, has been well within the top third of the countries surveyed, while Latin America has been somewhat below the mid-point of the 144 countries covered by the index. As in the case of the DBI, these results are broadly consistent with the trends one can observe in the strength of East Asia's industrialization drive over the past decades and the greater participation of the region's manufacturing sector in global export markets relative to that of Latin America.

What is particularly striking in the GCI results is that Latin America shows a marked discrepancy vis-à-vis East Asia in three categories, in particular, namely, the quality of its infrastructure, the strength of its macroeconomic environment, and its ability to innovate. The macroeconomic dimension needs no further comment in the light of the discussion in the previous chapter, but more can be said about infrastructure and innovation. The quality of infrastructure is a critical component of a country's developmental potential and capacity to participate in international trade. In this respect, surveys by the World Bank have shown that Latin America is particularly weak, in comparison with East Asia, in the quality of its trade and transport infrastructure, as well as other aspects of its logistics capabilities.[4] As discussed further below, this deficiency has prevented Latin America from participating to the same extent as East Asia in global production networks, which have become a key factor in determining opportunities for growth and development among emerging market economies.

One important reason why Latin America has fallen short with respect to East Asia in the quality of its infrastructure and logistics capabilities is that public investment in this area has been much lower than in the latter region. Unfortunately, this result can be traced to the fiscal consolidation effort that most countries in the Latin American region carried out during the second half of the 1980s and into the 1990s, which led to major cutbacks in public expenditure and tax increases, as governments had to respond to financial crises and the withdrawal of foreign financing. Unfortunately, public expenditure cuts were skewed toward infrastructure development, in part because of the political difficulties of curtailing public consumption in the form of wages and pension benefits. It has been estimated that cuts in public spending for infrastructure maintenance and development by Latin America accounted for roughly 40 percent of the improvement in its primary fiscal balance between the early 1980s and late 1990s.[5] In addition, studies carried out by the World Bank have estimated that cuts in public infrastructure investment in the LAC region were on the order of 2 percentage points of GDP and reduced public spending in this area by roughly half of what it was in the early 1980s. While these cuts had a short-term fiscal benefit, they also clearly have had a significant long-term economic cost in terms of foregone future output, as many studies have shown a strong correlation between infrastructure spending and the growth in real per capita income. In the case of Latin America, it has been estimated that the region's rate of economic growth 1980–2005 was reduced by around 2 percentage points below what it could have been, if public infrastructure spending had been maintained at its level of the early 1980s.[6] This estimate would account for around one-third of the gap in real per capita income growth between East Asia and Latin America during that time period.

One might think that a large part of the cuts in public infrastructure spending could have been offset by private investment in infrastructure either through direct privatization or concessions (i.e., public–private partnerships). As part of a general worldwide trend, private investment in infrastructure in Latin America surged in the 1990s, but this spending tended to be skewed toward certain sectors such as telecommunications where, because of the technology involved and growing demand for services, pay-back times for private investors were relatively short. Some infrastructural sectors thus have remained heavily dependent on public outlays, while in other cases ambiguities in contracts have left governments in many countries still burdened with significant commitments for infrastructure spending.

The other significant deficiency in the WEF's global competitiveness index for Latin America vis-à-vis East Asia that bears comment is in regard to its readiness for innovation. The establishment of a framework for promoting technological innovation has become an essential requirement for developing countries in a globalized economy because of the increasing technological basis of traded goods and services. More generally, technological improvements go hand in hand with the process of structural change and industrialization that is at the heart of economic development. As discussed in chapter 2, East Asia and Latin America have experienced very different patterns of productivity growth in the course of their recent economic development, which have been key drivers of their divergent paths of real output growth. Specifically, the component of productivity growth related to structural change in the economy has been significantly positive in the case of East Asia, whereas that same component has had a significantly negative effect on the overall productivity growth in the Latin American region.[7] This important difference between the two regions can be attributed, in part at least, to the impact of technological change and innovation in supporting the process of structural change. In this context, it is useful to recall from the discussion in chapters 2 and 3 that diversification over time in the scope of industrial production and in the shares of sectoral employment has been identified as a defining feature of structural change in the early stages of development.[8]

The capacity to support innovation needs to be placed within the broader scope of a country's development of technological capability. This latter concept relates to the set of arrangements (which often go by the name of "national innovation systems") that a country offers in terms of the strength of its tertiary educational facilities in science and technology, the skill base of its labor force, the strength of technological public goods required by industry, such as basic research, extension services, standards and metrology, and the ability of local businesses to adapt their internal production processes to accommodate new technologies.[9] Experience has shown that technological absorption and innovation by firms has been fostered most effectively by the development of clusters of related businesses and R&D facilities that create so-called agglomeration effects arising from the synergy and positive externalities associated with such arrangements. Often governments have a critical role to play in promoting technological clusters by facilitating business contacts with university-based research centers and by constructing high-class infrastructure for SEZs/EPZs and encouraging targeted forms of foreign direct investment.

The role of technological capability in the development process has received much attention from economists who have pursued a structural or evolutionist approach to economic development, in view of their dissatisfaction with the postulates of the neoclassical growth model. This contrast first came to prominence in the mid-1990s with the debate between the "accumulationists" and "assimilationists" on the causes for the so-called East Asian growth "miracle," as recounted in chapter 3. Essentially, as noted earlier, that debate pointed to the inadequacy of the neoclassical growth model as regards its implicit assumption that technological improvements were freely available to all countries and that each country faced few barriers or deterrents in their ability to absorb these public goods. A number of development studies have shown this assumption to be highly unrealistic, as it fails to recognize the range of tacit requirements that need to be satisfied in the process of basic technological absorption that makes industrialization possible.[10] Some technologies, for example, those associated with relatively low-tech, labor-intensive manufacturing production (e.g., for garments and leather goods), are mainly embodied in the equipment imported for factory use, which do not require extensive training and technological know-how to operate. However, the transition to a more sophisticated level of manufacturing (e.g., auto manufacturing) has a number of tacit elements of technological development beyond the acquisition of the required machinery and equipment that deal with the skill training of workers and the mastery of factory work procedures in areas such as quality management, procurement, inventory control, and outbound logistics. In addition, the ability to carry out and apply basic R&D processes becomes important as more complex technologies are involved. Over time, the process of technological absorption and development becomes a cumulative and path-dependent process.

By comparison with Latin America, East Asia has been far more successful in its development of technological capability, as reflected in international surveys such as those conducted by the World Economic Forum. These surveys typically identify a range of indicators that highlight certain aspects of technological capability, such as tertiary education enrollments in science and technology, telecommunication networks, outlays on R&D, and payments for licensing and royalties. In addition, the United Nations Industrial Development Organization (UNIDO) has devoted considerable resources to the collection of these kinds of data, which are summarized in the case of East Asia and Latin America in Table 6.2. These data show that East Asia already had a technological advantage over Latin America by the mid-1980s, which has increased since then.

Anecdotally, the superiority of East Asia's effort to acquire technological capability can be seen in the following description of the efforts by Hyundai factory workers in Korea to develop a command of automobile manufacturing and design:

Table 6.2 Drivers of technological capability

Group or region	Skills		Technological effort		FDI		Technology imports		ICT infrastructure	
	Tertiary technical enrollment (per 1000 of population)		R&D per capita (dollars)		FDI per capita (dollars)		Royalties and technical fees per capita (dollars)		Telephone mainlines (per 1000 of population)	Personal computers (per 1000 of population)
	1985	1998	1985	1998	1981–85	1993–97	1985	1998	1998	1998
Industrialized Countries	34.3	40.1	122.3	402.4	54.8	241.6	12	66.2	571.1	316.5
Developing Countries (o/w)	6.3	8.7	0.6	4.6	4.3	26.9	0.6	3.9	62.6	14.2
East Asia	4.6	9.2	...	8.7	4.3	39.7	...	7.1	82.7	19.3
East Asia excl. China	12.3	21.2	3.2	31.0	14.5	63.3	2.7	26.6	119.3	48.6
Latin America and the Caribbean	16.6	17.3	1.1	6.3	11.1	70.4	1.9	5.3	122.3	33.3

Source: UNIDO, Industrial Development Report 2004.

"Hyundai's efforts to develop a car began in the 1960s. It purchased foreign equipment, hired expatriate consultants, and signed licensing agreements with foreign firms. But the process was not a simple matter of adopting the technology. Despite the training and consultant services of a foreign consultant and three experts, Hyundai engineers repeated trials and errors for 14 months before creating the first prototype. The engine block broke into pieces at its first test. New Prototype engines appeared almost every week, only to break in testing. No one on the team could figure out why the prototype kept breaking down—casting serious doubts, even among Hyundai management, on the company's ability to develop a competitive engine."

"The team had to scrap eleven more broken prototypes before one survived the test. There were 288 engine design changes, 156 in 1986 alone. Ninety-seven test engines were made before Hyundai refined its natural aspiration and turbocharger engines. 53 more engines were produced for durability improvement, 88 more for developing a car, 26 more for developing its transmission, and 6 more for other tests, totaling 324 test engines. In addition, more than 200 transmissions and 150 test vehicles were created before Hyundai perfected them in 1992. In 2003, Hyundai sold more than 2 million vehicles around the world."[11]

By comparison with Korea's struggle for technological mastery captured in the quotation just cited, it is interesting to consider the case of Argentina in the 1960s and 1970s, one of the most industrialized countries of the Latin American region at the time. The main auto manufacturing facilities in Argentina during that time were dedicated to the assembly of completely knocked down (CKD) kits of Ford "falcon" sedans of a 1950s vintage, which were sold at relatively high prices in a heavily protected domestic market. This assembly operation required a relatively low level of technological skill, and did not lend itself to adaptation and upgrading in the manufacturing of automobiles, in part because of the lack of domestic competition and the absence of a government policy requirement to meet export market qualifications. Ideally, it was expected that elements of a domestic supply chain would be developed to support the existing assembly operations, but these linkages in practice proved difficult to establish. This experience, which was typical of many developing countries at the time, points again to the impressive example of Korea in mastering the development of a globally competitive auto manufacturing industry with its full supply chain, in much the same way that Japan did in an earlier decade.

The development of technological capability in practice is often guided by official industrial policy. This is a controversial topic in the study and practice of economic development, in that there are as many proponents, as opponents, for the use of such policy, depending on one's view of the relative importance of market failure and government failure in the development process. The case for industrial policy is usually advanced on the basis of various kinds of market failure in developing countries dealing with: (a) coordination failures in cases where complementary investments may be required for a project to be developed; (b) the appropriability of returns for a new business via rents where knowledge spillovers and/or significant scale economies are present; (c) access to finance for a new, unproven venture with significant potential for market development; and (d) information externalities. On the opposing side, the case against industrial policy rests uniquely on the practicality of implementing policies to meet the market failures identified above and the inevitability of errors on the part of government in "picking winners" in the context of targeted industrial policy.[12]

In the context of this discussion, it is useful to distinguish first between the so-called functional and selective aspects of industrial policy. Functional industrial policy is relatively noncontroversial, and refers to efforts of governments to provide critical physical infrastructure (ports, highways, etc.), as well as a variety of other public goods in the area of education, training, and innovation noted earlier, along with export promotion facilities. Government activity in these areas is nonspecific as to the kind of industry that is promoted, but can nevertheless be very effective in dealing with certain coordination failures in development by providing the communication, transport, and port facilities that make private sector industrial activity possible, by eliminating certain information deficiencies, or by facilitating contacts with foreign buyers and investors that would benefit export-oriented business activity. By contrast, selective industrial policy is more sector-specific and is intended to promote industrial activity in certain specific areas that meet a strategic policy objective of the government, such as auto manufacturing in the case of Korea. The challenge in the latter area is to design government interventions in a way that are consistent with a country's inherent potential for dynamic comparative advantage.[13]

More recently, there has been a revival of interest in the use of industrial policy, which tended to fade after the debt crisis of the 1980s and the growing influence of the "Washington Consensus." In its current formulation, which draws on some of the lessons from successful application of industrial policy in East Asia during its early period of export-oriented industrialization, the basic idea is that government can play a useful role in creating the conditions in which entrepreneurs can try out new ventures and discover the market potential for some of their manufacturing initiatives. One essential ingredient in this process of "self-discovery," as it has been called, is an institutional arrangement for close government–business consultation (through the use, e.g., of "deliberation councils" noted earlier) so that business entrepreneurs can identify key bottlenecks or constraints that they face in bringing a new manufacturing process into operation, and government officials can provide useful information on the marketing potential at home or abroad of products that are consistent with a country's endowment of resources, labor skills, and managerial experience.[14]

In the case of East Asia, governments initially favored import-substitution industrialization as a means of promoting economic development, but given the relatively small domestic markets of the four Asian NIEs, a shift was made in the 1960s toward export-oriented industrialization. To some extent, this shift was fostered by foreign direct investment from Japan consistent with the "flying geese" model discussed in chapter 4, as well as by a conscious imitation on the part of other East Asian governments of Japan's successful industrialization drive. In order to promote initially labor-intensive manufacturing with an export orientation that was followed by more capital-intensive manufacturing with a significant technological component, governments employed a variety of industrial policy instruments involving tariff protection, subsidized credit, and tax concessions. As a basis for these interventions, the authorities were clear about their strategic goals for export development, and ensured that essential intermediate inputs for manufacturing and final export goods were transacted at a competitive exchange rate and world market prices.[15] In more recent times, China has adopted this approach to the promotion of manufactured exports, while modifying it through the shift from a competitive to an undervalued exchange rate as a new form of industrial policy instrument.

By contrast, Latin America's early post–World War II industrialization effort was heavily weighted toward import substitution with nearly exclusive reliance on traditional commodity exports to offset the high costs of imports for the industrial sector. This approach was fully consistent with the structuralist ideology of ECLA and its suspicion of global market forces. Industrial policy was strongly supportive of this industrialization effort by means of large credit support from public development agencies, high tariff protection averaging over 100 percent in nominal terms (and much higher in effective terms), and a complex array of exchange subsidies and taxes that yielded a substantial degree of exchange rate overvaluation. The relative price distortions and economic cost of this kind of system were quite significant according to a number of historical accounts.[16] In addition, the burden on the balance of payments was increased by the fact that governments tended to neglect the needs of the agricultural sector, as noted earlier, in contrast with the experience of East Asia.

The difference across the two regions in their approach to industrialization was matched by different styles of industrial policy. In the case of the East Asian NIEs, industrialization was framed within medium-term development plans and managed by a lead agency with broad coordinating authority across government agencies. In order to minimize the risk of government failure, industrial policy for targeted sectors generally followed a certain set of rules that included the following elements: Special incentives and other government support were applied to new industrial ventures as distinct from existing ones; specific performance targets, usually in terms of export viability, were agreed between the administering agency and a local business seeking government support; strict monitoring of interim benchmarks consistent with agreed targets was enforced to allow for the suspension of government support in the event of major deviations; and clear sunset provisions were established to signal the termination of government benefits. In the case of Korea, the administration of industrial policy during the 1970s involving the kind of rules just described was accompanied by the assignment of special monetary awards for enterprises that exceeded export targets from a high-level government committee chaired by the president of the Republic. Such an arrangement left no doubt in the mind of participating enterprises of the strategic importance that the government, at the highest level, attached to the achievement of certain national export goals.

As a general proposition, the administration of industrial policy in Latin America in the period prior to 1980 followed a more haphazard pattern. While indicative, multiyear development plans were common, the criteria used in the selection of industries to be protected were not clear, and the range of instruments used were not well coordinated. In many cases, protection was open ended and not subject to the kind of rules described above. As a result, much of the protection degenerated into a form of rent seeking on the part of favored businesses that had close ties with government officials or significant political influence in industrial policy decision making.[17]

The early industrialization experience in the two regions led to a strong debate over the relative merits of import substitution and export orientation in the development of the manufacturing sector as a spur to sustained economic growth.[18] In the case of Latin America, some accounts provide a fairly positive assessment of its growth experience prior to 1980 during its phase of heavy import-substitution industrialization in view of the relatively high rates of real output growth that were sustained, even though they were lower than those of East Asia. However, in view of the strong dependence on imported inputs and foreign indebtedness of this industrialization phase in Latin America and the severe inefficiencies that it created, it is clear in retrospect that this effort was unsustainable. Major academic studies, such as that by Bhagwati (1978) and Krueger (1978), and then the impact of the debt crisis of the early 1980s, led to a major change in the prevailing policy debate to one of how developing countries could support export-oriented industrialization. This debate has been reinforced by the rapid globalization of trade and the growing phenomenon of GPNs that has led to a fundamental change in the way production for exports is managed, which is discussed later on in this chapter.

The degree to which East Asia's industrialization effort has been more successful than that of Latin America can be gauged by the fact that the pattern of structural change within the regional economy has been much more pronounced in East Asia than in Latin America. From 1965 to 2000, for example, the share of the agricultural sector in total GDP in East Asia declined, on average, from around 37 percent to 8 percent, while the share of value added in the manufacturing sector rose from around 16 percent to 26 percent. In line with the sequential pattern of development within East Asia, this shift occurred at a somewhat earlier date among the NIE or "tiger" economies than it did for the ASEAN-4 and for China. Nevertheless, the shift in the relative share of the two sectors in favor of manufacturing has continued into the first decade of the new century, albeit at a slower pace than before. By contrast, in Latin America, there was a decline in the relative shares of both agriculture and industry between 1965 and 2000, which has been followed by a gradual recovery in the case of agriculture attendant upon the sharp improvement in the terms of trade for agricultural exports during the first decade of the new century. The declining trend for manufacturing is suggestive of a process of deindustrialization, which has been particularly marked since 1980 in the case of South America. The shares of manufacturing for Mexico, Central America, and the Caribbean have tended to stabilize in more recent years, in part reflecting the preferential trade arrangements for these subregions within NAFTA and the Caribbean Basin Initiative (Table 6.3).

The contrast between the two regional economies in their industrialization experience can be more sharply drawn when one examines the

Table 6.3 Relative shares of agriculture and manufacturing: East Asia and Latin America and the Caribbean (in percent of GDP)

	1965	1980	2000	2005	2010
East Asia					
Agriculture	36.9	20.4	8.4	7.5	7.9
Manufacturing	16.5	24.8	25.9	25.6	27.2
China					
Agriculture	37.9	30.2	15.1	12.1	10.1
Manufacturing	29.2	40.2	32.1	32.5	29.6
NIEs (Hong Kong, Korea, Singapore, and Taiwan)					
Agriculture	13.1	5.9	1.6	1.2	0.9
Manufacturing	14.3	26.0	19.5	18.9	26.3
ASEAN 4 (Indonesia, Malaysia, the Philippines, and Thailand)					
Agriculture	36.0	23.7	11.8	11.1	12.6
Manufacturing	13.9	20.4	29.2	28.9	27.0
Latin America and the Caribbean					
Agriculture	19.8	14.0	9.1	8.9	10.1
Manufacturing	21.2	19.7	17.0	16.4	15.7
Mexico					
Agriculture	13.7	9.0	4.2	3.7	3.9
Manufacturing	19.5	22.3	20.3	18.4	18.0
Central America and Caribbean					
Agriculture	7.0	5.9	9.5	10.1	12.6
Manufacturing	14.0	13.7	17.2	15.8	14.6
South America					
Agriculture	10.3	7.6	6.7	7.9	7.5
Manufacturing	24.0	22.1	16.7	15.9	11.8

Source: World Bank, World Development Indicators.

technological content and export orientation of their manufacturing sectors. In this connection, the staff at UNIDO has developed an index of *Competitive Industrial Performance* (CIP), which captures these two dimensions by combining the following six measures of manufacturing capabilities into one index: manufacturing value added on a per capita basis, exports of manufactured goods on a per capita basis, the share of manufacturing in GDP, the share of medium- and high-tech goods in total manufacturing, the share of manufactured exports in total exports, and the share of medium- and high-tech manufactured exports in total exports.[19] Unfortunately, these data are only available since 1980, but already as of that date, the CIP index showed a clear superiority of the industrial sector in East Asia, with a composite CIP value double that of Latin America, reflecting particularly large differences

Table 6.4 Index of competitive industrial performance (CIP)

	1980	1990	2000	2005
East Asia				
CIP Index (average for the region)	0.323	0.394	0.465	0.378
Manufacturing Value Added (MVA) per capita (US Dollars)	770.9	1270.1	1911.0	2119.2
Manufactured exports per capita (US Dollars)	1507.7	3059.1	5826.5	8347.0
Share of Medium and High Tech activities in MVA (percent)	38.8	46.3	57.3	45.4
Share of MVA in GDP (percent)	24.7	26.5	28.6	26.2
Share of Medium and High Tech goods in manufactured exports (percent)	24.4	40.7	60.8	65.6
Share of manufactured goods in total exports (percent)	66.7	80.7	92.7	90.9
Latin America & the Caribbean	1980	1990	2000	2005
CIP Index (average for the region)	0.200	0.199	0.236	0.178
MVA per capita (US Dollars)	433.1	396.3	473.6	640.1
Manufactured exports per capita (US Dollars)	294.4	228.9	856.4	1266.7
Share of Medium and High Tech activities in MVA (percent)	25.6	27.4	27.6	25.7
Share of MVA in GDP (percent)	17.8	17.3	17.1	14.9
Share of Medium and High Tech goods in manufactured exports (percent)	26.3	27.8	35.8	33.9
Share of manufactured goods in total exports (percent)	37.0	40.6	59.3	64.3

Source: UNIDO Industrial Reports (2004, 2009).

in the components for manufacturing value added and exports on a per capita basis. By the end of the past century, the value of this index had expanded by nearly two-thirds in the case of East Asia, and was roughly double that for Latin America, reflecting a very rapid growth in medium- and high-tech manufacturing activities in sectoral output and exports (Table 6.4).

Clearly, one important factor that has been driving this disparate behavior of the manufacturing sector in the two regions is the weak performance and lack of competitiveness of Latin America's manufactured exports. This outcome has a lot to do with the impact of foreign direct investment and GPNs in the two regions, as well as the legacy of weak technological capability and industrial competitiveness of the ISI era, which became more of a burden for Latin America in the wake of the region's major efforts of external liberalization initiated after 1980. Latin

America's major opening to foreign trade and investment after 1980 also stimulated strong foreign demand for its natural resource-based commodities, in particular with the positive shift in the terms of trade for agricultural and mining exports in the first decade of the new century. These issues are discussed further in the final section of this chapter.

The External Sector

As in other dimensions of economic performance discussed above, there has been a marked divergence between the two regions in the extent of their integration with the global economy, which has had an important impact on the pace and quality of their economic development. The cumulative effect of research studies during the past 15 years has confirmed the fact that "trade is good for growth, and growth is good for poverty reduction."[20] The most recent official endorsement of this conclusion can be found in the report of the World Bank's Growth Commission (Growth Commission 2008). More recently, however, an important qualification to this renewed interest in trade and development has been added, namely, that "what you export matters for growth," which is highly relevant to an understanding of the sharp difference in the growth trajectories of East Asia and Latin America.[21] In a world of highly globalized trade, structural change in the composition of exports is as important for economic growth, as it is for the internal activity structure of the economy. Moreover, the increasing diversification of exports has been shown to be an important hallmark of high-growth economies, confirming the important finding of Imbs and Wacziarg (2003), noted earlier, that countries that had experienced high rates of economic growth also exhibited a significant diversification in the structure of their domestic sectoral production and employment.

This finding is at variance with the standard conclusion from traditional trade theory, which is that countries should specialize in the trade of commodities for which they have a static comparative advantage based on their endowments (both natural and technological). Instead, in a world of highly globalized trade, the challenge for developing countries is to discover how they can diversify their export structure by moving into sectors in which they may not have an existing comparative advantage, but which offer the potential for higher productivity gains from trade if they can master the associated technological component (latent comparative advantage). East Asia has generally been far more successful than Latin America in meeting that development challenge.

Table 6.5 East Asia (EA) and Latin America and the Caribbean (LAC) in global trade

	1980	1990	2000	2010
Share of World Exports (in percent)				
EA	6	9	15	21
LAC	3	3	3	4
Share of World Imports (in percent)				
EA	6	9	14	19
LAC	3	2	3	3
Ratio of Manufactured Exports to MVA				
Asia	1.74	2.41	3.05	5.65
China	...	0.37	0.52	1.14
NIEs	1.88	2.58	3.24	6.38
LAC	0.34	0.38	1.01	1.10
o/w Mexico	0.06	0.27	1.86	1.87

Note: For ratio of Manufactured Exports to MVA, the last year presented is 2009 instead of 2010.

Source: UN COMTRADE Data and IMF, World Economic Outlook, and World Bank, World Development Indicators.

According to a standard measure of trade openness (i.e., the ratio of exports and imports to GDP), East Asia has demonstrated far more dynamism in its trade development than Latin America, which has reflected the strength of its industrialization effort. Since the 1960s, the average share of trade in GDP for East Asia has nearly tripled until the past decade when it was roughly double that of Latin America (as noted in Table 2.2). As a result of these trends, East Asia's share of global exports and imports more than doubled between 1980 and 2000, while the comparable shares for Latin America remained relatively unchanged (Table 6.5).

Within the East Asian regional aggregate, the rise of China has been even more dramatic, starting from a very low base in 1980. Within global trade, the growth of exports from East Asia has been particularly strong, along with the competitiveness and expansion of its manufacturing sector. As the manufacturing sector of East Asia expanded, so too did the share of its manufactured exports in total exports, as well as the share of medium- and high-technology goods in its manufactured exports. These components of its export trade have been the main factors that have accounted for the substantial difference between East Asia and Latin America in UNIDO's measure of industrial competitiveness (CIP), as noted earlier. As a result, one can observe a very marked difference in the technological content of exports from the two regions, with a doubling of the share of manufactured exports in total exports for East Asia from 1983 to 2006, mainly on account of the rapid rate of growth in high-tech manufactured export goods. During this period, the largest components of Latin America's export trade have been raw materials and natural resource-based manufactures.[22]

In line with these export developments, one can observe a striking difference in Table 6.5 between the two regions in the ratio of manufactured exports to manufacturing value added, with that for East Asia rising from around 2 ½ in 1990 to 5 ½ in 2010. The only way such a ratio above the value of unity can make sense is by recognizing the significant growth in the role of global production networks in East Asian trade, as a result of which certain goods may transit customs borders more than once as they undergo different stages of processing in various country locations within the network. The only country in Latin America that has experienced a similar pattern of trade on a significant scale is Mexico as a result of its processing trade (e.g., via "maquiladoras") within NAFTA.

The marked difference in the structural shift of exports within the two regions is perhaps most striking when one compares countries in Southeast Asia, which have large natural resource endowments, with the resource-rich countries of South America. In the former case, in 1970, primary products and other natural resource-based exports accounted for an average of around 97 percent of the exports of Indonesia, Malaysia, the Philippines, and Thailand, whereas, by 2006, this share had declined to an average of 35 percent, with the strong growth in their exports of manufactured goods. By comparison, the share of primary commodities and other natural resource-based exports for South America remained above 50 percent throughout the same time period.[23] In this connection, it is interesting to note that South America's dependence on natural resource-based exports in fact expanded during the past decade as a result of the strong increase in the terms of trade for its agricultural and mining exports, in part because of the large demand for such goods from China.

It is also the case that export activity in East Asia has had a stronger effect on aggregate economic growth than in the case of Latin America because of a higher ratio of merchandise trade to merchandise value added, given the high export orientation of manufacturing in East Asia and the higher technological content of its manufacturing activity (see Table 6.5). In addition to the lagging behavior in the strength of its technological capability compared with East Asia, Latin America's export trade has been burdened by the weaker conditions of its infrastructure and logistics capability, as noted earlier. In this connection, it is note-worthy that Latin America scores substantially below East Asia in the quality of its port, customs and transport infrastructure, and logistical capacity, as measured by the World Economic Forum in its *Enabling Trade Index* (ETI).[24]

Consistent with their stronger export performance, the countries of East Asia have also been able to achieve a more diversified export struc-ture than is the case for Latin America. According to studies by Agosin (2007) using a standard measure of concentration (Herfindahl index), one can see a much sharper decline and lower index value for the exports of East Asia compared with those of Latin America, which implies a higher degree of export diversity in East Asia than in Latin America.[25] In this regard, it is worth noting that for a broader cross section of coun-tries, there is a strong inverse correlation between this export concen-tration ratio and the growth rate in real per capita income.[26] Building on these results, analysts at the Kennedy School of Government of Harvard University (Dani Rodrik and Ricardo Hausmann) have shown that both the diversification and increasing sophistication of exports by developing countries are particularly strong correlates and predictors of sustained growth in real income. In addition, the work of Ricardo Hausmann and his colleagues at the Harvard Center for International Development has combined and extended in a unique way the insights of Imbs and Wacziarg and the capabilities approach of Sanjaya Lall to show how the accumulation of useful knowledge that is embodied in export products of increasing diversity and complexity is a basic driver of economic development over the long term.[27]

What has been particularly unique about export trade in East Asia is the extent to which it has followed a sequential pattern, as suggested by the "flying geese" model that was discussed in chapter 4. In accor-dance with this model, the development of export capacity was linked to foreign direct investment from one country or group of countries to another. In the case of garments and textiles, for example, export pro-duction that developed in Japan in the immediate post–World War II period was subsequently transferred by Japanese manufacturers to Hong Kong, Korea, and Taiwan by way of foreign direct investment, as pro-ducers in Japan faced increasing production costs at home in that sector and were developing the capacity for light manufacturing and medium-tech export production in other sectors. In subsequent decades, as export producers in the NIEs moved up the production cost curve, producers in those countries, in turn, shifted production via foreign direct invest-ment to lower wage sites in Southeast Asia. By the late 1980s, certain producers in each of the three originating locations turned to sites in China as an attractive venue for locating labor-intensive manufacturing in the garment and textile industry. Sites outside of East Asia, such as Bangladesh, India, and Pakistan, were also the beneficiaries of this cascading effect of the "flying geese" model.

With the ICT revolution of the 1970s and 1980s, another important transformation of international trade began to take root in East Asia, similar to the impact of steamships, railroad, and telegraph in the late nineteenth and early twentieth century, as noted earlier. The impulse to foreign trade arising from the dramatic decline in trade costs associated with the introduction of steamships and transportation of freight by rail has been called the "first unbundling of trade," because it made possible the location of production in sites separate from that of consumers with enormous benefits in terms of scale economies. The "second unbundling" of trade began in the 1980s with the full effects of the ICT revolution made possible rapid communication and the coordination of business operations via digitization over long distances. One of the results of this revolution was the creation of GPNs/GVCs, through which it became possible to separate the process of manufacturing goods into subcomponents that could be located in different sites that were coordinated through electronic communication and production management techniques. This phenomenon has been described as "supply chain trade" by one of its most astute observers (Richard Baldwin). With this "second unbundling," developing economies did not need to develop an entire supply chain to make an industry viable, as Korea did in the case of automobiles for example, but rather they could specialize in one phase of a specific manufacturing process within an industry.[28]

In its initial phase, the emergence of GVCs managed by companies headquartered in the advanced countries (Japan in the case of East Asia) led to the creation of simple export processing zones (EPZs) with good logistics capacity in which relatively cheap labor could be trained for the assembly of one piece of a production process that was shipped back to the headquarters country for final sale, or to another developing country for further processing.

Within the garment industry, the emergence of GVCs created a new cascading or sequential development effect similar to the inter-industry trade effect of the "flying geese" model. As production of finished textile goods was decentralized within the East Asian region, so too was the production of the inputs, such as yarn and fibers, that are the inputs for the final product, first from Japan and then from the NIEs, as they developed the capacity to produce them. In addition, Japan developed the capacity to produce machinery for the manufacturing of garments and textiles, thus creating additional value added in its manufacturing sector. With the passage of time, this fragmentation of the production process was applied to automobiles and electronic equipment on a similarly large scale as in the case of garments, all of which have contributed to a dense network of investment, trade, and services in East Asia that has come to be known as "factory Asia."[29] The growth and expansion of GPNs/GVCs has created a nexus of foreign direct investment for establishing production sites, strong intra-industry trade patterns, and a decentralization of certain service functions such as logistics, transport, and accounting that is quite unique in international economic history.

In addition to Japan, leading manufacturers of these export goods from Europe and the United States have decentralized their production processes within East Asia to take account of the growing capacity and experience in the region, especially with the opening to trade of China. The counterpart of this "unbundling" process in the advanced countries has been the process of "off-shoring" and "out-sourcing," as major multinational consumer corporations have taken advantage of the significant differences in wage rates for labor services at home and abroad (i.e., in East Asia) to improve their profit position. As relatively low-cost assembly or production processes are shipped to low-cost labor sites abroad, the MNCs, which coordinate the decentralized process of production, at the same time maintain control of the high return functions of design and marketing, along with high-margin retail operations.

For developing countries, there are two challenges for economic development arising from the phenomenon of GPNs. The first is to be identified as a suitable destination for the off-shoring of labor services. By now, experience has shown that there are clear "framework conditions" that developing countries must meet in terms of establishing an attractive export processing zone, which include a good logistics function for ease of transporting goods and raw material in and out of the country, a disciplined labor force, and a stable macroeconomic and political environment. The second challenge over time is to move up the value chain in order to take on other functions within the GPNs, beyond the simple assembly of parts or final components of a consumer good, which offer higher value added and returns to labor. Significant investment and training is required to meet the quality and quantity standards of leading firms within the GPNs for this second challenge to be met, consistent with the development of a country's technological capability, as discussed earlier.

Generally, countries within East Asia have been more successful in meeting these two challenges than other regions of the globe where GPNs are active. One example of such a process within the garment and electronic industries has been the ladder of functions associated with the stages of original equipment manufacturing (OEM), original design manufacturing (ODM), and original brand manufacturing (OBM). The prior existence of these stages of the production process representing increasingly higher levels of competence in terms of technological capability and labor skills offered an incentive to producers, as well as government policy makers, in Korea and Taiwan in particular, to establish the training facilities and business management capacity to enable the development of globally competitive manufacturing enterprises over time. Companies such as ACER in Taiwan and Samsung in Korea emerged as globally competitive technology producers by moving up the OEM-ODM-OBM ladder.[30]

One measure of the strength of GPNs within East Asia can be seen in the growth in its trade of intermediate goods, which has expanded strongly along with final goods trade. During 1992–2003, global trade in intermediate goods more than doubled, and East Asia was the only region to experience a relative increase in its share of this trade; by 2003, the share of intermediate goods trade in East Asia was higher than that for any other region.[31] During this period, trade in intermediate goods typically represented more than 40 percent of exports and imports for most East Asian countries, reflecting the high degree of processing trade among these countries.[32] As a result of the growth of this kind of trade, as noted earlier, there has been a dramatic increase in the ratio of merchandise trade to merchandise value added, which in the case of the NIEs, for example, rose from a little more than 200 percent in 1980 to somewhat more than 500 percent in 2005. In the case of Mexico, this ratio peaked at around 100 percent in 2000.[33] Another direct measure of the impact of GPNs on production and trade in East Asia is the GVC participation rate, which has been developed by UNCTAD and shows that East Asia is the region with the highest participation of GVCs in its foreign trade.[34]

In contrast with East Asia, countries in Latin America and the Caribbean have participated in the growing force of GPNs to a far less extent, except for parts of Mexico, Central America, and certain Caribbean islands (in particular, the Dominican Republic), as noted earlier, which have been drawn into the orbit of North America producers. Generally, distance is a factor in determining the siting of GPNs, which can account for the limited reach of such operations into South

America. As a result, within the global economy, the four large orbits of GPNs and associated high intra-industry trade have been East Asia, the North American Free Trade Agreement (NAFTA), the Caribbean Basin Initiative area, and the EU and Eastern Europe. Where producers in the United States and Europe have linked into the GPNs in East Asia, it is typically in those areas of production where the item of final consumer trade, such as electronics, has a high value to weight ratio that makes transport by air freight feasible and competitive.

Patterns of External Sector Liberalization

As part of the process of promoting regional integration into global trade and financial markets, East Asia and Latin America have followed very different patterns of trade and financial liberalization. On the trade side, countries in Latin America traditionally maintained rates of nominal tariff protection that were far higher than those in East Asia; during the 1960s and 1970s, the nominal tariff levels in Latin America averaged around 154 percent, whereas in East Asia they were only 32 percent. After 1980, with the launch of major economic reform efforts in Latin America, tariff rates were reduced very sharply at first and then at a somewhat slower pace than in East Asia. By the beginning of the past decade, average tariff rates were at about the same level in the two regions.[35]

In the case of external financial transactions, East Asia has tended to follow a gradual process of liberalization since the 1970s, as in the case of trade, consistent with its export orientation and opening to FDI. By comparison, countries in Latin America tended to maintain external capital account restrictions at a much higher level than in East Asia during the 1970s and 1980s; however, beginning in the late 1980s, these restrictions were very sharply reduced to a level much closer to that of East Asia.[36]

This very divergent pattern of trade and capital account liberalization between the two regions created a certain anomaly for Latin America, in that during the last quarter of the twentieth century it tended to be less open on trade than other emerging market economies, but more open for capital account transactions, whereas East Asia was just the reverse.[37] Accordingly, Latin America was in a more vulnerable position than East Asia with respect to the problem of capital flow volatility and in a weaker position to sustain external indebtedness given its lower base of exports. According to a recent study by Daniel Gros and associates (Gros et al. 2013), Brazil is still relatively more open on its financial account and more closed on its trade account than other emerging market economies.

Within this process of liberalization, it is interesting to note that one can also see a different pattern of behavior for real exchange rates in the two regions, with much more volatility in the case of Latin America and periods of significant overvaluation. In 1980, at the point of major transition in Latin America's trade and financial policies, exchange systems were far more complex and distorted than was typically the case in East Asia (except in the case of Chile), consistent with the region's pronounced rate of trade protection. Accordingly, exchange rates in Latin America tended to be far more overvalued than was the case in East Asia. The problem of currency overvaluation continued into the 1980s, however, as the average black market premium for exchange rates in Latin America tended to be close to 50 percent, whereas it was less than 5 percent for East Asia. It was only by the end of the 1990s that these premia were roughly equivalent in the two regions.[38]

Consistent with this pattern of distortions in the exchange rate systems of Latin America, one can observe far more volatility in the behavior of real exchange rates in Latin America than in East Asia. Based on an index value of 100 for the year 2000, the average real effective exchange rate for Latin American countries peaked at a value of 150 in 1980, but then dropped to around half that level by 1985, after which it stabilized around the base year level during 1995–2005. By comparison, the real effective exchange rate index for East Asian countries appreciated steadily during the 1980s and then stabilized around the base year level from 1990 until 2005.[39] By way of summary, it seems fair to conclude that the management of trade, exchange rate, and capital account policies in Latin America was generally far less conducive to an orderly development of the trade and financial sectors of the regional economy than was the case in East Asia.

While both regions have pursued capital account liberalization, East Asia has been the greater beneficiary of foreign direct investment, which has been closely related to the development of its trade operations. In addition to a higher cumulative stock of FDI, much of the flow of FDI to East Asia has been related to the development of export trade platforms and has been efficiency seeking in the sense of seeking relatively low-cost sites for export production. By comparison, in the case of Latin America, FDI flows have tended to be market seeking, as they have been oriented to the privatization of public utilities and production for domestic consumer trade, or the exploitation of natural resources.

With the growing weight of China in global trade and investment, it is interesting to see how its impact on export activity in Latin America has grown in recent years. As noted earlier, China seems to be replicating the role that the UK played in South America during the latter part of the nineteenth century and early twentieth century, in that it has been a strong consumer of that region's agro-mining–based exports in exchange for its industrial goods, while being a source of both financial and direct investment inflows. In the case of Mexico and Central America, however, it should be noted that China has been a source of direct competition, as its high-tech exports have gained market share in the global trading system much faster than its competitors in the Western Hemisphere, thus representing a strong threat to their expansion.[40]

In the area of finance, the Chinese government has taken an active interest in Latin America since the start of the new century, consistent with its "Going Global" policy of being involved in the market and natural resource development of regions such as Africa, Central Asia, and Latin America. During the first half of the past decade, loans from the China Development Bank and the Export-Import Bank of China to Latin America totaled around US$75 billion, which exceeded the lending to that region from both the Inter-American Development Bank and the World Bank on a combined basis. During 2009–2010, half of China's overseas official lending was channeled to Latin America, in particular, to Argentina, Brazil, Ecuador, and Venezuela. In the latter two cases, some of this lending was linked to the purchase of oil exports. China's external financing has been directed primarily to sectors such as oil and gas exploration, mining and transport development, and housing.[41]

The continued dependence of South America on natural resource–based exports raises the issue and challenge of whether such resources can provide a sound basis for sustained economic development, which is an issue that is raised briefly at the end of chapter 10.

CHAPTER 7

The Role of Institutions and Governance

This chapter explores the third of the four major themes of the analytical framework that was laid out in chapter 1 as relevant for an understanding of the divergent development paths of East Asia and Latin America since the middle of the past century, namely, the role of institutions. This factor is one of the so-called deep determinants that has drawn the attention of development scholars, in particular, since the late 1990s, and was given a major impulse by the work of Acemoglu, Johnson, and Robinson (2001) in their work on the "colonial origins of economic development."

It is worth recalling at a conceptual level that institutions do not play any explicit role in the neoclassical growth model, which deals with the "proximate determinants" of economic growth, as noted earlier in the book. In a world of perfect markets and full information (as assumed in that model), economic agents can complete transactions in a mutually satisfactory manner without the accidental design of institutional arrangements that may vary over time and across countries, depending on cultural and historical antecedents. This consideration may help to account for the limited attention given by growth economists to the role of institutions in economic development until the nonquantitative work of Douglas North, which was grounded mainly in historical narrative, gained greater ascendancy and acceptance within the academy. Even within the "Washington Consensus," institutions were only covered within the narrow reference to "property rights" in the last of the ten elements listed in that framework, and in practical terms they played a relatively minor role in the applications of the Consensus, given its strong focus on the principles of sound macroeconomic policy management. The fact that institutions cannot be altered in the short run, whereas economic policies can be modified within a short- to medium-term time frame, may help to explain the major focus that was initially given to policy adjustments, rather than institutional reform, in efforts to implement the Consensus.

In any event, with the triumphant declaration of "Institutions Rule!" by scholars such as Dani Rodrik (2004), building on the work of Bill Easterly, Robert Hall, and Ronald Jones, by the turn of the new century institutions had become a central focus of development economists within the triad of the "deep determinants." In the comparative study of East Asian and Latin American economic development, it is therefore appropriate to ask what role institutions have played in the divergent economic outcomes of the two regions. The quick answer to this question is that they have played a critically important role, in particular as regards the dimension of bureaucratic effectiveness that one would need to evaluate in trying to understand the impact of public policy intervention. More generally, however, institutions should be understood in a broader sense as the "rules of the game," or the set of incentives, constraints, and enforcement mechanisms that allow mutually satisfactory economic exchange to take place and investment to be undertaken. As such, institutions can be informal in nature, as embodied, for example, in the idea of "social capital" or "social infrastructure," which relies on the notion of interpersonal trust as the basis on which markets can develop and function effectively, or they can be identified with formal arrangements such as private or public organizations that shape human interaction in accordance with certain prescribed rules of behavior.[1]

In the remainder of this chapter, the role of institutions in the economic development of East Asia and Latin America will be examined from three perspectives. The first is to consider the role of two informal institutional arrangements that were important in the economic development of East Asia, but which have no counterpart in Latin America. One of these is the concept of "guan-xi," or Chinese business networks, that played an important role in promoting commercial activity throughout many parts of East Asia. The other is to consider how governments in East Asia, in the absence of a formal legal system of property rights that underpinned economic development in Western Europe and the United States, dealt with the issue of the "commitment problem," which Chinese business networks satisfied at an informal level through norms based on interpersonal trust. That is, what surrogates or substitutes for a formal legal system of property rights did governments in East Asia use to give confidence to investors, both domestic and foreign, that the profits arising from their economic activity would not be confiscated. The second perspective to be explored in this chapter is how the success or failure of government economic policies across the two regions depended on the critical role of bureaucratic effectiveness, which generally was stronger in East Asia than it was in Latin America. In this connection, the chapter will also compare the two regions against a set of "governance indicators" that have been developed in recent years as a means of assessing the role of governmental institutions in implementing economic policies. Finally, the chapter will consider the obstacles that governments in Latin America have faced in promoting institutional reform and in reducing the scope of the informal economy that has developed as a consequence of poor institutional development in that region.

Informal Institutions in East Asia

This section deals with the informal institutional arrangements such as guan-xi that allowed governments in East Asia to deal successfully with the "commitment problem," which all governments face in promoting economic development. Guan-xi, which broadly refers to social or business networks, is an excellent example of social capital at work in the development context. Beginning in the late 1990s, the role of social capital was given increased emphasis by a number of development scholars as an essential element for successful economic and political development.[2] In more specific terms, social capital refers to the informal arrangements of social organization or networks that facilitate coordinated or collective action, as exemplified by the mutually beneficial exchange of market transactions. Trust or some other form of social norm is seen as the core element of social capital. In the absence of a specific framework of legal norms, sanctions, and procedures, interpersonal trust is the basis for reciprocity and contract fulfillment that are at the heart of successful, or mutually beneficial economic transactions. More generally, the existence of social capital provides efficiency gains by means of reduced transactions cost and increased information sharing that allows profitable investment to take place.

A number of attempts have been made to identify the quantitative impact of social capital on economic growth in the context of cross-country growth regressions on the basis of measures of interpersonal trust drawn from surveys such as the World Values Survey.[3] In one study by Zak and Knack (2001), variations in the measure of social capital were estimated to have a statistically significant impact on investment and economic growth: a 7 percentage point rise in the measure of social capital was associated with a 1 percentage point increase in the ratio of investment to GDP, while a 15 percentage point increase in that measure was causally identified with a 1 percent higher rate of growth in income per capita. Generally, according to measures of trust as compiled by the World Values Survey, countries in East Asia have scored at a relatively high level (with the exception of the Philippines), in comparison with those of Latin America. Accordingly, these differences could account for some of the divergence in economic development outcomes between the two regions.

In the context of East Asia, guan-xi is grounded in certain principles of Confucian tradition related to interpersonal trust as a basis for promoting a harmonious social order. In this sense, the concept of guan-xi is a good example of the role of cultural forces in economic development, as discussed in chapter 4. Confucian culture as a moral code of behavior emphasizes the norms of social obligation and the collective good as expressed in the practice of fulfilling duties toward others or meeting certain standards of interpersonal behavior and group solidarity within a social network such as a family, business organization, or community (e.g., nation). In the business context, these norms have played a vital role in promoting mutually beneficial economic exchange because they embody certain unwritten rules dealing with contract fulfillment, reciprocity, and sanctions for noncompliance with agreed commitments. The business networks rooted in guan-xi usually have some shared sense of identity related to geographic sites of residence or native origin, common dialect or ethnic origin, or ties of family and kinship. It is worth noting that a number of authors have cited the important role that informal institutions including guan-xi, as well as other forms of informal social or cooperative arrangements, played in the success of some of the early reform initiatives by the Chinese government. Some of the highlights of these studies are summarized in Box 7.1.

Box 7.1   The Institutional Features of China's Successful Economic Reforms

The early institutional history of economic reform in China, beginning under Premier Deng Xiaoping in 1978, is important to understand, as there was no blueprint for making a transition from a centrally planned to a more decentralized, market-based economy. Moreover, the process of transition was potentially highly destabilizing from a social and political standpoint if not managed well, as became evident during the "big bang" approach to economic reform adopted by the countries of the Former Soviet Union in the early 1990s. What is unique in the case of China is that the early process of economic reform beginning in the late 1970s was managed through a set of adaptive or transitional institutional arrangements that included both "top-down" and "bottom-up" approaches, while being both experimental and gradual in nature. Three institutional innovations can be identified as having been particularly important in making the process of early economic reform successful in China: One was the creation of Special Economic Zones; the second was the reform of certain provincial and local economic activities; and the third was the development of an emergent business community through informal institutional arrangements.

Special Economic or Export Processing Zones (SEZs/EPZs), which have become ubiquitous in developing countries, were invented in China as a means of attracting foreign investment in the development of manufacturing facilities for export activities, initially in the coastal regions of Guangdong Province that were near trading centers in Hong Kong and Taiwan. As an example of a "top-down" approach to development, the central government intended SEZs to provide all the features of an attractive investment site in terms of modern infrastructure, logistics capability, trade facilitation, property rights, and disciplined labor force in a dedicated location, which could not be found generally in China given its relatively low level of development. Special tax incentives and duty-free imports were also attached to SEZs. Given the government's clear signals of commitment to these facilities, they were successful in attracting significant flows of foreign direct investment, employing millions of rural migrants, and expanding China's manufacturing and export activities. Between 1980 and 2007, more than 200 SEZs were created in Guangdong and neighboring provinces, which in the latter year accounted for nearly 22 percent of national GDP, 46 percent of FDI, and 60 percent of exports, while generating in excess of 30 million jobs.

The second example of transitional institutional arrangements, which have been credited with significant development impact, was associated with a decentralization of governmental decision making to the local and provincial levels, beginning in the early 1980s. One of these institutional reforms allowed local government fiscal authorities to exercise control over certain revenues and expenditures that had previously been subject to central government mandate. This reform created an incentive for local authorities to develop new sources of revenue for the expansion of local public goods that could attract new forms of economic enterprise. One example of the latter was township and village enterprises (TVEs), which were also authorized under the decentralization reforms. While maintaining a collective identity, the TVEs operated outside the formally planned economy and offered the incentive of local profit making for the benefit of their owners. The creation of TVEs was accompanied by other decentralized reforms in the form of "dual-track pricing" and the "household responsibility system," which allowed firms and farmers, respectively, to allocate any surplus in their production to private market activity, once certain quota allocations to the planned system were satisfied (Qian 2003).

Within the framework of decentralization, a third example of institutional innovation emerged with the creation of an informal business/commercial community of private entrepreneurs. While this aspect of economic development was not explicitly intended under the period of early economic reform, private entrepreneurs came to realize during the 1980s that existing sanctions against private enterprise activity were not being strictly enforced by governmental authorities, which reduced significantly the risk of such activity (Nee and Opper 2012). The emergence of a private enterprise economy, in particular in zones of traditional commercial activity such as the Yangzi delta region, was a uniquely "bottom-up" approach to economic reform that was strongly supported by informal social norms associated with "guan-xi" business networks that are rooted in traditional Confucian culture. These norms call for reciprocity in business dealings based on mutual trust and reputational credibility that are embodied in principal–agent relationships, buyer and seller agreements, and the enforcement of sanctions for the nonfulfillment of business contracts. In the absence of a formal rule of law for private enterprise activity in the early phase of economic reform in China, these informal social norms were indispensable in the creation of self-organized networks of private producers, suppliers, and distributors. These norms constituted a form of "social capital" that was critical in helping entrepreneurs to start a business enterprise, to safeguard commercial transactions, to monitor and punish cheating, and to develop sustainable, mutually beneficial business relationships. Over time, the growth and success of this kind of informal business activity led state reformers to put in place a regulatory and legal framework to legitimize private enterprise as a formal organizational model for economic development in China.

From the beginning of the reform process, the Chinese leadership believed that it needed to be managed on a gradual basis, for a number of reasons. One was to avoid or minimize the risk of social and political disruption that would be likely to accompany a major, top-down overhaul of the communist system. In addition, it was recognized that the reforms needed to be interest-compatible in the sense of not threatening certain existing economic arrangements of the planned economy to which many political interests were allied. A gradual process of reform was also seen as appropriate in view of the lack of unanimity about the pace of reform within the Politburo, which needed to endorse the changes that the reformers wished to make. Given the experimental aspect of many aspects of the reform process, a gradual pace of institutional change was seen as important in order to ensure that the government could learn from the success or failure of reform initiatives. In this connection, special institutes were created to carry out technical studies and the evaluation of key aspects of the reform process. By and large, the gradualist approach to reform adopted by the Chinese leaders has been vindicated by the successful economic results that have been achieved.

While guan-xi or business networks are obviously important for understanding the success of market transactions and the fascination with markets associated with Confucian culture, they have also played an important developmental role in many other countries of East Asia where large communities of the Chinese diaspora have developed, as native Chinese have fled the mainland at different phases of domestic turmoil there. Such communities have been an important segment of society and the business sectors in Indonesia, Malaysia, Thailand, and, of course, in Singapore and Taiwan. In certain cases, however, the power and influence of Chinese business communities have been a source of political friction, as in the tensions that led to the break-up of the Malaya Federation in 1965 and the creation of an independent Singapore, and during the financial crisis in Indonesia in 1998. Nevertheless, in each of the five countries outside mainland China mentioned above, Chinese business communities grounded in guan-xi have played a positive role in mobilizing investment and expanding foreign trade. More recently, with the evolving economic reforms in China since the late 1970s, these networks of successful business organizations have played a critical role in channeling investment into EPZs or forging trade links that have fostered the growth of intra-industry trade within East Asia.

A number of writers have pointed to the particular role that Chinese business networks have played in the countries of Southeast Asia, for example, in helping to build the automobile manufacturing industry in Thailand, which is one of its critical industries. In the case of Malaysia, business organizations run by ethnic Chinese have dominated certain segments of the electronics industry in that country and helped to forge important trade links with major suppliers in Taiwan. Within Indonesia, Chinese business firms have been a dominant force in real estate transactions and all aspects of export-import trade.[4]

Within Latin America, one cannot find any comparable phenomenon within the social fabric that has fostered the same kind of positive business dynamics with both national and intra-regional effects. Traditionally, levels of social trust have been judged to be relatively low in many countries of Latin America, as noted above, in part because of the extreme inequality and high levels of social, ethnic, and political tension that have been endemic for many decades.[5] In this connection, Brazil is a striking example, as its scores on the World Values Survey are one of the lowest in the region, as well as in the global context. One of the strong manifestations of social and economic inequality in Latin America has been the widespread phenomenon of nepotism, which has been a strong guiding principle of business relationships, with success often linked to patron–client ties with government officials. One product of such ties has often been a license to build a monopoly position in certain industries that has created great wealth for certain family-run business empires, such as Bunge and Born in Argentina, the Cisneros Group in Venezuela, and Carlos Slim in Mexico, which has served to perpetuate the problem of economic inequality in Latin America.

Dealing with the "Commitment Problem"

The "commitment problem" was a major challenge for governments in both East Asia and Latin America during a formative period of their post–World War II development, as prior to 1980 most of the governments in these two regions were autocratic in nature or dominant one-party states. In the advanced countries, this problem has been solved through various kinds of checks on executive power in the form of legal frameworks and arrangements, court procedures and enforcement, and representative government based on popular sovereignty. However, in East Asia and Latin America during much of the second half of the twentieth century, most of these protections could not be said to have existed in a workable or predictable manner, even though there was definite progress toward institutionalizing them during the last quarter of the past century.

In East Asia, however, there were a number of common features of successful developmental states that provided a surrogate for the kind of formal institutional protections that commonly exist in developed economies to deal with the commitment problem. One was the political stability that most autocratic governments provided, which was grounded in a long-term commitment to economic development as a strategic goal of government expressed from the very top leadership down. National leaders such as Park Chung Hee of Korea, Mahathir Mohamad of Malaysia, and Lee Kuan Yew of Singapore exemplify this kind of leadership. A second attribute of successful governments in East Asia was a strong commitment to macroeconomic stability as an essential condition for sound investment and the creation of an independent bureaucracy to manage economic policy. In some states, the concept of an independent bureaucracy can be identified with the prestige attached to public administration by a mandarin class in Confucian tradition, but even in non-Confucian countries such as Indonesia, Malaysia, and Thailand, governments recognized that in respect of fiscal and monetary policy, even if not in other spheres of economic policy management, central banks and ministries of finance should be operated generally according to technocratic rules and procedures, and free of political interference. This aspect of government management would have provided some assurance to domestic and foreign investors that a sound macroeconomic environment would exist for their business operations. More specifically, the creation of Special Economic Zones or Export Processing Zones, which were characterized by special rules of operation along with good logistics and infrastructure, as discussed in chapter 6, could provide another concrete example of the government's strong institutional commitment to investment.

The existence of a professional and independent public administration was essential for the success of industrial policy, which could be seen as providing another signal of the government's commitment to the promotion of sustained investment. This commitment was reinforced by the establishment of "deliberation councils" comprising representatives of business and government that served as important channels to validate the government's goals for business development and economic growth and to promote dialogue between business and government leaders on the means by which those goals could be accomplished.[6] These councils, which were often chaired by the head of government, played a particularly important role in countries such as Korea, Malaysia, Singapore, and Thailand in helping to promote business investment in economic sectors of priority interest for national development by reducing coordination problems and issues of asymmetric information, and by stabilizing expectations about economic policies. In this manner, they would have helped to deal with some of the uncertainty and the potential problems of market failures that could encumber the development process. They also served as an effective constraint on government policy makers from engaging in arbitrary changes in policies. In an effort to identify a key, defining characteristic that the councils exhibited in dealing with the commitment problem and promoting development, Peter Evans (1995) coined the term "embedded autonomy" to capture the nature of the government's involvement. At first glance, this term is something of an oxymoron, but it is meant to convey, on the one hand, the government's independence from the influence of business ("autonomy") that would be identified with rent-seeking behavior in its administration of industrial policy, and, on the other hand, the close involvement of government officials ("embeddedness") in consulting with business representatives to understand the obstacles that businesses faced or the critical support they needed in meeting economic targets set by the government. Without autonomy, embeddedness could become rent-seeking, and without embeddedness, autonomy could become unproductive dialogue.

In dealing with the commitment problem, Latin America provides a sharp contrast with East Asia, if only as measured by the relatively low and unchanging level of investment as a ratio to GDP. However, it is also possible to identify a number of deficiencies within the institutional environment for public policy in Latin America that until recent times have undermined the ability of governments in the region to deal successfully with this problem. One deficiency that must be given great weight, as discussed in depth in chapter 5, is the general environment of macroeconomic, financial, and political instability that plagued the region for most of the second half of the past century. In such an environment, governments would be focused more on short-term policy objectives than on medium-term development goals, and investors would have had to deal with a high degree of uncertainty about government policies in making medium-term business plans and projections. Another important deficiency that has characterized Latin America is the absence of any tradition of a professional or meritocratic public administration. To an important extent, as noted earlier, this problem is rooted in Iberian culture in which one of the government's principal tasks was to grant certain privileges and rights to individuals or groups who held favor with the crown by virtue of their social status or official rank. The history of Latin America has also shown that there was a very weak boundary between the private and public spheres in the political culture of the region, as many autocratic leaders have viewed government leadership as primarily a means of personal or group enrichment. (Again, the Philippines has shared with Latin America some of this political culture and history.) Corruption, more generally, has been a continuing problem in the hemisphere, and a concern raised in many contemporary surveys of the business environment. Finally, one must point to a continuing problem of poor government–business relationships as an impediment to dealing with the commitment problem. In addition, rent-seeking rather than constructive dialogue between business and government leaders has been a typical pattern and determinant of economic policy on the part of many businesses.

The Key Role of an Independent Public Administration

Max Weber was the first scholar to point to the key role that a professional bureaucracy played in the development of a number of Western nations. Certain specific traits or characteristics can be identified with a "Weberian" bureaucracy, which have an important bearing on the effectiveness of policy formulation and implementation.[7] One is a clear commitment on the part of the civil service to the public interest or strategic goals that have been established by the government. Another is recruitment by means of competitive exam or other rigorous selection process according to strictly professional criteria. The French civil service with its specialized career paths, such as the "Inspecteur de Finance," which draw many of their candidates from the prestigious "Grandes Ecoles" on the basis of a rigorous examination process, is one example of professional recruitment for an independent bureaucracy. Similarly, in East Asian societies such as China and Japan, the government has traditionally recruited young career officials from among the "best and brightest" graduates from Beijing and Tokyo Universities, respectively. For such a recruitment process to be successful in attracting high-quality candidates, there must be clear, meritocratic principles that guide advancement within the civil service and incentives for long-term service in order to provide stability and the accumulation of practical, institutional know-how in matters of policy application. A strong public commitment to these characteristics of a professional bureaucracy will minimize the risk of political interference in the activities of the public sector, except at the most senior level where it is appropriate that ministerial leadership be determined in accordance with the political process established for selecting government leaders.

Most governments in East Asia have tended to subscribe to the general principles of a professional civil service, at least with respect to the administration of economic policy and programs. Singapore, in particular, from the very beginning of its independent statehood, set a high professional standard for its civil servants and very low tolerance for corruption, which has become a model for other emerging market countries. It has also set its compensation levels for public servants on a scale commensurate with that of the private sector, as both a signal of the high professional standards that it expects of its civil servants and as a means of limiting incentives for corruption.

By contrast, Latin America did not have the benefit of a strong cultural tradition, such as Confucianism, that placed a high value on the development of a learned mandarin class of public administrators, or the colonial tutelage under the British crown, which also fostered a professional "esprit de corps" within the ranks of its public administration. Instead, government office holding has traditionally been viewed as a privilege offered to friends of the ruling elite or as temporary employment subject to the winds of political change. Unfortunately, too, employment in the government sector has often in the past been largely determined by nepotism or political clientelism as a reward to supporters of a particular political party that has taken control of government operations at the regional or national level. Notwithstanding gains in recent years by many Latin American countries in establishing more professional standards for critical parts of the government service, the evidence for the more typical historical pattern described above can still be seen in countries such as Bolivia, Ecuador, and Venezuela, where populist governments have come to power and have made major personnel changes in the rank and file of the civil service in order to use public sector employment as a reward for their political supporters. In certain cases, such as the Central Bank of Venezuela and PDVSA (the National Petroleum Corporation of Venezuela), this practice has meant that institutions, which enjoyed a reputation for meritocratic management or high standards of professional business practice in the past, have been corrupted and converted into political instruments of the national leader.

The traditional lack of professionalism within public sector institutions in Latin America also has had an effect on the business climate. As noted in the previous chapter, a number of contemporary surveys reflect concerns on the part of domestic and/or foreign investors about delays in the processing of licenses, permits, or other bureaucratic requirements to open or close a business and handle foreign trade transactions. The burden of excessive government procedures has often been cited as an impediment to doing business in Latin America, and this burden is made worse if government administrators are not adequately trained in handling these procedures, nor viewed as capable of expediting them. The overregulation of economic activity in the region was highlighted in a celebrated study in 1986 by Hernando de Soto ("The Other Path") of his native country Peru, which has become a clarion call for economic reformers who view a major reduction in regulation and in the scope of government as central elements for promoting economic development.[8]

The Role of Public Sector Governance in Regional Economic Development

Given the importance that sound public administration has received in the development literature, institutions such as the World Bank have made an effort to establish specific criteria of "good governance" against which to evaluate governments represented in their membership. The Governance Indicators of the World Bank have been assessed on a biannual basis since 1996 and provide a valuable benchmark against which to measure a country's position over time or relative standing with respect to other developing and emerging market countries. The indicators are assessed according to a reasonably objective set of criteria covering the following six dimensions of governance: voice and accountability, political stability, government effectiveness, regulatory quality, rule of law, and control of corruption.[9] Countries are ranked according to their percentile rank in fulfilling the criteria for each dimension. East Asia, on average, scores well above the 50th percentile for most of the dimensions, and Hong Kong and Singapore, in particular, have consistently been among the top 10 percent of all countries surveyed for most of the dimensions. By contrast, Latin American countries have typically scored well below the mid-point for all dimensions except one (voice and accountability), where it is marginally above (Table 7.1). The rankings for Latin America have also shown a tendency to weaken since 1996 in most of the dimensions. The largest difference in the rankings of the two regions is exhibited in the dimension of government effectiveness,

Table 7.1 Governance indicators (percentile rankings)

	1996	2000	2004	2008
East Asia				
Voice & Accountability	44	50	50	43
Political Stability	46	48	48	48
Government Effectiveness	74	68	72	74
Regulatory Quality	73	68	68	69
Rule of Law	69	60	63	62
Control of Corruption	65	60	61	60
Latin America				
Voice & Accountability	56	53	52	52
Political Stability	37	40	36	34
Government Effectiveness	42	46	45	44
Regulatory Quality	61	54	49	47
Rule of Law	42	38	35	32
Control of Corruption	42	43	42	41

Note: The data are average country percentile ranking for each region, with a score of 100 being the highest.
Source: World Bank, Worldwide Governance Indicators.

with East Asia ranked considerably higher than Latin America, which tends to confirm many of the observations presented in the previous section of this chapter.

The results of the Governance Indicators are confirmed by a set of similar rankings that have been compiled by the Political Risk Services Group since 1985, which cover measures of state institutional capacity as reflected in the control of corruption, law and order, democratic accountability, and bureaucratic quality. Again, the average scores for East Asia have been consistently higher than those for Latin America in the period since 1985, and in particular for the measure of bureaucratic quality. As one might expect, Latin America's only advantage in these comparisons is in the area of democratic accountability.[10]

It is interesting to note that a clear pattern of correlation can be identified between the relative rankings of countries according to the Governance Indicators and their levels of real income per capita, which is consistent with the statistical evidence for "institutions rule" in accounting for the divergence of income levels within the global economy. More specifically, differences in the quality of governance should be seen as an important factor in explaining the divergent development paths of East Asia and Latin America since the middle of the past century.

While it may be possible to assess the extent to which countries are deficient with respect to certain measures of public sector governance or institutional capacity, it is far less clear what are the remedies for these deficiencies. Institutional development is a path-dependent and context-specific process in terms of being rooted in certain historical and political processes that may vary from one country to another. Certain countries may provide examples of institutional excellence in the area of public administration, but it is unlikely to be the case that the practices and procedures related to those examples can be transferred without adaptation, modification, or experimentation to make them relevant to another country. Thus, while it has become fashionable in development policy and practice to prescribe a number of "best practice" standards of institutional behavior over a range of bureaucratic functions within the public administration, it is much more difficult to identify pathways and timetables for countries to meet those standards. In this connection, sociologist Peter Evans (2004) has warned development practitioners about the dangers of "institutional mono-cropping" involved in the evaluation of governance and institutional standards by international agencies, and has argued instead for a much more eclectic approach in promoting home-grown efforts at institutional innovation that are tailored to a country's specific needs and capabilities.[11] Nonetheless, benchmarking is a useful exercise in enabling countries to identify areas of institutional weakness in their public administration and to focus on potential areas of improvement in consultation with various stakeholders at the national level.

Just as it is difficult to make rapid changes in institutional capacity, it may also be the case that there are serious impediments to institutional reform because of political economy considerations. This is an issue of serious concern for development, as it is the large majority of people that are impoverished in developing countries who would gain from institutional reform, but who have little or no influence in bringing about such change because they lack political power. At the same time, those groups or institutions that are in a more privileged position may gain from weak tax administration in order to escape direct levies on wealth and income, or poor financial regulation that allows banks to engage in connected lending, or individuals and firms to bypass restrictions on foreign investment abroad. In these conditions, the rise of populist political or clientilistic regimes may only serve to perpetuate weak institutions by using patronage and public employment as a basis for political support, or by using the government budget for income redistribution mechanisms at the expense of more durable solutions to development. In this connection, income inequality in Latin America has represented an important obstacle to institutional reform and development, as it has fostered some of the syndromes and political behavior just described.

As noted in chapter 2, one of the consequences of Latin America's deficient economic institutions is that a large parallel or informal economy has developed in many countries, in particular in those countries where large native Indian populations exist and social cleavages have been present for a long time, such as in Bolivia, Ecuador, and Guatemala. The phenomenon of an informal economy exists in many countries throughout the developing world, but in no region is it as deep and prevalent as in Latin America. By contrast, the size of the informal economy is relatively small in most countries in East Asia. Analysts have used various measures to gauge the size of the informal economy, such as the extent of self-employment (i.e., the number of workers outside the retirement pension schemes), or the number of businesses that do not register for tax purposes as garnered from Business Climate Surveys. These indicators give a range of estimates for the size of the informal sector in Latin America, which, on average across the region, represent 30 to 70 percent of the economy. Bolivia is an extreme example of the size of the informal economy, and stands at the top of various measures, whereas some of the Southern Cone countries (e.g., Chile) fall at the lower ranges.[12] The case of Bolivia is particularly noteworthy, as it exemplifies many syndromes of political, ethnic, and regional conflict that have been common in Latin America and are grounded in a history of land, income, and educational inequalities. The result has been a strong pattern of clientilistic politics, patronage systems of public employment, and weak central government administration that have frustrated the hope of sustained economic development.[13]

At the level of individual worker or firm, the choice between the formal and informal sectors of the economy is essentially one of costs and benefits of each sector. The higher the burden of regulation and red tape and the lower the perceived benefit of public services, the greater is the likelihood of joining the informal sector. In countries where social cleavages have been large because of ethnic differences, such as Bolivia and Guatemala, the cost–benefit calculation for many firms and individuals has favored participation in the informal sector. Informality is also a result of institutionalized mechanisms that have excluded large segments of the population in many Latin American countries from national educational and health systems and the scope of the judiciary function. These exclusionary mechanisms, together with low levels of trust, as noted earlier, have created what has been called a "dysfunctional social contract" in Latin America, whereby the state is perceived not to be providing essential goods and services for all of its citizens, and, therefore, large segments of the population choose not to play by its rules. In this regard, the problem of informality has represented a major challenge for Latin America's economic development, which will require a long-term agenda of reform to overcome. The rise of left-of-center political parties with strong ties to the labor movement in countries such as Brazil, Mexico, and Uruguay in the past decade or so with a strong focus on programs of social and educational reform, which have yielded significant benefits for some of their excluded citizenry, offers some hope that the problems of informality and inequality can be reversed on a sustainable basis.

CHAPTER 8

The Political Economy Factor in Comparative Economic Development

This chapter considers the role of political forces in determining economic policy choices, as well as the nature of political regimes and their impact on economic development, as key determinants of the divergent development outcomes of East Asia and Latin America. The chapter concludes with some reflections on the role of the state in economic development and on how academic and policy views on that role have changed recently, largely in the light of the experience of East Asia and Latin America.

The role of political economy factors is often neglected in analytical studies of economic development, where emphasis is mainly placed on understanding how different economic policies have been applied in a comparative or cross-country context, and what has been the nature of their effects on development outcomes. However, the success or failure of economic development strategies in a specific country or regional context cannot be fully understood without some consideration of the influence of political forces on the choice of those strategies and on their implementation. For example, the conclusion that East Asian countries generally adopted sound macroeconomic and external sector policies because of strong economic advice from national and foreign experts, while Latin America adopted a more inward-oriented development strategy with less emphasis on macroeconomic stability because of the strong advice from UNECLA advisors, would be of little analytical value from a comparative perspective, if it was not grounded in an understanding of the role that internal political and institutional forces played in the adoption of those policy frameworks. In addition, in this context it is important to understand the interplay of political forces that either foster or frustrate economic policy reform at a key juncture in a country's development path.

The Nature of Political Regimes and Economic Development

Given that there has been a mix of autocratic and democratic regimes in East Asia and Latin America since the middle of the twentieth century, it is natural to ask if there has been any association between the nature of the political regime in the two regions and development outcomes. Prior to 1980, most regimes in the two regions were of an autocratic nature, whereas after that date, there has been a shift to more democratic political systems, with Latin America moving more strongly in that direction than East Asia. Nevertheless, the experience of East Asia would tend to give general support to the view that economic development is a prior condition for political development, which was a thesis (the so-called modernization thesis) popularized by Seymour Lipset some years ago.[1] The Lipset thesis generalized on the observation that most economically advanced countries were democratic, while most poor countries tended to be autocratic or authoritarian. One factor in support of this thesis is the role of the middle class, which expands with the growth of aggregate income and opportunities for education, and becomes a source of political pressure by means of various civil society networks for greater participation in governmental decision making. In fact, such a process may be unfolding in mainland China, as the number of civil protests has increased sharply in recent years signaling a stronger interest on the part of the growing middle class in that country for more transparency in government decision making and the participation of civil society representatives in that process.

Recently, however, this evolutionary view of political development has been challenged by Daron Acemoglu and James Robinson (2012) in their widely acclaimed book, *Why Nations Fail*, which argues that the development of inclusive political institutions is a prerequisite for sustainable economic growth. While this thesis would appear to be consistent with the development of capitalism in the West, it does not accord well with the experience of East Asia. In addition, Acemoglu and Robinson seem to disparage the role of strong leadership in helping to unleash the forces of modernization in the course of a country's development, but again this position is defied by the experience of East Asia as, for example, in the cases of China, Korea, Malaysia, and Singapore.

Apart from the experience of East Asia and Latin America, it is not clear on *a priori* grounds whether dictatorships or democracies are generally preferable from the point of view of fomenting economic development. Dictatorships solve the problem of a stable political order, which is a favorable and necessary condition for sustained economic growth, but they can also be predatory and thus destructive of growth. In the language of Mancur Olson (1993), dictators can be "roving" or "stationary" bandits; the former are predatory, while the latter are developmental, at least in the sense of wanting to provide some improvement in the general well-being of the population in order to avoid popular unrest.[2] What determines which of these two categories apply in a given country case is an issue to be taken up later on in this chapter in the context of East Asia. In preference to dictatorships, democracies can more easily solve the commitment problem, which is a necessary condition for sustained investment, but they can also be too focused on redistributive policies at the expense of economic growth.

Adam Przeworski and Fernando Limongi (1993) provide a somewhat different perspective on this antecedent choice between dictatorships and democracies by posing states and markets as alternative mechanisms for allocating resources for growth or redistribution. Citizens participate in both mechanisms: in the former through the decisions of elected officials on fiscal policy via one vote per person, and in the latter through decentralized decisions of the market for resource allocation via one dollar per vote. In dictatorships, these two mechanisms can be aligned in support of economic growth, whereas in democracies they are often in conflict or misaligned.[3] In the latter case, political scientists have argued that the possibility of conflict depends on the "median voter" theorem: that is, if income distribution is skewed upward and the median voter is poor, then the political contest of democracies will favor redistribution; whereas if the median voter is in the middle class, then democracies will tend to favor economic growth.[4]

Consistent with these *a priori* ambiguities, Przeworski and his colleagues (2000) in a major study of political regimes and economic development for the period 1950–1990 report the following results, as summarized in a study by Stephen Haggard (2004):

- "Controlling for income and a number of other variables, regime type has no effect on investment, the growth of the capital stock, or overall income growth;
- Dividing the sample into wealthy and poor countries (above and below US$3000 per capita income), there is no evidence that regime type affects growth in poor countries;

- There is no significant difference in the aggregate economic performance of wealthy dictatorships and wealthy democracies, but the nature of growth differs. Wealthy democracies exhibit somewhat slower growth in the capital stock and much slower growth in the labor force, but use labor more productively, pay higher wages, and show higher productivity growth;
- The standard deviation of growth in the sample of dictatorships is much larger than in democracies (6.08 vs. 3.87, controlling for a number of confounding factors), suggesting that dictatorships include both high-growth "miracles" and low-growth "debacles";
- Dictatorships that experience high growth for some period—even an extended period—revert to the mean or even experience disastrous growth collapses; Nigeria, Iraq, Romania, and Ecuador provide examples."

One possible way of sorting through these ambiguities of regime type and development outcomes has been suggested in a study by Robert Barro (1998), which concludes that there may be a nonlinear relationship between democracy (as measured according to the Gastil index of political rights) and economic growth.[5] Accordingly, in the case of dictatorships, a strengthening of political rights tends to foster investment and economic growth as this change in political power helps to resolve the commitment problem; whereas in regimes with a moderate degree of democracy, a further gain in political rights tends to dampen investment and growth due to a growing concern with income redistribution. Based on the quantitative results of Barro's statistical study, there is an inverted U-curve between economic growth and political rights that reaches a maximum or turning point at a measure of democracy that corresponds to the level achieved by Malaysia and Mexico in 1994. It is also interesting to note that other parts of Barro's study tend to confirm the strong regularity of the Lipset hypothesis noted earlier, namely, that increases in the standard of living of poorer countries tend to foster a gradual improvement in democracy. By contrast, democracies that emerge without the support of prior economic growth tend not to be sustainable.

"Developmental States" in East Asia and Latin America

Given the prevalence of autocratic or authoritarian regimes in East Asia and Latin America during the third quarter of the twentieth century and the strong bias at that point in time in both theory and practice toward government intervention in development policy, the notion of "developmental states" was created to identify those cases of autocratic governmental regimes that were associated with sustained economic growth.[6] Except for a period of time under the administration of Getulio Vargas in Brazil's early post–World War II history, most of these cases were found in East Asia, in particular among the four Asian "tigers" (Korea, Taiwan, and Singapore), followed later by Indonesia, Malaysia, and Thailand, and more recently China.

The first question that needs to be asked is why was there such a concentration of "developmental states" (or "stationary bandits" in Olson's terminology) in East Asia. The answer to this question is rooted in both political culture and the international political context of East Asia. The early post–World War II and postcolonial period in East Asia was one of considerable social and political tension, with the outbreak of war on the Korean peninsula in 1950 and the military demarcation between Communist North Korea and republican-based South Korea, the takeover of mainland China by the Communist Party in 1949 and the movement of the former nationalist government to Taiwan, the expulsion of Singapore from the Malaya Federation in 1962, and guerilla warfare in Indonesia in the late 1960s. These events created an environment in which there was a strong view of political competition between two different economic systems in the division of Korea and a formerly unified China, as well as within countries such as Indonesia and Malaysia (not to mention the Philippines) that faced the threat of internal insurgencies favorable to communist ideology. Thus, throughout East Asia in the early post–World War II period, there was a sense of urgency expressed by the newly independent states in achieving rapid economic development as a key strategic goal of government. For this objective, there was strong economic and political support from the United States, which provided significant flows of economic aid and policy advice to the nominally democratic regimes of the region, as well as an important military umbrella for the region.

Political mobilization for development was achieved by either military rule in the case of South Korea under Park Chung Hee or by the creation of large multi-interest or corporatist political parties such as the UMNO in Malaysia, the Kuomintang (KMT) of Taiwan, the People's Action Party (PAP) in Singapore, and Golkar in Indonesia. Most of these parties expressed a strong commitment to social values and a broad distribution of the benefits of economic development, and viewed the government as playing an essential role in guiding national development; indeed, the charters for the KMT and PAP were rooted in certain socialist ideals that fostered an activist role on the part of the government in promoting the general welfare. One model within the region for these new governments was Japan, which prospered economically from 1870 to 1930 under the guidance of a strong state and again in its early post–World War II economic recovery. Within the traditions of a Confucian political culture, which had a direct influence in a number of countries in East Asia, one can also find a model for benevolent or paternalistic leaders, as well as for a technocratic or Mandarin-like bureaucracy to support them. That tradition, as noted earlier, was rooted in the idea that leaders are legitimized not so much by the process through which they are chosen, but rather by the favorable impact that their national stewardship has on the general welfare of the population. This notion is the foundation stone for what has been called the "authoritarian bargain," in that autocratic leaders have sought a limitation on the exercise of certain political rights that could challenge their legitimacy, in exchange for the promise of improvements in the general economic welfare. As a result of these forces and factors in the early post–World War II period in East Asia, an environment emerged with relatively strong states and independent bureaucracies, which (except in the case of the Philippines) did not face resistance from entrenched rural oligarchic forces or powerful labor unions in building alliances with business interests to promote industrialization.

None of the factors just noted that favored the emergence of developmental states in East Asia can be found to be at work in the case of early post–World War II Latin America. Under the tutelage of ECLA, governments in Latin America assumed an important role in development policy, which led to a sharp rise in public investment and public sector employment through a vast network of state enterprises. However, notwithstanding a common regional orientation to indicative planning for industrialization, governments were often oriented to short-term policy goals because of various pressure groups and the clientilistic demands associated with a fragmented political culture rooted in economic and social inequalities. Also, as discussed in chapter 7, government bureaucracies tended to be lacking in independence because of endemic political instability and the impact of patronage systems on civil service employment. More generally, given the history of strong concentration of political and economic power in most Latin American countries, there was little incentive to invest in state capacity or an independent public administration that would serve the public interest.[7] Most political parties in the period prior to 1980 tended to be patron-clientilistic in orientation, rather than programmatic, thus serving the narrow redistributive interests of a particular region, economic sector, or segment of the working class. Rent seeking was a prominent focus of political discourse, given the strength of various business interests in the region and the relatively weak stance of government in state–society relationships. In a climate of political conflict and instability, entrenched oligarchic interests associated with traditional agricultural pursuits often supported military intervention and control of government as a means of stabilizing economic and political affairs. The one country that avoided this political syndrome was Mexico, which throughout the second half of the twentieth century was ruled by a large corporatist or multi-interest party (*el Partido Revolucionario Institucional*—PRI) that shared many of the autocratic tendencies of similar parties in East Asia, such as the KMT of Taiwan or the PAP of Singapore. This brief summary of the political climate that prevailed during much of the second half of the twentieth century in Latin America provides the backdrop for the common occurrence of pro-cyclical fiscal policy (fed by the "voracity" effect and the "commons problems") and populist business cycles that drove much of the traditional macroeconomic instability in the region that were discussed in chapter 5.

Developmental states in East Asia displayed certain common attributes that may make them hard to replicate in the modern world of developing countries.[8] One is that they exhibited a high degree of political stability reflected in a strong executive power with a major commitment to long-term economic development as a key strategic objective of the government, with little challenge from parliamentary forces. Another common attribute was the articulation of a coherent program of macroeconomic and industrial policies coordinated by a lead government agency with broad oversight and coordinating functions. The Economic Planning Board of Korea and the Economic Development Board of Singapore are examples of these kinds of agencies. More generally, ministerial functions in Asian developmental states tended to be technocratic in nature and insulated from societal interest groups. This was an essential characteristic for them to have been able to exhibit "embedded autonomy," as discussed in chapter 7, or to manage effectively "deliberation councils" in close consultation with business organizations. While exhibiting a favorable attitude toward business interests as a means of promoting industrialization, these developmental states also suppressed the rights of workers to organize within industrial sites, as well as the political rights of the citizenry, more generally, consistent with their authoritarian character. East Asian developmental states that were not managed by military regimes were often associated with large multi-interest political parties (such as the KMT or UMNO) with a corporatist structure that accommodated most of the major interest groups of society (e.g., business organizations, industrial labor groups, and rural workers) as constituent members in order to represent their interests.[9]

In more recent times, military dictators or autocratic political figures in the developing world have often declared the formation of a developmental state with their assumption of power in order to signal their strong attachment to economic development, but without the apparatus of a technocratic government structure and close working relations with business groups. These governments have tended to serve the interests of some dominant economic group or close political associates of the head of government through biased policies and corrupt practices, in the manner of a neo-patrimonial state, which, over time, have often fostered social unrest and political conflict. Ferdinand Marcos of the Philippines, Daniel Ortega of Nicaragua, Rafael Correa of Ecuador, and Hugo Chavez of Venezuela provide examples of this kind of political leader.

More generally, the discussion of developmental states suggests certain criteria that may be useful in differentiating the nature of state power in East Asia and Latin America during a formative period in their post–World War II development. These criteria may be seen as linear characteristics or dimensions with strong polarities at one end and the other and countries positioned along a continuum ranging from a high degree of association at one end and a low degree at the other. One of these dimensions along which countries could be ranked would be the strength or weakness of political stability. Another would be the strategic orientation of the government with a High value associated with economic development as a long-term goal at one end and a Low score associated with short-term redistributive goals at the other. A third dimension would be the professional character of the government bureaucracy with a High incidence suggesting technocratic orientation at one end and a Low value pointing to a patronage-based system at the other. A fourth characteristic would be the degree of insulation that government functions exhibit with respect to social and political pressures with a High degree of insulation at one end and a Low degree of insulation at the other. Finally, one could qualify countries according to their High or Low manifestation of policy consistency in government decision making. As a general matter, East Asian governments have tended to fall closer to the High range for each of the five polarities described above, while Latin American governments have tended to fall closer to the Low end. If correct, these characterizations would go a long way toward defining the strength or weakness of government institutions as a deep determinant of economic development in each region.

Other writers have tended to focus on a subset of the five characteristics or dimensions identified above as a means of differentiating the role of government institutions in development. For example, Przeworski (2004) has suggested a 2×2 classification of states according to the dimension of state capacity on one axis and insulation from private interests along the other, with states ranked as displaying low or high features of each dimension. Many of the East Asian developmental states would fall in the northeast quadrant of this 2×2 classification device, displaying high degrees of state capacity and high degrees of bureaucratic insulation. Neo-patrimonial states would fall in the southwest quadrant (low capacity and low insulation), with Nicaragua under Somoza and the Philippines under Marcos as examples. In the boxes of mixed characteristics, one can also find examples, with Hong Kong, as a modern regulatory state, exhibiting high capacity and low insulation, and Indonesia and Mexico, as proto-developmental states during the 1980s and 1990s, exhibiting high insulation but low state capacity.

Francis Fukuyama (2004) has offered a more refined version of the classification device just described by focusing in his 2×2 classification on the strength and scope of state/governmental activity. Again, East Asian developmental states would fall into the northeast quadrant of his classification with high attributes of state strength (on the vertical axis) and state scope (on the horizontal axis), with Latin America tending to fall in the southeast quadrant of high state scope but low state capacity. Neo-patrimonial or failed states would fall in the southwest quadrant with weaknesses along both dimensions, while modern regulatory states subject to lobbying interests, such as Hong Kong and the United States, would fall into the northwest quadrant.

State–Society Relations and Economic Policy Choices

Another important aspect of the political economy factor in development is the role of political forces in economic decision making and in the promotion or frustration of economic reform. In the latter context, economic analysts and practitioners often simply question whether a government has the "political will" to implement certain policy reforms that are judged to be favorable to economic development, or if it is limited by the power of "vested interests" in pursuing beneficial economic reforms, without any effort to define the nature of political forces that make "political will" possible or that need to be accommodated for policy reforms to be acceptable. In this respect, the role of an economic analyst or advisor is incomplete, if some effort is not made to understand how political forces influence economic decision making.

One perspective that can be useful in understanding this aspect of the political economy factor is the balance of political power within the realm of state–society relations, which can be a determining factor in the adoption of certain policies. One example of how the balance of power between the state and societal interest groups played a role in economic decision making can be seen in the shift away from import-substitution industrialization (ISI) in East Asia toward export-oriented industrialization (EOI) and the continuation of ISI in Latin America during the 1960s and 1970s.[10] In the case of East Asia, the four Asian Tigers relatively early on in their development process exhausted the scope for ISI based on labor-intensive manufacturing, and did not face entrenched interests in the rural sector that would have wanted to preserve natural resource rents from commodity exports. Given the relatively weak power of labor groups and rural landholders vis-à-vis the state, governments in these countries had a relatively free hand in orienting business operations through policy incentives and the promotion of FDI toward manufactured exports, which over time could adapt to the growing demand for industrial sites that could be accommodated within Global Production Networks. Countries such as Korea and Taiwan did not abandon the use of import tariffs to protect certain domestic industries, but such a policy was usually applied on a strictly temporary basis and only for those industries that had the potential to become internationally competitive. The important shift from ISI to EOI by these states was also consistent with external advice they received from the US government and the World Bank, and was seen as necessary in order to provide foreign exchange earnings to meet the growing import demand of a rising middle class.

Over time, however, the balance of power in state–society relations in these countries began to shift in favor of societal groups with the growth of the industrial sector and under the impact of political reforms that gave greater voice to civil society organizations in national leadership selection and government decision making. Large industrial conglomerates (such as the Chaebols in Korea) began to exercise undue influence on the political process through intense lobbying and corrupt practices, which were not checked by appropriate regulatory frameworks and accountability mechanisms for elected representatives.

In this environment, it was easy for risky business and financial deals to be mounted with the explicit or implicit guarantee of the state that became one of the leading factors in the onset of the regional financial crisis in the late 1990s.

In the case of Latin America, a different dynamic within state–society relations helped to perpetuate the region's attachment to ISI.[11] Throughout most of the second half of the twentieth century, the state was generally weak as an independent political force and was heavily influenced by a complex of societal groups that held significant influence in political life throughout much of the past century. State power was weakened, on the one hand, by the absence of a strong independent bureaucracy, which was crippled by nepotism and patronage systems of civil service employment and the lack of an institutional model in Iberian political culture to guide the development of professionalism in public administration. On the other hand, state power was also weakened by persistent conflict within the central government function over the primacy between executive and legislative powers, and in many countries over the appropriate distribution of fiscal authority between central and local governments. Notwithstanding this background, it is important to recognize that gradually over time, in response to the frequency of financial crises in the region, a more technocratic policy orientation has been developed within the central banking and budgetary functions, in particular in states such as Brazil, Chile, Colombia, and Uruguay where democratic rule has been consolidated and the general public through the political process has come to demand a strengthening in public administration in order to deliver important public goods, such as macroeconomic stability.

Within Latin American civil society, there have traditionally existed strong poles of political power originating with rural oligarchic groups in control of major traditional exports and labor unions attached to urban sites of industrialization throughout the region. Prior to World War I, rural elites promoting the export of grains, beef, and minerals to international markets, and foreign investors involved with developing those exports, combined with the state to form a "triple alliance" in support of a liberal international regime in the region that was open to trade and foreign direct investment. With the beginning of industrialization on a major scale after the Great Depression, however, a different coalition of political forces emerged with the expansion of trade unions, which developed a strong vested interest in ISI. During the 1960s and 1970s, the power of industrial trade unions was amplified by a new "triple alliance" of industrial groups, labor unions, and the state that perpetuated the region's attachment to ISI even in the face of growing balance of payments problems. During the 1950s, this orientation to ISI was strongly reinforced by the views of the early "structuralists" associated with ECLA, as noted earlier. Within the changing dynamics of state–society relations just described, the state was not a leading, independent force of decision making; rather, it was the instrumentality of prevailing political interests within the domestic and international economy.

In some cases, policy determination in post–World War II Latin America could be understood as the result of contests between traditional rural export interests, on the one hand, and urban business and labor interests of the industrial sector, on the other. Exchange rate policy, for example, was often determined by the balance of power between these two opposing sectors. Rural export groups were attached to a realistic and competitive exchange rate that would sustain a strong flow of income from sales abroad of grains, beef, or minerals. The industrial sector, however, was more favorably disposed to an overvalued exchange rate that would provide protection for domestic ISI and subsidize a source of cheap consumer goods imports. After a balance of payments crisis, if the industrial interests had prevailed, rural export interests and the state, often with the assistance of foreign official agencies, would gain influence with a sharp devaluation of the currency in order to restore export growth and limit unnecessary imports. Over time, however, as pressures from urban labor and industrial groups mounted for an expansion of aggregate demand through public sector spending, and incomes started to rise, the fixed value of the exchange rate following devaluation would become overvalued again, and a new cycle of balance of payments deficits and foreign borrowing would begin, which ultimately would threaten the viability of the exchange rate. This contest of opposing political forces was one of the driving mechanisms behind the so-called populist business cycle discussed in chapter 5, which was so common within the region prior to 1980 and in Argentina, in particular.[12]

Even today, the exchange rate policy in Latin America continues to be strongly influenced by the nature of the political regime in power in certain countries. For example, in countries with a strong populist orientation such as Argentina, Bolivia, and Venezuela, the governments in power and their political supporters mainly in the large urban centers have been strongly attached to an overvalued exchange rate to support the purchase of essential imports and to contain inflationary pressures, especially if the terms of trade for their traditional exports have been favorable. With a growing dependence on capital inflows to cover trade imbalances and any softening of the terms of trade, the conditions for a balance of payments crisis, typical of Latin America in the past century, will surely develop in these countries at some point in the future.

This traditional pattern of exchange rate politics has been supplanted more recently by a more technocratic orientation in other countries such as Brazil, Chile, and Mexico, which are highly integrated into global trade and financial markets. In these countries, more centrist or center-left governments have supported a new tradition of independence and insulation of central banks from political interference in their management of exchange rate and monetary policies, as noted earlier, which has promoted macroeconomic stability and allowed the exchange rate to maintain a reasonably competitive level in line with market forces and balance of payments developments. This pattern of technocratic management of exchange rate and monetary policies has also been typical of governments in East Asia, which have largely escaped the political economy dynamics described above for Latin America, except in the case of the Philippines.

The dynamics of state–society relations are also relevant for examining the failure or success of economic reform, for example, in dealing with the problem of macroeconomic instability that has been so endemic within the Latin American region. This is of particular interest for Latin America where state power has been relatively weak vis-a-vis entrenched sociopolitical interests, and various privileged groups have been able to control the government for their own benefit or enrichment. As noted earlier, this feature of Latin America is grounded in the high incidence of income inequality in the region, which has given rise to a disproportionate political influence of certain small segments of society traditionally associated with oligarchic rule. In countries such as Bolivia, Ecuador, and Venezuela, which have a history of oligarchic rule or ineffective political institutions, in recent years populist forces have been able to mobilize and take control of the government through the ballot box under the charismatic leadership displayed by political leaders such as Evo Morales, Rafael Correa, and Hugo Chavez. However, the result of these movements has not been economic reform with a view to the long-term development of the country, but rather a short-term focus on redistributive mechanisms to deal with the immediate nutritional and medical requirements of the vast, underprivileged majority of the population that have been neglected by previous governments.

In other cases where populist forces have not taken control of the government, economic reform has often been stymied by other kinds of factors, which have frequently been cited by political economy experts. One is the "logic of collective action" made famous by Mancur Olson (1965), which is based on the notion that the smaller the size of the group with a vested interest in a certain policy or government benefit, the easier it is for that group to organize in its defense, and the more difficult it is for the majority to organize for its removal, even if they would clearly benefit from such action. This model is particularly relevant for countries in Latin America, where political power has traditionally been concentrated in the hands of certain elite economic groups. Within this framework, one can even imagine that positive economic reform is frustrated simply because the beneficiaries, being poor, do not have the resources to organize themselves, or may not understand how and why a particular economic reform may be in their benefit, as the benefits of such reform are latent or unknown.

Another political economy framework that has been developed to explain the difficulty of introducing reforms to deal with sources of macroeconomic instability, which is very relevant for Latin America, is the "war of attrition" model (Alesina et al. 2006). In this model, stabilization reforms are delayed because of political conflict among heterogeneous groups as to how the costs of reform are to be allocated. This conflict arises because different groups each bear a different cost of reform, which is only known to each group involved in the negotiation of a reform package. In these conditions, agreement is delayed, and one group concedes only when it recognizes that the cost of delay is greater than the benefit of reform.

On the positive side, one political economy framework that has been conceptualized to show the potentially beneficial effects of political and economic reform is that of "deliberative development" (Evans 2004). This model has been associated with efforts at decentralization in Latin America since the mid-1980s, and in Brazil in particular, where a number of budgetary and governmental functions have been devolved to the urban level in cities such as Porto Alegre beginning in the late 1980s, in order that those citizens who are most directly affected by governmental programs can have a determinative voice in their design and implementation. The term "deliberative development" was applied to these experiments in decentralization as a means of capturing the participatory role of citizens through the democratic process in the framing of policies to improve local societies. It is also noteworthy that these experiments in local political control were managed by the Brazilian Workers Party in municipal elections, which helped it to become a national political force that ultimately gained the presidency of the country with the election of Luiz Inacio Lula da Silva ("Lula") in 2002. A brief discussion of how the Workers' Party has broken a historical pattern of income inequality in Brazil is provided in Box 8.1.

Box 8.1 The Political Economy of Income Inequality in Brazil

Brazil has traditionally had one of the highest measures of income inequality in Latin America and the world, as measured by the Gini coefficient, which fluctuated between 0.52 and 0.63 for most of the second half of the twentieth century. This box attempts to explain briefly the main political economy factors that can account for the persistence of this inequality, and then for its decline since the late 1990s.

As with the rest of Latin America, income inequality in Brazil has deep historical antecedents associated with its colonization experience under Portugal (and also the Netherlands), which was primarily focused on the extraction of natural resource rents derived from the cultivation of sugar and cotton and the mining of gold. The assignment by the Portuguese crown of large tracts of land and mineral rights to privileged nobility, together with the importation of literally millions of African slaves, established the foundations of profound inequality in land and income, which have endured since the sixteenth century. This colonial system has been examined extensively by Charles Boxer (1962) and Gilberto Freyre (1946).

During the modern era since the end of World War II, a number of political economy factors have served to perpetuate inequality in Brazil. These factors have manifested themselves in the fragmentation of the political party system, the weakness of public administration and the fiscal mechanism, in particular, and the development of a large informal economy.

A high degree of income inequality in Brazil has traditionally led to a fragmented system of political parties, many of which are clientilistic in nature rather than programmatic or reform-oriented. Such a pattern of politics, which emphasizes the distribution of public favors in terms of public sector employment or special transfers in return for political loyalty, has served to perpetuate patron-clientilistic bonds and special interests in Brazilian society, which remained largely unaffected by the constitutional reform of 1988, following a long period of military rule (Roett 1999). Such a pattern of politics has frustrated the delivery of public goods at the micro-level dealing, for example, with the provision of primary and secondary education and good urban infrastructure. It has also prevented the implementation of serious land reform despite numerous legislative initiatives. As a result, in the mid-1980s, when an estimated 10 percent of landowners still controlled 80 percent of the land in Brazil, the Landless Workers Movement (MST) was founded to support direct action by peasant workers in the occupation and seizure of parcels of large estate holdings. In recent times, the MST has become one of the largest social movements in Latin America.

The absence of a strong middle class in Brazil and sharp divisions between rich and poor have led to an underinvestment in public administration to serve the social welfare and a weak fiscal system, in particular. The level of tax collections remained well below the equivalent of 18 percent of GDP throughout the second half of the twentieth century, as powerful elite groups have resisted direct or progressive taxation with the result that indirect taxes in the form of a value-added tax and taxes on bank transactions and imports have been predominant. Traditionally, pubic administration has been weak in Brazil because of the influence of special interests and corruption, and as a result, tax administration has been poor, and public expenditure management inefficient and subject to influence peddling. Notably, there have been some pockets of excellence within the public sector, such as the national development bank (BNDE). Nevertheless, the general lack of professionalism in the public service, together with the influence of special interests, has led to an undersupply of the critical public good of macroeconomic stability, until recently when greater independence and a technocratic orientation have been given to the central bank. Brazil's history of high inflation has also exacerbated income inequality, as the real wages of poor income groups have been eroded more than those of unionized or upper income groups. In addition, skill premia related to the educational level attained by workers have increased the wages of unionized and skilled laborers, who have been favored by access to primary and secondary schooling (World Bank 2004).

Even with the pattern of poor fiscal management, public expenditures have been biased in favor of upper income groups, as around 18 percent of public spending on social programs is allocated to tertiary education, which has tended to be free. This arrangement favors disproportionately upper income groups (e.g., the 5 percent share of the population with incomes above the equivalent of US$50/day on a purchasing power parity basis) who can afford good private education at the primary and secondary levels. In addition, public pensions have favored unionized, public sector workers, as distinct from large numbers of workers in the informal sector. The privileged position of public workers, which was established under the regime of Getulio Vargas, was recognized in the constitutional reform of 1988.

Since the late 1990s, there has been a steady and significant decline in the measured rate of income inequality, with the Gini ratio falling from 0.593 to 0.539. This change has been fostered by, among other things, social policies of the Workers' Party, which was founded in 1980 as a grass-roots social movement in reaction against the traditional party system in Brazil. Its early success in supporting successful experiments in decentralized government budgeting programs in the southern state of Rio Grande do Sul established the base from which the Party was able to become a force in national politics. Under the administration of President Lula da Silva, a number of public expenditure reforms were introduced to promote wider access to primary and secondary education and to support low-income poor families through programs of conditional cash transfers ("bolsa familia"). The conquest and maintenance of macroeconomic stability since the late 1990s has also supported the expansion of economic activity and a reduction in the size of the informal economy, along with improvements in the minimum wage (Lustig et al. 2012). These positive effects on income growth and an expansion of the middle class were reinforced by favorable changes in Brazil's external terms of trade in recent years.

This same process of "deliberative development" could be said to have been at work in the initial reform efforts of the Chinese government that began in the late 1970s with the decentralization of political authority for the management of township and village enterprises and the household responsibility system (see Box 7.1). It is important to note, however, that the Chinese experiment in decentralization only improved local decision making for economic institutions and did not lead to more broad-based political reform, as in the case of Brazil.

In the conditions that traditionally have prevailed in Latin America, where there have been strong political factors that have often frustrated economic reform, as suggested above, a common catalyst for reform has frequently been a systemic crisis in the form of banking, currency, or external debt crisis, or some combination of the three. One of the most important examples of this catalytic effect was the regional external crisis of the early 1980s, which ushered in a region-wide economic reform effort that broke a pattern of balance of payments and inflation problems that had been endemic in the region prior to that date. Unfortunately, such crises have continued well into the current decade on a more individualized basis as countries in the region have adapted to the demands of globalization and have made efforts to integrate their economies into the global trading and financial system. The incidence of these crises has been a severe impediment to sustained economic development for many countries in the region.

The Role of the State in Economic Development—Revisited

The previous discussion points to the critical role of state capacity in supporting and guiding economic development, and the changing role of government policy at different stages of a country's development. In the light of the experience of East Asia and Latin America, there has also been a clear evolution of views about the proper role of the state in economic development. This latter issue is taken up first in the discussion that follows, which is followed by some reflection on the changing role of government policy as economic development proceeds.

As recounted in chapter 3, mainstream thinking about the role of the state in economic development has followed a traditional, historic dialectical pattern that mimics the sequence of thesis, antithesis, and synthesis. The first (thesis) phase prevailed from the early 1950s through the late 1970s, while the second was dominant during the past two decades of the twentieth century. A period of synthesis has begun to emerge since the beginning of the new century. This historic intellectual debate about the proper role of government in economic development can also be characterized as one about the proper balance between the role of the state and market forces in promoting economic development. During the first (thesis) phase, market failures were seen as predominant in economic development, and thus a large, important role was envisaged for direct government intervention to help overcome those failures and constraints on development. This phase was grounded in what Paul Krugman has called the period of "high" development theory that originated with the writings of economists such as Albert Hirschman, Arthur Lewis, and Paul Rosenstein-Rodan, who focused on the essential role of government in promoting industrialization by means of overcoming problems of coordination, asymmetric information, and missing financial markets in development. The idea of the "big push" in industrial planning and government investment epitomized this school of development thinkers, which influenced a generation of development practitioners that sought to find an effective means of closing the income gap between developing and advanced economies. This phase of development thought also gave rise to the practical notion of import-substitution industrialization, which gained particular currency in Latin America through the work of ECLA, as noted earlier. Quite often in practice, however, this approach resulted in a neglect of agriculture, the emergence of significant macroeconomic imbalances, and the build-up of gross inefficiencies in a large public enterprise sector.

By the late 1970s, the elements of a strong reaction to this government-led approach to development began to form with the publication of a number of important cross-country studies that showed the perverse economic effects of ISI.[13] These studies pointed to the huge economic cost of government policies geared to heavy tariff protection for domestic industry, subsidies for loss-making state enterprises, and the stifling of export potential. These studies began to sow the seed for the idea that government failure was more of an impediment to economic development than market failure. As a result, a broad-based appeal for trade liberalization, fiscal consolidation, and the domestic deregulation of business and financial activities was launched, which was crystallized during the 1980s in the concept of the "Washington Consensus" that represented the second (antithesis) stage of thinking about the proper role of the state and market forces in economic development. This framework envisaged a much more limited role for government in the development process, and a greater reliance on market forces and private initiative. As a region, Latin America embraced the principles of the Washington Consensus perhaps more than any other region of the world in formulating its policy responses to the devastating effects of the external debt crises that engulfed the region in the first half of the 1980s. By the late 1990s, however, it became clear that the policy reforms based on this approach had had very mixed results, as macroeconomic stability was gradually restored, but the pace of economic growth had been very weak. The region also fell behind in terms of its penetration of global trade markets, as export diversification was weak, and participation within global production networks was relatively limited.

To a great extent, this mixed record on the part of the Latin American region has given rise to a reassessment of the Washington Consensus, and the development of a third stage in the evolution of thinking about the role of the state in economic development. This third stage of synthesis, which is still evolving, has sought to combine in a more balanced approach a role for both active government policy and a strong reliance on private initiative in the development process. In this regard, the new synthesis regards the old debate about the state versus the marketplace in economic development as a false debate or dichotomy. The simple truth embodied in the synthesis stage of evolutionary thinking is that one needs both elements for successful development. Two particular approaches to development policy that can be associated with this latest stage of thinking about the role of the state and market forces in economic development can be identified as the new "structuralist" approach and "growth diagnostics." Both of these approaches point to the critical importance of industrialization in the growth process; they also focus on the constraints that may be impeding or frustrating investment and entrepreneurial activity in developing countries, and on the role of government in overcoming those impediments or constraints as an independent force within the concept of state–society relations, without the influence of rent seeking.

The new structuralist approach, which has been most recently articulated by Justin Lin (2012), the first economist from a non-Western country to hold the position of Chief Economist of the World Bank, sees a clear role for industrial policy by the government in supporting industrialization, as did the old "structuralist" school of the 1950s/1960s. However, where the new version deviates from the old is in the selection of industries to be promoted, and in limiting the role of government in its use of tariffs and subsidies or through the heavy involvement of state enterprises. The lessons from the experience of ISI clearly indicate that in many cases government involvement by way of tariffs/subsidies or state enterprise investment was targeted for industries for which the country had no actual or latent comparative advantage. As a result, many of the industries supported by government intervention during the ISI phase ended up being inefficient and uncompetitive at prices determined in international markets, thus giving rise to a gross misallocation of economic resources and sizeable fiscal losses. In the light of this experience, the new structuralist approach advocates a more modest and consultative role of government in identifying local entrepreneurs who are initiating new business ventures consistent with a country's given endowment of labor, capital, and natural resources, but who may be facing constraints because of inadequate infrastructure that government investment could resolve, or a lack of access to technology that foreign investors could provide through government facilitation. In other cases, the government may play a role in encouraging private investment by providing "seed money" to support technical experiments in a new industry that was successfully developed by other countries with a similar endowment structure in the past. The development of the salmon industry in Chile with the initial support of a government investment fund is an example of this latter approach.[14] Once new industries are established, the government can continue to play a role in facilitating the upgrading of industrial capacity by promoting labor training and by providing improvements in the technological and physical infrastructure of the country.

The second approach that combines a role for both government and private investment in spurring successful industrialization is the program of "growth diagnostics," which was developed by economists associated with the Kennedy School of Government at Harvard University (Hausman, Rodrik, and Velasco 2005). As with the new structuralist approach, the pursuit of growth diagnostics envisages a highly consultative role on the part of government in working with businesses and other organizations to discover the particular impediments that may be frustrating or preventing productive investment activity. Analytically, growth diagnostics developed out of a conceptual framework that identifies investment behavior as being determined essentially by (a) an appropriate cost of capital; and (b) the presence of certain key complementary investments or public goods. A decision tree can be constructed in which each of these two basic determinants are used to diagnose the key impediments that may be frustrating private investment, given the specific conditions that apply to a country in relation to its peer group. Since the time academic papers outlining this approach were first circulated (around the middle of the past decade), a number of "growth diagnostic" case studies have been elaborated by the Asian Development Bank, the Inter-American Development Bank, and the World Bank from among its low- and middle-income borrowers.

In defining the proper role for the government in the current synthesis phase of development thinking, it is interesting to note that some defenders of the new synthesis have adopted the notion of "embedded autonomy," as discussed in chapter 7. This concept, which was originally developed by a political sociologist (Peter Evans) in the mid-1990s as a means of trying to identify a critical feature in the behavior of East Asian governments in promoting industrialization during the

1960s/1970s, has been cited as an appropriate model for defining government–business relationships more generally in the development process (Rodrik 2007b).

The new synthesis on the role of the state has also been influenced by an appreciation of the growing impact of the forces of economic and financial globalization on low- and middle-income countries, and the important role that global governance plays in determining states' participation in the process of globalization. As writers such as Rodrik (2012) have pointed out, the growing impact of globalization has not diminished the important role of the state in economic development; rather it has refined and expanded its role, and placed a greater premium on appropriate safety nets to mitigate the impact of external shocks and on technical competence in the management and administration of public programs.

CHAPTER 9

Three Cross-Regional Case Studies

This chapter examines the comparative development of East Asia and Latin America through the lens of three comparative case studies that illustrate or highlight particular themes raised in the preceding chapters, and are important in explaining the divergent development trajectories of the two regions. These are: Jamaica and Singapore, Chile and Malaysia, and Indonesia and Venezuela. In each case study, an attempt is made to focus on a key turning point in the economic development of the country that was rooted in a problem common to both countries, but which provoked a different policy response and had an enduring impact in terms of promoting or retarding economic growth. Each of the case studies is analyzed in terms of the four dimensions or factors that were identified in previous chapters as key differentiating characteristics for the development outcomes of the two regions, namely, (a) initial conditions, (b) policy choices, (c) institutions, and (d) political economy factors.

The first case study (Jamaica vs. Singapore) features an example of two countries that shared much in common in terms of initial conditions as regards colonial background, income per capita, and population size and geography, which nevertheless have displayed one of the most dramatic cases of divergence in income per capita within the developing world since the time of their independence in the early to mid-1960s. The case study attempts to show that different policy choices made during the late 1960s and early 1970s have had an enduring impact on the economic fortunes of the two island economies, with very positive effects in the case of Singapore and substantially negative ones for Jamaica. Singapore today stands as one of the most successful examples of the transition from a low-income to high-income level economy, whereas Jamaica represents an extreme case of frustrated development.

The comparison of Chile and Malaysia is intended to demonstrate how the latter country was relatively successful at promoting a long-term process of growth with equity based on export diversification, whereas the former country was not. Both countries have traditionally been reliant on natural resource–based exports (copper in the case of Chile and rubber and tin in the case of Malaysia), and yet Malaysia has been more successful than Chile in promoting rapid economic growth and improving income distribution through a process of export diversification and manufacturing development. The role of institutions and political economy factors has been particularly important in accounting for this case of economic divergence, in particular during the decade of the 1970s when each country was responding to a political crisis grounded in concerns of significant income disparities among different social or ethnic groups.

In the final of the three case study comparisons (Indonesia and Venezuela), which involve two oil-producing economies, one can see an example of how one country (Indonesia) avoided the natural resource "curse," whereas the other (Venezuela) did not, with pronounced implications for the long-term economic development of the two countries. As a result, Indonesia has been relatively successful in promoting a sustained growth in its income per capita through economic diversification, whereas Venezuela has experienced a decline in real income per capita, sharp income volatility, and recurring bouts of balance of payments crises. The striking divergence in development outcomes for the two countries is grounded in important differences in policy choices, institutions, and political economy factors.

Jamaica and Singapore

The choice of Jamaica and Singapore is motivated by the fact that both countries share a number of similar initial conditions, such as colonial origin, income per head, and population size; nevertheless, each country has followed a radically different path of economic growth since its independence in the mid-1960s, in an attempt to pursue a strategy of state-led development. By the end of the past decade, real income per capita in Singapore was roughly eight times that of Jamaica. Singapore has sustained one of the most rapid rates of economic growth among the newly industrializing economies (perhaps only to be surpassed by China), whereas real income per capita in Jamaica has largely stagnated over the past 30 years, clearly one of the weakest records of economic performance in the Western Hemisphere (along with that of Venezuela), if not the developing world. In the sections that follow, an attempt is made to explain this different economic outcome in terms of initial conditions, policy choices, political economy factors, and institutions. Through each of these dimensions, both cases can be seen as paradigmatic for the larger region they represent.

Initial Conditions

As noted already, Jamaica and Singapore shared a number of similarities just prior to independence in 1962 (for Jamaica) and in 1963 (within the Malaya Federation in the case of Singapore). Both were island economies in the tropics, and shared a common colonial administration under the British government.[1] In 1960, the population size was about the same (2.1 million), and real income per head was somewhat higher in Jamaica (US$2670, or 23 percent of the US income level) than in Singapore (US$2310, or 20 percent of the US level) (Table 9.1). Literacy rates and average years of schooling were also very similar.

Strong ethnic differences in Singapore (Chinese, Malays, and Indians) and racial and class differences in Jamaica posed similar problems for political leaders in terms of social cohesion and nation building. Those leaders who have dominated political life in the two countries (Lee Kuan Yew in Singapore and Michael Manley in Jamaica during the 1970s and early 1990s) shared much in common, in that both were members of an elite class and trained in British universities, and each was sympathetic to the traditions of Fabian socialism that was popular in British academic and political life in the 1940s.

Significantly, natural endowments differed in each country. Jamaica had a large proportion of its workforce in rural agriculture (bananas and sugar), while enjoying attractive beaches for tourism and becoming, by the late 1950s, the largest producer of bauxite in the world (which is used in the production of aluminum). Singapore, by contrast, had no natural resources, being less than one-quarter the size of Jamaica, although it had one important natural geographic advantage in terms of its strategic location along the major shipping routes from Asia to the Middle East and Europe. In its higher land/man ratio, Jamaica shared certain characteristics of natural resource abundance and dependence on agriculture, typical of Latin America, along with a relatively high level of inequality. Singapore's much lower land/man ratio implied a relatively high cost for the production of non-tradable goods (because of the relatively high cost of land), which made it similar to other East Asian economies, such as Hong Kong, Korea, and Taiwan.

Table 9.1   Comparative data for Jamaica and Singapore

	1960	1970	1980	1990	2000	2010
Per capita real income in relation to the United States						
Jamaica	0.23	0.26	0.17	0.16	0.13	0.12
Singapore	0.20	0.30	0.49	0.61	0.74	0.95
Shares of Exports						
Natural resource-based (% of exports of goods and services)						
Jamaica	30.5	17.9	16.6	6.1	1.9	11.1
Singapore	38.9	34.1	30.6	18.1	6.7	14.1
Manufactured Goods (% of exports of goods and services)						
Jamaica	5.1	34.1	44.1	36.2	29.8	12.8
Singapore	24.8	17.7	37.7	58.9	64.0	58.3
Exports of goods and services/GDP						
Jamaica	33.3	33.2	51.1	48.1	32.8	31.3
Singapore	123.3	126.1	202.6	177.4	192.3	207.2
Poverty Rate (in percent)						
Jamaica	...	...	30.5[a]	27.5[b]	18.7	17.6
Singapore	...	...	...	...	...	...
Gini coefficient (in percent)						
Jamaica	57.7[c]	45.7[d]	44.8	44.5	38.5	45.5
Singapore	49.8[e]	40.0[f]	43.0	46.0	48.1	48.2[g]

Notes: [a]1989; [b]1995; [c]1958; [d]1975; [e]1966; [f]1972; [g]2007
For shares of exports in 1960, data for Jamaica refer to 1963, and data for Singapore refer to 1965;
Singapore does not have an official poverty line.

Sources: Maddison (2010); World Bank, World Development Indicators; Department of Statistics of Singapore (2011); UNU WIDER Database.

By most accounts, the economic prospects of Jamaica were considered far more favorable for economic growth and development at the time of its independence than those of Singapore, because of its rich natural resources, strong political institutions, and good social indicators. Singapore, notwithstanding its long history as an entrepot trade center, had the strong characteristics of a traditional, dual economy and was not seen as viable economically outside of the Malaya Federation.

Policy Choices

Initially, after independence, both countries pursued a similar strategy of import-substitution industrialization. In this connection, the development plans for both Jamaica and Singapore of the mid-1960s were remarkably similar, emphasizing the need for labor-intensive, low-technology manufacturing production to deal with the problem of high urban unemployment. Tax incentives for local and foreign investment, coupled with import protection, were the main policy instruments. In this respect, each economy was following the popular development paradigm of that time.

By the mid-1960s, Jamaica was farther along this path than was Singapore, and it had enjoyed, as well, several years of high foreign direct investment for the development of its tourist and bauxite resources. This course of development, however, had created a much distorted wage structure with very low wages being paid in the rural sector and relatively high wages being paid in the capital-intensive mining and manufacturing sectors. These conditions created strong incentives for the migration of rural workers to the cities searching for higher wage employment in local manufacturing or foreign mining enterprises, which resulted in high unemployment and the symptoms of "dutch disease" (as reflected in a high relative price of non-tradable goods and an overvalued exchange rate), as well as a relatively high level of inequality, as noted earlier.

In the early 1970s, with the coming into power of the People's National Party (PNP) under Michael Manley, Jamaica made a decisive turn to a more inward development model with a growing role for the state in the economic affairs to deal with the country's unemployment problem. Given its strong nationalistic bent, the PNP government adopted an aggressive stance vis-à-vis the multinational mining corporations by imposing a six-fold increase in government levies on bauxite production and establishing majority government control of foreign mining operations in Jamaica. It also increased government intervention in the economy through expanded public employment and the nationalization of local banks, hotels, and some local manufacturing enterprises, while increasing the scope of price and import controls and introducing a minimum wage. In 1974, the Manley government formally announced the adoption of a "democratic socialist" model of development and affirmed the importance of government control of "the commanding heights of the economy."

Over the course of the 1970s, the scope of public sector operations and the size of the overall public sector deficit expanded substantially.[2] As a result, most (75 percent) of the bauxite levy receipts were used to finance government consumption, even though all of the tax proceeds were initially transferred to a capital development fund for long-term investment projects. At the same time, the economic policies of the

Manley government increasingly alienated the private sector, with the result that private investment dropped sharply and local financial assets were shifted abroad. By the end of the decade, massive macroeconomic imbalances had developed and a change in government was decided in a bitterly contested national election.

Beginning in the early 1980s, Jamaica began a slow, difficult process of undoing the economic effects of the Manley government under a more private, business-oriented government led by Eddie Seaga of the Jamaica Labor Party. That government, given its close foreign relations with the Reagan administration, enjoyed many years of substantial foreign assistance; however, it made only slow progress toward installing a more market-based, outward-oriented development model. By the end of the 1980s, the overall public sector deficit had been reduced to more manageable levels; a unified, flexible exchange rate had been reestablished; and quantitative import controls were eliminated, while high tariff levels were reduced. Jamaica also made an initially successful attempt to develop export-processing zones for garment manufacturing in an effort to diversify its export base.[3]

In 1989, Michael Manley was returned to power, but this time in the figure of a liberal economic reformer.[4] Under the new PNP government, trade and financial reforms were intensified, and privatization efforts were stepped up. Notwithstanding the relatively high "scores" that Jamaica received for these efforts in evaluations of the Inter-American Development Bank and UNECLA, the government was not able to promote sustained growth during the 1990s.

Jamaica has encountered a number of problems since the 1990s, which have severely hampered its growth prospects. First, because of a hasty process of financial liberalization and bank privatization without adequate regulatory safeguards, the country suffered a massive banking crisis in 1994–1995, which involved fiscal outlays on the scale of Indonesia during the Asian financial crisis of 1997–1998 (40 percent of GDP). This crisis expanded substantially the public sector debt burden and significantly reduced credit availability for local businesses. Domestic interest rates were also maintained at a high level in order to mitigate the effects of the crisis on the balance of payments. A second inhibiting factor for growth has been continued pressure from strong labor unions for wage increases in excess of productivity improvements, which, coupled with an overvalued exchange rate, has weakened export incentives.[5]

The combination of banking problems, high wages, and an uncompetitive exchange rate severely weakened export-processing industries (i.e., for garments and small manufacturing assembly), with the result that many of these have moved to the neighboring islands or countries in Central America, which are more competitive. Thus, by the end of the past decade, the value of exports from these zones was less than half of its peak level of around US$500 million in the early 1990s. More recently, Jamaica has tried to spur the development of a new information and communication technology (ICT) sector built around call centers, data processing, and software development, but it is far from clear that this initiative will lead to fruition given the weak technological infrastructure in place and continuing problems of competitiveness and crime.[6] In addition, the domestic linkages of these export processing activities, as well as tourism, the major export service industry of Jamaica, have tended to be weak.

Singapore also reached a critical turning point in its economic development strategy in the late 1960s. By then, it had suffered two severe economic shocks: One was the breakdown of the federation with Malaya in 1965 due to ethnic differences between the dominant Chinese in Singapore and the majority Malay group in Malaysia; the second was the withdrawal of British naval forces from the island in 1968, the servicing of which had been a key source of foreign exchange earnings and employment for Singapore. In the face of these shocks, the government formed by the People's Action Party (PAP) under Lee Kuan Yew adopted a strong export-oriented development framework based on foreign direct investment. In contrast with Jamaica, which adopted a confrontational attitude toward foreign direct investment, Singapore embraced it. Singapore, in effect, became one large, export-processing zone: The government established world-class infrastructure to support foreign enterprises and provided generous tax incentives to encourage the reinvestment of profits. It also introduced legislation to restrict labor stoppages, which had been a serious problem in the island's earlier history, and established a National Wages Council involving government, business, and labor representatives to reach consensus on wage restraint and employment objectives. The latter objective was reinforced by strong efforts on the part of the government to develop labor skills training programs, in concert with multinational corporations operating in Singapore, and by the introduction of special tax incentives for these enterprises to upgrade the skill base of their local employees in order to promote the transition to higher value-added manufacturing activities over time.

Singapore did not pursue a passive policy vis-à-vis the participation of foreign multinational corporations in its economy. Industries were carefully targeted to establish operations in Singapore as regards their potential for promoting, over time, high-technology, capital-intensive manufacturing, and worker training. Initially, the government established training institutes to ensure the supply of necessary skills in the local workforce to support foreign industry. In addition, it promoted linkages between foreign business and local universities to provide further support for the development of local technological capability.[7]

The government also pursued very conservative fiscal and monetary policies to maintain macroeconomic stability and to make Singapore attractive to foreign business and financial institutions. Prime Minister Lee, like his counterpart in Jamaica, also believed that the government should have a significant role in the "commanding heights of the economy," and thus government control and administration was established in transport, communication, banking, and other industries. However, unlike the case of Jamaica, the government of Singapore ensured that each of these public sector operations was run on a strictly commercial basis with no subventions from the national treasury. In fact, they were generally the source of revenues for the central government budget.

The Singaporean government was also able to reduce pressures for government expenditure to support public sector employment and social welfare services through its emphasis on worker training, local industrial development, and the provision of basic housing and health care facilities. National savings were promoted through a mandatory Central Provident (pension) Fund (CPF) to which both workers and employers were required to contribute in equal proportion. The CPF was a private-based, defined contribution scheme operating outside the central government. Contributions to the fund reached a peak of 50 percent of wages and salaries paid in the mid-1980s, when the fund contributed around 25 percent of national savings.

Institutional Factors

In the area of institutions, clear differences between Jamaica and Singapore can be seen in terms of political stability, the strategic vision of government leaders, and the strength of the administrative arm of government. In the case of Singapore, the continuity of the PAP as the dominant political party, the consistency of policies pursued by the government, and the clear strategic vision of its leadership that was focused on economic development as the primary goal of government policy have strongly underpinned Singapore's successful development outcome. As regards policy planning, programming, and implementation, the Economic Development Board played an indispensable role as a lead, coordinating agency for the government's economic program, which was critical for maintaining policy consistency over time and across agencies.[8] More generally, within the government bureaucracy, the PAP fostered the development of a strong, professional career service, with a very low tolerance for corruption. One expression of this commitment, as noted earlier in chapter 7, is that Singaporean ministers and civil servants are among the highest paid in the world.

By contrast, Jamaica has been characterized through much of the period since independence by a lack of consensus on economic goals and the means of achieving them, as well as policy inconsistency and political instability. Within the institutions of government, while it is true that Jamaica began its postcolonial development with the strong attachment to a professional civil service consistent with the values of its British colonial administration, this professionalism has been eroded over time. In part, this outcome not only has reflected budgetary constraints, but it also has been the result of the development of a patron–clientilistic style of politics and the impact of political patronage in an economic climate of relatively high unemployment.

The different approaches to the style of government discussed above have had clear implications for the quality of governance of government institutions in the two countries. According to the governance indicators assembled by the World Bank, which are similar to those of the Political Risk Services Group discussed earlier in the book, Singapore has consistently scored near the top of all countries surveyed in terms of government effectiveness, regulatory quality, the rule of law, and control of corruption. Jamaica is closer to the middle range of countries surveyed. The one dimension where Singapore scores below that of Jamaica, not surprisingly, is in regard to voice and accountability. Clearly, parliamentary democracy is more vibrant and contestable in Jamaica than it is in Singapore. The long-standing constraint on political freedoms in Singapore has clearly been a defect in its development model, and is only now beginning to be addressed by the government and civil society groups.

Political Economy Factors

Both the PNP in Jamaica and the PAP in Singapore had similar origins in the labor movement. Both parties also espoused socialist principles of development and were members of the Socialist International until 1976, when the PAP withdrew. Despite these similarities, both political parties adopted radically different styles of governing when their elected leaders first became head of government.

The PNP under Michael Manley pursued a strongly patron-clientilistic style of government, which had developed in Jamaica because of intense competition between the two major parties and public concerns over issues of equity and unemployment. In this sense, the PNP shared a common orientation and pattern of behavior with many other labor-based parties in Latin America. Accordingly, the PNP government pursued very populist economic policies, and viewed the state as a major player in economic affairs. As noted earlier, this approach created an unmanageable fiscal burden for the government and created a bloated state bureaucracy. In order to advance its economic agenda, the PNP government also weakened the independent and professional status of the civil service by using government employment as a reward for party loyalty and placing key party officials in charge of strategic areas of economic policy. The PNP's espousal of democratic socialism during the 1970s was also influenced by the attachment of some of its leadership to the tenets of Caribbean "dependency theory," which had strong similarities to the ideology of the same name that developed within the early days of the UNECLA.[9]

When a change in political power was brought about by an economic crisis at the end of the 1970s in Jamaica, it became very difficult to adjust economic policies in the face of strong entrenched interests and the availability of foreign assistance. Households became reluctant to give up the protection of price controls, businesses were strongly wedded to interest rate subsidies and import protection, and workers were resistant to government downsizing or the privatization of state enterprises. At the same time, because of strong local industrial elites, both the PNP and JLP were vulnerable to rent-seeking behavior on the part of local business groups in order to win their support.

In contrast with Jamaica, the PAP under Lee Kuan Yew adopted in response to the crisis Singapore faced in the late 1960s a corporatist or authoritarian-bureaucratic style of government. Within the region, there were clear models for this approach in the experience of South Korea and Taiwan; in addition, the concerns about Singapore's economic survival convinced PAP leadership of the need for strong executive control of national affairs. Lee's strong personal respect among labor groups, his actions to expel the extreme left-wing faction within the PAP, and the weakness of local business organizations also gave him scope for this style of government.

The establishment of the National Wages Council in Singapore in the early 1970s, as noted earlier, was particularly important in helping to forge a consensus among business, government, and labor on the government's medium-term economic objectives, and employment and wage levels consistent with those objectives. By contrast, relations among government, business, and labor representatives were far more conflictive in Jamaica during the 1970s, with deleterious effects on investment, employment, and growth.

In economic affairs, the PAP administration pursued a very pragmatic approach to policy making, in contrast to the more ideological approach of the PNP. In addition, as noted earlier, economic policy in Singapore was administered by an elite group of civil servants, with a lead agency (the Economic Development Board) given clear, coordinating authority to ensure full implementation of the government's export development model based on foreign enterprise operations.

The PAP government also asserted influence across a wide range of national affairs in order to forge a national identity and to weaken ethnic rivalries that were very strong prior to Singapore's independence. In addition, political opposition was strongly resisted. The considerable range of interventions of the government in the lives of local residents appears to have been generally accepted by the citizenry at large, as long as the government was able to deliver employment and real wage gains for workers. In this sense, the political history of Singapore provides an example of the "authoritarian bargain" that has been characteristic of other countries, which have shared a Confucian tradition in East Asia.[10]

Chile and Malaysia

The case study of Chile and Malaysia has certain parallels with that of Jamaica and Singapore, in that each country went through a decisive turning point or transition in its economic development at the end of the 1960s and in the early 1970s, which was motivated by concerns about high unemployment and income distribution and provoked a very different pattern of policy responses and development outcomes for the two countries. However, neither country has replicated the retardation of Jamaica or the accelerated advancement of Singapore. In fact, both Chile and Malaysia have tended to converge in their development paths, with Malaysia growing more rapidly as a result of its polices focused on structural transformation and social equalization.

Initial Conditions

Chile is well endowed with natural resources, which have supported traditional economic pursuits in agriculture, fishing, forestry, and, in particular, mining (mainly copper). Copper mining alone accounted for around 45 percent of GDP and 40 percent of exports, on average, during 1950–1970, with some tendency to decline attendant upon the expansion of manufacturing. However, the mining sector has accounted for a significant share of economic activity and exports (more than 40 percent) up to the first decade of the current century, in particular with the strong demand for industrial raw materials emanating from rapidly growing, emerging economies such as China and India.

Chile does not share with some of its Andean neighbors an important indigenous heritage, with people of native-American ancestry (Araucanians) comprising less than 5 percent of a fairly homogeneous population comprising mostly white settlers whose descendants have been primarily engaged in traditional economic activities. Unlike the other Latin American republics with a large indigenous population (such as Bolivia, Peru, and Guatemala), there was relatively little miscegenation in Chile, in part because the Araucanians lived in fairly concentrated geographical areas. Given its Spanish colonial background, the control and ownership of Chile's natural resources have been highly concentrated among residents who are the descendants of European white settlers and immigrants, as distinct from other residents of more mixed heritage. This legacy has given rise to significant class differences within the population, with a relatively small agro-mining aristocracy controlling a major share of natural resource wealth, and the large majority of the population represented as agricultural, mining, and industrial workers. Land reform has been a continuing issue of public policy concern, with a major, lasting effect on ownership patterns only becoming a reality since the return of democratic rule in 1989.[11]

In the early post–World War II era, Chile pursued a policy of import-substitution industrialization as the main element of its development strategy, as was typical of Latin American governments more generally at the time. This policy initially was formulated as part of a response to the breakdown of the global economy in the 1930s, but was given a major new impetus by the postwar doctrine and policy recommendations of ECLA, headquartered in Santiago, that was grounded in "structuralist" and "dependency" thinking, as discussed earlier in chapter 4. This policy of inward development in Chile was buttressed by a system of high protective tariffs, import controls, and multiple exchange rates, which supported an inefficient domestic manufacturing sector and also created strong disincentives for exports and natural resource–based activities. Together with a pattern of lax fiscal and monetary policies, Chile during the 1950s and 1960s experienced an average annual growth in GDP per capita of around 2 percent in real terms, with persistent inflation of around 30 percent, and relatively high unemployment of 10 percent, along with periodic balance of payments crises and a series of failed stabilization attempts.[12]

Against the backdrop of these mediocre economic results and particular concern about high unemployment and the distribution of income (with a Gini coefficient in excess of 50 percent), the national political campaign of 1970 yielded the election of an avowedly Marxist politician (Salvador Allende) as head of government, for the first time by a Western democracy. The program of his parliamentary coalition ("Unidad Popular") was strongly oriented to bring about the "Chilean road to socialism" through widespread nationalization of mining and manufacturing activities, agrarian reform, and the creation of a People's Assembly. While initially there was a surge in the growth of real GDP in 1971 on account of a massive expansion in government activities and public outlays, over a period of three years, the policies of the Allende government led to accelerating inflation, widespread scarcities of basic commodities, a sharp decline in private investment, and a massive public sector deficit that could only be financed through large-scale central bank credit expansion. The impact of these policies also led to rising social and political unrest, with the result that Allende was removed from office by the leader of the armed forces (Augusto Pinochet) in a coup d'etat in September 1973. The economic reforms introduced by the Pinochet regime have had an enduring effect on Chile's development path since then.[13] In this regard, the Pinochet government set certain precedents in the conduct of economic policy and political rule that were imitated by a number of other countries in the region during his reign through the end of the 1980s.

The initial conditions of Malaysia share an important similarity with Chile insofar as natural resource–based commodities have traditionally accounted for the major share of the country's domestic economic production and exports. During 1950–1970, rubber and tin accounted for around 60 percent of Malaysia's exports. As a result of active government intervention beginning even prior to Malaysia's independence from Great Britain in 1965, it is interesting to note that palm oil production had been promoted for purposes of agricultural diversification and has gradually overtaken the export shares of the other two commodities. However, on a combined basis in the past decade, these products have come to represent less than 20 percent of Malaysia's exports, which are now overwhelmingly based on domestic manufacturing. Malaysia's industrialization drive was successful in raising real income per capita on a purchasing power parity (PPP) basis from a level that was around 14 percent of that of the United States in 1970 to one that was nearly double that in relative terms in 2000; during this same period, the relative real income position of Chile remained basically unchanged (Table 9.2). At the same time, absolute poverty and income inequality have been reduced more sharply in Malaysia than in Chile.

Unlike the case of Chile, Malaysia has traditionally been a racially mixed society, with native Malays comprising around one-half of the

Table 9.2 Comparative data for Chile and Malaysia

	1960	1970	1980	1990	2000	2010
Per capita real income in relation to the United States						
Chile	0.38	0.35	0.31	0.28	0.36	0.46
Malaysia	0.14	0.14	0.20	0.22	0.27	0.33
Shares of Exports Natural resource based (% of merchandise exports)						
Chile	89.1	91.0	75.4	63.7	56.8	70.4
Malaysia	84.6	80.0	65.9	34.2	13.3	20.5
Manufactured Goods (% of merchandise exports)						
Chile	3.5	4.3	9.1	11.3	16.2	12.7
Malaysia	5.2	6.5	18.8	53.8	80.4	67.2
Merchandise Exports/GDP						
Chile	9.6	13.9	17.1	26.5	24.2	32.8
Malaysia	38.1	39.4	52.0	66.9	104.7	80.5
Poverty Rate (in percent)						
Chile	...	17	45.1[a]	38.6	20.2	15.1[b]
Malaysia	...	52.4	29	16.5	5.5[c]	3.8[d]
Gini Coefficient (in percent)						
Chile	46.1[e]	46.0	53.2	53.2	59.5	52.1
Malaysia	56.6	49.8	50.5[f]	44.2	40.3	46.2

Notes: [a]1987; [b]2009; [c]2004; [d]2009; [e]1968; [f]1984
For shares of exports in 1960, data for Chile refer to 1962, and data for Malaysia refer to 1964.

Sources: Maddison (2010); World Bank, World Development Indicators; Malaysia Development Plans, Ministry of Finance; UN WIDER Database; ECLAC Statistical Yearbook for Latin America and the Caribbean.

population and the other half split between Chinese (33 percent) and Indians (17 percent). At the time of independence in 1963 as the Malaya Federation of Malaysia and Singapore, economic power was concentrated in the hands of Chinese residents, who traditionally had held dominant positions in retail and manufacturing activities. Notwithstanding the existence of a coalition government representing the three ethnic groups of society, there was early tension between the economic and political aspirations of the Malays and Chinese that led to the break-up of the Federation and the expulsion of Singapore in 1965, which was perceived as a threat to the economic aspirations of the Malays because of its dominant Chinese population. Nevertheless, while the economic policy of the new government of Malaysia was focused on rural diversification and infrastructural development that would have favored the Malays, who represented the main rural working class, it was viewed overall as essentially laissez-faire in protecting the dominant interests of the Chinese business groups that remained in Malaysia. The poverty rate in 1970 was around 50 percent, while income inequality during the 1960s as measured by Gini coefficients was relatively high in the low- to mid-50s. By 1969, discontent among the Malays had risen to the point of major civil and political protests, which led to a change in government and a major restatement of government economic policy in 1970, which took the form of the New Economic Policy (NEP). Among other things, the NEP represented probably the most radical affirmative action plan implemented by a government in the second half of the twentieth century.[14]

Policy Choices

Under military rule that extended from the end of 1973 through 1989, Chile introduced a program of economic reform radically different from that of Malaysia, which was aimed at institutionalizing as fully as possible the hallmarks of a pure free market economic system. Initially, the effort of the government was focused on restoring domestic and external equilibrium, as the rate of inflation had reached in excess of 400 percent during 1973, while the external current account deficit rose to 6 percent of GDP in that same year. In this stabilization effort, the government began to rely extensively on the advice and policy inputs of a group of well-trained local economists, who came to be known as the "Chicago Boys," as some of them had been educated at the University of Chicago and were assigned key leadership positions in the central bank and ministry of finance.

During 1974–1976, the economic equivalent of shock therapy was administered by the Pinochet government, with the elimination of price controls and interest rate ceilings and the dismantling of elaborate exchange and import controls. With the liberalization of the exchange rate, the Chilean peso experienced a major devaluation in both nominal and real effective terms (well in excess of 300 percent), thus signaling the substantial extent to which economic distortions and imbalances had built up during the Allende government. The domestic impact of these stabilization measures was severe, as real GDP fell by more than 10 percent in 1975, while the rate of unemployment rose to more than 15 percent.[15]

During this initial period of economic reform, the focus of the government was mainly on reestablishing the macroeconomic foundations for economic growth, with relatively little concern for poverty reduction and income redistribution. During 1977–1980, the government's objective of restoring the conditions for economic growth appeared to have been met, as real GDP grew at an average annual rate of around 8 ½ percent. Unfortunately, however, in the relatively unregulated financial environment that had been created, the seeds of a bubble phenomenon had also been sown, as domestic bank credit with significant external funding began to grow at unsustainable rates. The excessive reliance of local banks on foreign financing was strongly encouraged by the authorities' decision to fix the exchange rate in 1979, which became significantly overvalued and a source of moral hazard. When Chile experienced a combined, negative external terms of trade and interest rate shock in 1981, partly induced by the anti-inflationary policies of the US Federal Reserve, nonperforming loans and bank losses began to mount, which led to a collapse of the banking system in 1982. During 1982–1983, the growth in real GDP again turned sharply negative, while the stock of government debt rose by around 40 percent of GDP with government assistance to official banks and support for recapitalization efforts by private banks.[16]

The banking crisis of 1981–1982 was a major blow to the prestige of the "Chicago boys" and the government's economic reform program; nevertheless, the reform effort was continued with the reduction and simplification of external tariffs; a further strengthening of monetary and fiscal policy management that would pave the way for central bank independence and fiscal policy rules; and a major reduction in the size and scope of public sector operations with pension reform, the expansion of private-public partnerships, and privatization. As noted in Box 5.1, Chile has been at the frontier in many areas of macroeconomic policy reform and an example in this regard for many other emerging market economies. Over the medium term extending beyond the period of military rule, these reforms have been solidified by democratically elected governments and have laid the groundwork for a period of sustained economic growth of around 6 percent in real GDP a year from1985 to 1997. However, unemployment remained in the double digits through 1989, while the poverty ratio had only been marginally reduced below 40 percent by then. In addition, Chile has not experienced any significant degree of economic and export diversification or reduction in income inequality, which has remained in excess of 50 percent, after having increased above that level during the early years of military rule. To a large extent, these results can be attributed to the extreme neutrality of the government's economic policies, which can be encapsulated in the notion of "getting the macro policies right, and growth will follow." In this context, there has been little room or support for active industrial policies that would rely on the use of government incentives to influence or facilitate economic restructuring and diversification or income redistribution.

In contrast with the Chilean economic model, Malaysia represents an example of the active use of industrial policy to promote economic restructuring, consistent with the maintenance of a stable macroeconomic environment based on sound fiscal and monetary policies. The NEP was framed within a long-term time horizon stretching from 1970 to 1990, and established explicit medium- and long-term targets for the growth in real GDP, poverty reduction, and lower income inequality, as well as specific objectives for the Malay (or "bumiputera") share of income and economically productive assets.[17] The NEP program of growth with equity was to be achieved through the promotion of export-oriented industrialization by means of a variety of government initiatives, with an increasing focus on high-tech manufacturing. These initiatives included an active program of infrastructure development, the creation of export processing zones, and the promotion of foreign direct investment. In addition, various tax incentives and selective credit mechanisms of official banks were used to channel private and foreign investment into manufacturing industries. Malaysia also followed the example of Singapore in sponsoring government programs, in cooperation with foreign multinational corporations operating in Malaysia, for labor training and skills upgrading with a view to inducing industrial restructuring and the development of local technological capabilities.[18]

By and large, the NEP objectives were achieved within the context of a stable macroeconomic environment. The growth in real GDP averaged around 5 ½percent from 1970 to 2000, while domestic price inflation was minimal at around 1 percent. At the same time, the poverty ratio was reduced from around 50 percent in the former year to 17 percent in 1990 and to 8 percent in 2000, while the Gini coefficient was lowered from a peak of 57 percent in 1976 to around 40 percent in 2000. In addition, the "bumiputera" share of corporate stock ownership was raised from 1 ½ percent in 1969 to 18 percent in 1990 and to 30 percent in 2000. The results in terms of economic restructuring have been equally impressive, as the share of primary commodities in total exports was reduced from around 80 percent in the 1960s to less than 15 percent in 2000, while the share of manufactured goods rose to around 80 percent in the latter year, with an increasing weight carried by higher value-added products, such as electronic equipment and machinery.

However, not all the industrial initiatives of the NEP have been an economic success. In 1980, the government embarked on a program to build industries oriented to the domestic market, in partnership with Japanese investment under its so-called HICOM (Heavy Industries Commercial Enterprise) initiative. The most important of these enterprises (PROTON) was dedicated to the production of automobiles for the domestic and regional markets. Notwithstanding significant tariff protection and government subsidies, this car manufacturer has not been able to become a viable commercial operation on a large scale with export competitiveness. In this effort, the government of Malaysia thought it would be able to replicate Korea in establishing the basis for a viable automobile industry; however, it has not been able to develop the plant and scale efficiencies nor the technological skills for such an industry, in part because of strong vested interests in an inefficient, protected market.[19]

As in the case of Chile, Malaysia experienced a period of financial distress in the mid-1980s, although not as severe as that of Chile, with the emergence of a bubble phenomenon in real estate, which was abruptly ended following an adverse terms of trade shock. However, the government avoided taking on the kind of debt burden that was assumed in Chile through an adroit coordination of private sector–led financial restructuring (via mergers and acquisitions) and bankruptcy proceedings. The government was also able to implement countercyclical fiscal and monetary policies during the banking crisis in order to minimize its impact on economic activity. During 1997–1998, Malaysia suffered a more serious bout of financial distress as a result of the spillover effects of the Asian regional financial crisis emanating from Thailand and Indonesia. Again, the government relied on central bank and regulatory intervention, and the temporary use of capital controls, to minimize the effects of the crisis on domestic economic activity, with reasonable success.[20]

Institutions

Institutional factors played a critical role in bringing about a successful outcome of the NEP in Malaysia. One of these factors was the stability of the political regime and the long-term strategic leadership and orientation of the government. From the time of its independence through the end of the past century, Malaysia has been governed by a political alliance comprising the three main groups of the domestic polity, which included the United Malay National Organization (UMNO), the Malay Chinese Association (MCA), and the Malay Indian Congress (MIC). After the ethnic riots of 1969, this alliance was formalized through the creation of a coalition government ("Barisan Nasional") that operated on the principle of elite cooperation and proportionality of representation (which was captured by the term "consotionalism"). Each of the first three leaders of the Barisan Nasional government were of Malay descent, with Mahathir Mohamad serving the longest term as prime minister from 1981 to 2003. Throughout the period of the NEP, each of these leaders has firmly championed the growth and distributional objectives of the government's development program, while strongly advocating the virtues of hard work, personal discipline, and Islamic moral values among the local population. As a visible sign of the government's commitment to the economic and social objectives of the NEP and its strategic orientation, the prime minister has often chaired important committees charged with the oversight or implementation of key aspects of the government's development program.

Along with strong political leadership for the NEP, the government of Malaysia created a lead agency (the Economic Planning Unit) in the Office of the Prime Minister with primary responsibility for overseeing and coordinating activities related to the NEP, in a manner similar to that of Singapore's Economic Development Board. In addition, the long-term vision of the NEP was translated into one-, five-, and ten-year indicative plans in order to ensure consistency, follow-up, and the effective monitoring of results against the objectives and targets of the NEP. Macroeconomic policies were managed by the Ministry of Finance, which was usually headed by a minister with the rank of deputy prime minister, and closely coordinated with the NEP.

For this bureaucratic apparatus to function well, Malaysia required a professional civil service, for which it received tutelage and training under British colonial rule. By and large, a meritocratic government service was established prior to independence that has been protected from patronage politics by each head of government since then. As in the case of Singapore, government ministers and the top civil servants have routinely been paid on a salary scale similar to that of private business leaders in order to attract the "best and the brightest" and to reduce incentives for corruption and bribery.

In addition to strategic leadership, policy consistency, and sound program implementation, Malaysia has demonstrated another important institutional factor in the form of "deliberation councils" to ensure popular and business support for the NEP and effective cooperation and consultation between government and business in the implementation of the Program. In the design and implementation of major initiatives under the NEP, the government has created special coordinating committees with representation from civil society and business groups in order to seek effective input and feedback from the private sector. In addition, the government has established various monitoring groups to seek feedback from the business sector on the obstacles or problems they may be encountering in trying to fulfill specific economic targets set under the NEP, in a manner similar to that now espoused under the new "structuralist" approach and "growth diagnostics," as discussed in chapter 8. While the government maintained a sound framework of property rights protection in part given its common law heritage from Great Britain, this regime was reinforced by various other institutional devices noted above, which acted as strong surrogates for dealing with the "commitment problem," as discussed in chapter 7.[21]

Within the scope of government-business relationships, some critics have raised concerns about the cronyism and favoritism that developed under the regime of Prime Minister Mahathir, which came to be known as "Malaysia Inc." In effect, however, the title just cited can also be seen as a symbol of the close government-business collaboration and strong pro-business posture of the government that developed in Malaysia under the NEP. In that regard, Malaysia has scored relatively strongly in the World Bank's *Doing Business Indicators* and the World Economic Forum's *Global Competitiveness Indicators*. Since 2005, Malaysia has ranked within the top 15 to 20 percent of all countries covered by these assessments, being surpassed in East Asia only by Hong Kong and Singapore, which consistently are among the global leaders in these listings.

Institutional factors have also played an important role in Chile's period of economic and political transformation since the early 1970s. Political stability was obviously achieved by means of military rule and political repression to a significant extent as a result of institutional changes aimed at consolidating General Pinochet's control of government. The process of policy making, while providing consistency over time for private agents and business organizations, was freed of any of the normal constraints of consultation with domestic stakeholders and the building of consensus that operate on democratically elected regimes. Moreover, any potential opposition from political groups was suppressed through large-scale violation of human rights and the harsh repression of political activity. Given the strong commitment of the military regime to the establishment of a free market economic system, considerable effort was devoted to strengthening the governmental institutions involved in economic policy making, in particular the central bank and ministry of finance. Unlike Malaysia, however, Chile did not have a strong tradition of a professional civil service to draw on during much of its post–World War II development effort, as prior to the military regime civil service appointments were significantly influenced by political patronage and nepotism. However, as reflected in the World Bank's *Governance Indicators*, Chile has been near the top of its regional rankings in terms of "governmental effectiveness" since the late 1990s, suggesting that the professional quality of the government bureaucracy has been improved significantly over time.

Political Economy Factors

Political economy factors must be given substantial weight in accounting for the success of Malaysia's development effort under the NEP. The revision of the arrangements for a coalition government under the Barisan Nasional in response to the civil unrest of 1969, with clear rules for power sharing and parliamentary representation among the three constituent groups, provided a firm political base for the implementation of the government's development program. In addition, the legitimacy of the government was enhanced by the extent to which it was able to address the material needs of society under the NEP, in particular for those members (largely of Malay descent) who had been in a disadvantaged position. Clearly, in retrospect, the consultative mechanisms that the government established to seek public input into the design of its development programs and to foster close collaboration with business were critically important for securing public support for the NEP, as well as for fulfilling its economic targets and objectives. Notwithstanding the existence of consultative mechanisms among government, business, and labor, it must also be recognized that certain labor rights and union activities were suppressed by the government, mainly with a view to eliminating opportunities for radical political action. However, the impact of these restraints was offset to a large extent by the government's successful efforts in improving the economic welfare of the working class, and of Malays in particular.

The period of military rule in Chile offers a stark contrast to the description of Malaysia provided above. Under the government of Salvador Allende, Chile had become virtually dysfunctional in both economic and political terms given the marked conflict that permeated political life and the abysmal failure of economic policy management. The economic reforms of the Pinochet government were a direct threat and attack against traditional business interests that had thrived on rent seeking and other forms of government protection under the regime of import-substitution industrialization. With the passage of time, the reforms of the military regime began to draw support from new business interests that could thrive in international markets. At the same time, however, the military government's suppression of labor unions and workers' rights, as well as serious violation of human rights, represented a direct assault on an important base of support for previous governments, which would undermine its legitimacy.

In more dramatic terms, the balance of power between labor, on the one hand, and the owners of capital and land, on the other, was sharply reversed before and after 1973. Prior to that date, there had been a gradual ascendancy of labor's effective power through the process of industrialization and labor union organization against the traditional oligarchic interests in agriculture and mining, which culminated in the election of Salvador Allende. Under the traditional developmental model of ECLA, there had been a reduction in poverty through industrialization and the promotion of social benefits through the government budget. However, these trends were sharply reversed with the coming to power of Pinochet (who fits the mold of a traditional *caudillo* of the colonial era) and the sharp suppression of labor rights and social expenditures through the budget. A new business ascendancy began to take hold under the radical neoliberal reforms of the Pinochet dictatorship. It is only with the return to democratic rule under the *"concertacion"* governments beginning in 1989 that workers have been able to organize again and play an active role in the political life and policy debate within Chile.[22]

Indonesia and Venezuela

The comparison of Indonesia and Venezuela provides a striking contrast in the way each country handled the problems of managing the oil boom of the 1970s and the oil bust of the 1980s, such that the former country was able to avoid the so-called resource curse, whereas the latter was not. In fact, following a period of sustained and rapid growth through the late 1970s, Venezuela has been in a period of implosion in which its real income per capita has returned to where it was in 1960.

Initial Conditions

Following its independence from the Netherlands in 1949, Indonesia established its first government under the presidency of Sukarno, a leader of the pro-independence forces. Indonesia is a diverse and widely scattered archipelago, with a vast array of natural resources, including oil. Most of its residents are of Malay descent, with the dominant social and economic group occupying the island of Java.

During the early postcolonial period, Sukarno and other local elites saw economic development as a critical task for asserting Indonesia's rightful place as a great power. With this objective, the government followed a typical state-led development model of import-substitution industrialization, relying mainly on the export of its natural resources for foreign exchange earnings. This program was not effective in supporting the economic growth of Indonesia because of poor economic policy management, which ultimately led to a period of hyperinflation and political turmoil that crystallized in an attempted communist-led–insurgency in the mid-1960s.[23]

The economic and political crisis associated with these events led to a change in government and the assumption of power by Suharto under his "New Order Regime." What was unique about this change was the installation of a group of technocrats from the Faculty of Economics at the University of Indonesia as leaders of the key macroeconomic institutions, that is, the central bank, the ministry of finance, and the ministry of planning (BAPPENAS). Because each of the key officials recruited into the government had studied at the University of California, Berkeley, they came to be known as the "Berkeley Mafia," in somewhat analogous fashion to "the Chicago Boys" of the Pinochet regime in Chile.[24] In both of these cases, it is interesting to note that the technocrats could trace their professional training to exchange programs with US-based universities, which US donor agencies and private foundations had supported beginning in the mid-1950s. In the case of Indonesia, it is also significant that the technocratic group maintained their positions of influence through the early 1990s, which provided an important underpinning and long-term continuity for the conduct of macroeconomic policy. An important reason for the appointment of this group of economists to government positions is that they had provided training sessions to leaders of the military high command prior to Suharto's takeover. These sessions were organized in response to the latter group's interest in learning more about the problems of economic development for a low-income country, such as Indonesia, with great power aspirations.

Following the implementation of a successful stabilization program in 1966 engineered by the "Berkeley Mafia," during which the rate of inflation was substantially reduced from more than 1000 percent a year to less than 10 percent by 1970, the prestige of this group was enhanced, and the management of macroeconomic policy remained relatively insulated from political interference. This arrangement was reinforced by the fact that both a unified exchange rate, free of any restrictions, and a liberalized system of capital account restrictions were introduced in 1970, which were highly unique commitments for a developing country to adopt at the time.[25] These measures had been advocated by the technocratic group as a means of ensuring the maintenance of macroeconomic stability. In other areas of economic policy, such as trade and industrial policies and the operations of sectoral ministries, which remained under the influence of the so-called engineering nationalists or technologists, the government pursued a more interventionist stance. One of the first moves by the latter group under the New Order Regime was the creation of a special rice logistics agency (BULOG) to ensure the stability of rice prices and the distribution of seed for the production of rice, which was a staple food source for the majority of Indonesians both working in the agricultural sector and as urban residents.

As in the case of Indonesia, Venezuela is a country richly endowed with natural resources, including bauxite, iron ore, and petroleum. However, since the 1920s, oil production has been the dominant extractive activity; in fact, during the 1930s, Venezuela was the largest oil producer in the world. Notwithstanding a period of political instability with both democratically elected and military regimes, Venezuela enjoyed one of the longest periods of sustained economic growth in Latin America from 1920 to 1975, during which real income per capita grew at an average annual rate of 4 percent. As a result, it achieved by 1960 the highest level of per capita income in Latin America, and one that was 85 percent that of the United States, measured on a constant purchasing-power-parity basis. Initially, this period of income growth was powered by an expansion in oil production, mass consumption, and infrastructure development. Then, during the 1960s and 1970s, Venezuela followed the rest of South America in pursuing a program of import-substitution industrialization.

The latter period of economic growth was accompanied by a power-sharing arrangement between the two major political parties, the social democrats (*Accion Democratica*-AD) and the Christian democrats (COPEI), which was solidified by the endorsement of the peak labor and business organizations, as well as the Catholic Church in 1958 (under the so-called *Pacto de Punto Fijo*). Under this arrangement, an elite group of party elders would play a major role in selecting candidates for public office, and each party was ensured a share of ministerial positions, government contracts, and public sector employment. Major decisions on budgetary allocations were worked out in advance among the leaders of the political parties and other peak associations. During a period of relatively stable oil prices, prior to the oil price shock of 1973–1974, this arrangement provided an environment of strong growth and macroeconomic stability, as there was an implicit understanding that government spending would be kept in line with government revenues (mainly based on oil), somewhat akin to a balanced budget rule, while a fixed, unified exchange rate and interest rate stability were maintained.[26]

Policy Choices

During the oil price boom of the 1970s, Indonesia expanded significantly its public expenditure, mainly for rural infrastructure and agricultural development, on which most of the population depended, as well as for health and educational facilities. In addition, the government established a number of state enterprises to develop natural resource–based industries. At the same time, under the influence of the "Berkeley Mafia," some of the oil windfall was sterilized as official international reserves, and downward adjustments were made to the exchange rate for the rupiah in order to maintain the competitiveness of non-oil exports.

During the 1980s, in particular, following the first of the oil price declines in 1982, the government began an aggressive campaign to promote non-oil exports. In addition to further exchange rate adjustments, the government embarked on an ambitious program of foreign direct investment to promote the assembly of labor-intensive manufacturing for export, in part through the creation of export-processing zones. As the decade progressed, this initiative coincided with a major wave of foreign direct investment emanating from Japan and the Newly Industrializing Economies of Northeast Asia, which were interested in off-shoring some of the production related to their major industries to regional destinations with lower wage costs. As a result of these policies, Indonesia was able to bring about a major restructuring of its exports in the face of a dramatic decline in oil export prices, while maintaining the share of exports in GDP roughly unchanged. During the period from 1980 to 2000, the share of oil exports dropped from around 70 percent of total exports to only 25 percent, while that of manufactured exports rose from less than 3 percent to nearly 60 percent (Table 9.3). During this period of export transformation through 1997, Indonesia was able to maintain a relatively steady growth in real GDP per capita averaging

Table 9.3 Comparative data for Indonesia and Venezuela

	1960	1970	1980	1990	2000	2010
Per capita real income in relation to US						
Indonesia	0.09	0.08	0.10	0.11	0.11	0.15
Venezuela	0.85	0.71	0.55	0.36	0.29	0.32
Shares of Exports						
Natural resource-based (% of merchandise exports)						
Indonesia	72.7	79.0	89.9	53.4	33.9	46.1
Venezuela	92.6	96.8	97.9	87.7	89.4	95.5
Manufactured Goods (% of merchandise exports)						
Indonesia	2.1	1.2	2.3	35.5	57.1	37.5
Venezuela	6.1	1.4	1.7	10.4	9.1	4.3
Merchandise Exports/GDP						
Indonesia	14.1	11.5	28.1	22.4	39.6	22.3
Venezuela	23.7	24.4	28.6	37.2	28.6	16.7
Poverty Ratio (in percent of population)						
Indonesia	...	40.1[a]	28.6	17.6[b]	18.2[c]	13.3
Venezuela	...	25.0	22.0	34	46.3	32.5
Gini Coefficient (in percent)						
Indonesia	33.3	30.7	31.8	31.9	33.9[d]	39.4
Venezuela	54.6	61.1[e]	47.5	44.0	45.8	47.6[f]

Notes: [a]1976; [b]1996; [c]2002; [d]2002; [e]1971; [f]2005
For shares of exports in 1960, data for Indonesia refer to 1967, and data for Venezuela refer to1963.

Sources: Maddison (2010); World Bank, World Development Indicators
UNESCAP; UNU WIDER Database; ECLAC Statistical Yearbook for Latin America and the Caribbean.

around 5 percent, while the share of manufacturing value-added in total GDP more than doubled.[27]

Venezuela's management of the oil boom and bust was much more problematic than that of Indonesia, and ushered in a period of economic and political deterioration from which the country has not been able to escape. During the oil boom of the 1970s, the government of Venezuela headed by Carlos Andres Perez (1974–1979) greatly expanded its program of ISI by creating large state enterprises to develop the production of aluminum, petrochemicals, and iron and steel, drawing on the country's rich stock of bauxite, iron ore, petroleum, and hydroelectric power. At the beginning of the oil boom, the government also created a Venezuelan Investment Fund (FIV) to invest some of the windfall oil profits in overseas assets for future generations to draw on, but this program was soon reversed as the scale of its public investment began to outpace the government's stepped-up oil income stream, in somewhat similar fashion to the experience of Jamaica. As a result, the overall public sector deficit as a share of GDP reached the high single digits during the second half of the 1970s, and Venezuela tapped into the newly-established sovereign debt market that large international banks had created, mainly for the purpose of recycling deposits of oil surplus funds from OPEC producers to oil consumer nations.

As a result of these developments, Venezuela was woefully unprepared to handle the shock of oil price declines that came in 1982. The government defaulted on its commercial bank borrowings in that year, and established rigid exchange and import controls to ration foreign exchange and limit the demand for imports. It also created a complicated, multiple exchange rate system for the first time, in which three, different, fixed official rates for the bolivar were set for essential goods and services, which began to deviate significantly from a fourth exchange rate for nonessential transactions that was allowed to fluctuate freely. For the balance of the 1980s, leaders and advisors of the two-party system were unable to formulate a coherent, alternative economic model to the one that existed prior to the oil shocks of the 1970s, which was heavily reliant on import and price controls to protect inefficient domestic industries and the award of public sector employment and contracts to party loyalists. Notwithstanding some scaling back of public sector outlays in response to a lower stream of oil tax income during the balance of the 1980s, the government of the time continued to run an overall public sector deficit, which resulted in greater reliance on central bank borrowing and the accumulation of arrears. With this relatively lax fiscal and monetary environment, the rate of domestic inflation began to exceed single digits for the first time in Venezuela's post–World War II experience, while large-scale private capital flight occurred as a signal of a growing lack of confidence in the ability of the political system to manage the country's economic affairs.[28]

This pattern of stagnation was broken in 1989 with the election of Carlos Andres Perez as president, for a second time, and his adoption of a bold experiment in macroeconomic adjustment with the advice of a technocratic group of US-trained economists, some of whom were associated with a local school of business administration (IESA). In similar fashion to the cases of Chile and Indonesia, this academic affiliation prompted critics of the policy changes to refer to the technocratic group, two of which assumed key ministerial positions for planning and trade, as the "IESA boys." Unlike the technocratic orientation of Chile and Indonesia, the governorship of the central bank was assigned to a leading private banker who had been an important campaign supporter of Perez and link for the business community to the AD party.

With the benefit of hindsight on a decade or so of macroeconomic adjustment programs in Latin America and aware of the economic transition programs under way in the former Soviet Union, Perez's technocratic group advocated the equivalent of shock therapy for Venezuela with the liberalization of price controls and the unification of the exchange system at a freely fluctuating value for the bolivar, along with the initiation of a rapid program for dismantling import controls and duties, some of which exceeded 900 percent. Apart from some vague and nonspecific campaign references to the need for economic adjustment, Perez and his economic team made no effort to seek the input or reaction of major domestic stakeholders to some of the key elements of his reform program, which was a major departure from the traditional pattern of wide consultation among the leaders of the political parties and the peak business and labor associations that was established after 1958. The surprise and suddenness of some of the price liberalization moves, in particular for urban bus fares, immediately following Perez's inauguration, provoked a violent reaction, as public riots erupted in many cities across the country in late February 1989. These events set in motion a pattern of political resistance to the Perez administration and public criticism of his reform program, some of which emanated from political appointees within the president's own cabinet. While the economic team implemented as many aspects of the program as they could through executive decree, some critical aspects of the program, involving a major tax reform and privatization that required legislative approval, were not approved. Despite these problems at home, the economic reform program received strong support from the IMF and World Bank and foreign investors, and Venezuela was able to secure an important program of foreign public debt relief under the so-called Brady Plan (named for US Treasury Secretary Nicholas Brady) in 1991. Nevertheless, public criticism of the reform program persisted throughout the Perez administration, and crystallized in two attempted military coups in 1992 (the first of which was led by Lt. Col. Hugo Chavez with the support of certain leftist political groups) and congressional impeachment of the president in 1993.[29]

Institutions

Differences in institutional strength between Indonesia and Venezuela can account for much of the divergence in their economic trajectories after 1975. Indonesia clearly had the benefit of sustained executive leadership in the figure of Suharto, who was unambiguously committed to economic development as a strategic priority for his country. Given the strong collective identity of the Malay people and the prestige of Javanese leaders within their polity, an autocratic style of government was tolerated as long as improvements in general economic welfare and the standard of living of the rural population were provided. To a large extent, the government's economic program was successful because it was grounded within a framework of macroeconomic stability. The relative insulation from political interference in which macroeconomic policy was designed and implemented, which was symbolized by the prestige and influence of the "Berkeley Mafia," provided an important assurance to foreign investors about the long-term stability and prospects for Indonesia. This group also provided a valuable link with the foreign aid community, which formed a consultative forum (the IGGI) to channel foreign aid and policy advice to Indonesia throughout the period 1967–1991. A positive signal to foreign investors and creditors was also conveyed by the government's decision to maintain an open regime for capital account transactions, as noted earlier, which the economic team saw as a commitment device for the maintenance of macroeconomic stability, as well as a proxy for the protection of property and profit repatriation rights in the eyes of foreign business operators and financiers.

Another important aspect of institutional strength in Indonesia was the formulation of medium-term development plans beginning in 1974, which set out a coherent framework within which the government could identify and articulate its development goals. These five-year plans (or so-called Repelitas) were elaborated on the basis of wide consultation with private and public stakeholders and were publicly communicated before their implementation. Behind the scenes, there were often conflicts between the "technocrats" (who guided macroeconomic policies) and the "technicians" (who guided industrial and trade policies) that had to be resolved. While the plans that resulted from these internal debates provided a relatively coherent framework for guiding a successful period of economic growth in Indonesia, it is also the case that the public investment and industrial policy initiatives associated with these plans became a source of enrichment for Suharto, and over time for his family and close Sino-Indonesian business associates (known as "cukong"), through the award of government contracts and new business licensing. Nevertheless, this corruption did not overwhelm the planning system, as the Planning Ministry (BAPPENAS) in charge of its oversight maintained a program of monitoring and evaluation to ensure that development goals were generally fulfilled. In some cases, however, technical misjudgments were made, for example, in the design and development of a national aircraft industry, for which Indonesia was not well suited by virtue of its engineering skill base or domestic supply chains.

By contrast with Indonesia, Venezuela did not have the benefit of an independent, professional bureaucracy and strong governmental institutions to guide economic policy formulation and implementation. The two exceptions to this generalization, as noted in chapter 7, were the central bank, which enjoyed a reputation of institutional integrity mainly due to its careful stewardship of the country's historically strong international reserve position, and the national oil company (PDVSA), which was created in 1976 following the nationalization of the oil industry in Venezuela. Notwithstanding these pockets of bureaucratic professionalism, the rest of the public sector in Venezuela was subject to strong intervention by the two main political parties for purposes of maintaining a patronage-based system of employment and political influence in the administration of a widespread system of price controls, import licensing, and quotas that had developed in support of a very inefficient program of import-substitution industrialization.

Even in the area of social policy, where the Venezuelan government spent in the range of 10 to 14 percent of GDP (or around 40 percent of the government budget) during the 1970s, one could find clear evidence of political capture and corruption. According to one World Bank study, it was estimated that less than 50 percent of the basic staples that were heavily subsidized by the government were consumed by the poor, as the rest was consumed by middle- and upper-income groups, used by industry, or exported for private gain.[30] As a result of the waste and abuse in the administration of social programs, the available evidence suggests a significant increase in the incidence of poverty in Venezuela during the last quarter of the twentieth century.

A large part of the challenge in the economic adjustment program initiated by the Perez administration in 1989 was that, beyond the immediate phase of macroeconomic liberalization and stabilization, its ultimate success required a complex and time-consuming redesign and organizational strengthening of major parts of the bureaucracy in order to support, among other things, a program of tax reform, decentralized budgeting, privatization, non-oil export development, and a reform of the social service delivery system. This program of major economic and social reform was much different from the government's policy orientation in the past, and proved impossible for a weak bureaucracy to sustain in a climate of political conflict, and without the support of Congress and the main labor union confederation (CTV).

Political Economy Factors

From the late 1950s to the mid-1970s, Venezuela was seen as an island of relative economic progress and political stability, in a region in which many democratic regimes had fallen prey to military autocracies because of an increase in political conflict and a fragmentation of the political party system. Under the *Punto Fijo* system, noted earlier, Venezuelan political leaders had developed a system for the distribution and management of oil rents, in concert with the leading business and labor organizations, that provided economic benefits for the vast majority of the population and maintained economic and political stability for a period of 15 years. This system was first challenged by the oil boom of the 1970s, when the growth of oil rents proved to be too large for the political system to manage wisely. One manifestation of this problem was that a decision to allocate a portion of the oil "windfall" receipts for future generations, by means of a sovereign wealth fund in the manner of Chile, as noted earlier, could not be maintained in the face of pressure by the national executive to carry out an ambitious capital development program, which quickly exceeded the country's capacity to finance.

During the 1980s, as difficult adjustments had to be made in response to a sharp decline in oil export prices, the two-party system began to lose popular support, as it was seen as increasingly isolated from the concerns of the working and middle classes, which were beginning to take an interest in new political parties, and too dominated by the influence of an elite group in the formulation of the government's economic and social programs. Carlos Andres Perez was aware of this growing popular discontent in his 1988 presidential campaign and formulated an important program of political deconsolidation and decentralization, along with his program of economic reform. In effect, the program of political reform that Perez introduced in 1989 allowed for the direct election of state governors and mayors (instead of their appointment by the national executive and party leaders) and a significant delegation of budgetary authority from the central to the state governments. In the climate of political protest that the Perez economic program provoked, these political reforms accelerated the formation of new political parties and candidates for national office, who previously had been chosen by the leadership of the two main parties.[31] By the end of the 1990s, with continuing problems in economic policy management, the two main political parties had effectively ceased to function due to their loss of popular support, with the result that Hugo Chavez was elected president in December 1998 as head of a new party (MVR), on a strong anti-establishment and populist platform.

The political culture in which Indonesia's drive to development took place was significantly different from that of Venezuela. Traditionally, there has been a greater sense of collective identity within the dominant ethnic group and respect for strong leaders. Thus, in a guided democratic system, where there were controls on political activity and the national executive exercised significant influence over legislative branch activity, the dominance of a government-sponsored party (Golkar), which was organized to aggregate the interests of major stakeholders in society, allowed an effectively authoritarian style of political system to be maintained. The legitimacy of this regime, however, depended to a large extent on the degree to which the interests of the poor rural working class were served. This orientation to the welfare of the rural poor was also accepted by Suharto as a matter of political survival, given the potential appeal of Communist organizers who had launched insurgencies in many regions of the country during the 1960s. As a result of this concern, programs for the rural and urban poor, including the promotion of labor-intensive manufacturing for export, featured prominently in the development plans of the government. Accordingly, public expenditure has traditionally included significant allocations for programs of rural education, health services, and economic infrastructure to attract foreign direct investment in manufacturing facilities. Notably as a result of these efforts, the poverty ratio was reduced between 1976 and 1996 by more than half, from an estimated 40 percent to 17.6 percent.

Notwithstanding the effective delivery of certain public goods, there was growing public concern during the 1990s with the extent of corruption in public sector operations and the repression of political activity under the Suharto regime. This loss of public confidence reached a climax during the financial crisis of 1997–1998, which, among other things, ushered in an important political reform that allowed for a more open democratic system and political oversight of governmental functions.

Some Closing Observations

The three case studies presented above illustrate a number of key factors that were highlighted in the general discussion of chapters 4–8. Countries were selected from each region to demonstrate in one way or another some of the critical features that were common in the successful economic development of East Asia, on the one hand, and the more problematic development path of Latin America, on the other. Each country pairing was based on an important common identity in terms of initial conditions, such as colonial origins or economic structure, but where a critical turning point was reached that set in motion a significant divergence in the development paths of the two countries concerned. The following general points are raised here as a preface to the next, concluding chapter of the book.

1. Many of the country studies point to the important role that macroeconomic stability played in laying the foundation for a period of sustained high growth in real income per capita. This was true for Indonesia after its hyperinflation of the mid- to late 1960s and for Chile after the chaos of the Allende government of the early 1970s and the financial crisis of the early 1980s, and as evidenced by the generally sound macroeconomic stewardship demonstrated by Malaysia and Singapore during most of the second half of the past century.

2. Financial crises involved a heavy economic cost in all of the countries except Singapore, in terms of foregone output and a significant debt burden assumed by the public sector. Generally, such crises have been more of a problem for Latin America than East Asia in view of their frequency in the former region, as illustrated by each of the three cases chosen for this exercise.

3. The advent of an economic or financial crisis was often the catalyst for an important program of economic reform that initiated a significant period of output growth. This was demonstrated by Indonesia in the mid-1960s and late 1990s, Malaysia in the early 1970s, Chile in the mid-1970s and early 1980s, Jamaica in the late 1970s, and Venezuela in 1989.

4. Concerns about income inequality and entrenched poverty were often another form of catalyst for a change in government and the direction of economic policy. Examples of this political economy factor, which has been more typical of Latin America given the unique historical roots of inequality in that region, can be found in the experience of Chile in the late 1960s with the election of Salvador Allende, in Jamaica with the election of Michael Manley in the early 1970s, and in Venezuela with the election of Hugo Chavez in the late 1990s. Malaysia in the early 1970s is an interesting example for the East Asian region.

5. Each of the East Asian pairings in the three case studies illustrated the key role played by structural transformation and economic diversification tied to export development as a basis for positive and sustained economic growth. By contrast, the economic development of each of the Latin American case studies has been characterized by relatively little structural economic change in terms of the growth of manufacturing as a basis for new export development. In each of the successful cases of economic diversification, the government played an active role in terms of providing strong infrastructure development, a good business climate, and a combination of tax and trade incentives to attract targeted industries with the potential to develop export-oriented manufacturing.

6. Many of the country case studies illustrated the important role that political stability and strategic leadership can play in successful development outcomes. In each of the East Asian cases, as has been typical of the region more generally, strong political leadership grounded in economic development as a key strategic, long-term goal of the government can be identified with Lee Kuan Yew in Singapore, Mahathir Mohamad in Malaysia, and Suharto in Indonesia.

7. Each of the leaders just identified was supported or sponsored by a dominant political party or coalition with corporatist characteristics (the People's Action Party in Singapore, Barisan Nasional in Malaysia, and Golkar in Indonesia) that sought to encompass the main class, ethnic, or functional groups in society. These

regimes were quasi-autocratic or "soft" authoritarian in nature. The one case in Latin America that had some obvious similarity with the East Asian experience was Chile under Augusto Pinochet, although this case was much less grounded in political legitimacy than the others. Despite their authoritarian character, the East Asian cases demonstrate the important role that consultative mechanisms can play in seeking the input, and addressing the concerns, of business and labor groups. By contrast, the Latin American cases demonstrate the obstacles to sustained economic development that can arise from conditions in which there is intense political conflict at work in society, as illustrated by the struggles between the Peoples' National Party and the Jamaica Labor Party in Jamaica, Accion Democratica and COPEI in Venezuela, and the polarized political landscape that preceded the election of Salvador Allende in the late 1960s.

8. The case samples drawn from East Asia serve to illustrate the critically important role that an institutionalized, professional civil service can play in supporting sustained economic development. This feature of the institutional dimension of successful development not only is demonstrated preeminently by Singapore, but is also exemplified by Malaysia and, to a lesser extent, by Indonesia. Even in the last-mentioned case, where corruption was well known, there was commonality with the other two regional cases in that the design and coordination of economic policy making and planning was conducted, by and large, according to technocratic standards, with a lead government agency assigned a key role in coordinating the implementation and monitoring of economic policy. The examples chosen from Latin America show how patron-clientilistic political parties and patronage-based systems of public sector employment can weaken a critical institutional component of government, with a major loss in terms of long-term planning capability, continuity in economic decision making, and bureaucratic independence. Notably, Chile is an interesting example of how institutional reform has come about with the struggle to gain macroeconomic stability, in part through the strengthening of the institutional foundations for decision making and program implementation in the monetary and fiscal areas.

CHAPTER 10

Conclusions and Lessons for Development Policy

This chapter attempts to bring together the different strands of thinking and approaches laid out in the previous chapters in order to provide a coherent and concise response to the basic question raised in the title of this book, namely, why did East Asia surge ahead in its economic development during the second half of the twentieth century while Latin America fell behind, in relative terms. At one level, this response can be provided in terms of a set of propositions or theses related to the four "deep determinants" that were examined throughout the discussion of this book, which provide a fairly clear diagnosis of the factors that have favored East Asia, on the one hand, and that have hindered Latin America, on the other. At another level, the response to the basic question examined in the book can be provided by delineating the key features of the development process of East Asia, which account for its exceptional record of economic growth and, at the same time, sharply differentiate its experience from that of Latin America. Many of the positive features about successful development that emerge from the analysis of comparative regional development in this book reinforce, or have contributed to, current thinking at a more general level about the essential features of the development process and the challenges for developing countries in the twenty-first century. Within this context, the chapter identifies some of the key elements that are missing from the "Washington Consensus" as a framework for development. In this connection, the chapter then closes with a few thoughts about the main challenges facing Latin America in its development quest, notwithstanding the significant macroeconomic gains that it has registered since the end of the past century.

The four dimensions of the development process that were identified earlier in the book in regard to initial conditions, economic policy choices, institutions, and political economy factors can be recapitulated in terms of five theses about the divergent development process of East Asia and Latin America. The **first thesis** can be called the *"regionalist"* *thesis*, and argues that East Asia's more successful development outcome can be attributed to a significant extent to certain critical features of its colonial and cultural traditions, ideological traits, and integrative forces that were quite distinct from those that pertain to Latin America. In this context, a central argument in this book has been that Latin America has carried a heavy burden of history from its Iberian colonial and cultural heritage that has had a profound and negative impact on both the distribution of income and wealth and class and social differences, as well as on the quality of public administration and attitudes toward government. Both historical and ideological factors also oriented the Latin American region toward an inward model of development in the immediate post–World War II era that proved to be very entrenched and inefficient, and difficult to modify in an increasingly globalized economy. By contrast, East Asia's colonial heritage was much less pernicious than that of Latin America in terms of the economic and social conditions that it established for the region's post–World War II development, whereas the region's historical, cultural, and social forces created more homogeneity and a stronger collective identity in East Asian societies, which were reinforced by economic and regional ties. While sharing some of the integrative forces within East Asia, the Philippines is an interesting case in that its strong similarity with Latin America in terms of its colonial and cultural heritage created for that country some of the same burdens and constraints on its development process as in Latin America.

The consideration of economic policy choices in comparative perspective gives rise to **second** and third theses that contribute to an understanding of the divergent development experience in the two regions. One could be called the *"macro fundamentals" thesis,* which argues that East Asia was able to sustain a stronger pace of economic growth and development than Latin America during the second half of the twentieth century because it was more successful in establishing and maintaining the basic conditions of macroeconomic stability. The maintenance of a relatively sound macroeconomic policy framework in East Asia, as evidenced by a relatively low rate of inflation, fiscal discipline, the maintenance of a competitive exchange rate and interest rates that were generally positive in real terms, and a moderate level of protection, created an environment that encouraged private savings and investment, both domestic and foreign, as well as an expansion of the financial and external sectors in relation to the overall size of the economy. These conditions created a strong environment for private sector business activity and sustained economic growth. By contrast, macroeconomic conditions in Latin America were generally far less stable than in East Asia, as evidenced by a high and variable rate of inflation, the frequent occurrence of financial crises, and substantial variability in the rate of tariff protection, as well as in the level of interest rates and the exchange rate in real terms. Such an environment was far less conducive to the promotion of private financial savings and sound investment on a sustained basis, with the result that the rate of economic growth was relatively low and fairly volatile during the second half of the twentieth century. Within the context of this thesis, it is clear that in strictly quantitative terms the explanation for the sharply divergent path of economic growth of East Asia and Latin America during the second half of the twentieth century is overdetermined. The basis for this claim relies on independent statistical estimates cited in chapters 3 and 4 of the impact across the two regions arising from differences in the scale of investment, the "demographic dividend," financial depth, public spending on infrastructure, and the extent of output and policy variability, not to mention differences in the levels of social trust and bureaucratic quality cited in chapter 7.

The **third thesis** (and second aspect of economic policy) relevant for the comparative development of East Asia and Latin America can be called the *"structuralist" thesis*. This thesis maintains that getting the macro fundamentals right would not have been sufficient for generating East Asia's relatively high rate of economic growth without the benefit of industrial policy and other government interventions that promoted significant structural transformation and a rapid pace of industrialization in the East Asian economies. Even though Latin America entered into its phase of industrialization at an earlier stage than East Asia, it was mainly oriented to the domestic market and did not alter the region's significant reliance on traditional agricultural and mining pursuits for exports. As a result, there was relatively little structural transformation of the Latin American regional economy in the post–World War II era and only modest labor productivity growth, such that a rapid rise in real incomes could not be achieved as in the case of East Asia. Consistent with the "structuralist" thesis, one can point to significant differences between the two regions in terms of the strength of technological capabilities within the domestic manufacturing sector and the industrial labor force, the quality of infrastructure and logistics for investment and trade, and the competitiveness of local manufacturing in external markets, with clear advantages for East Asia in each of these dimensions.

These positive characteristics of the East Asian regional economy did not arise spontaneously or by private initiative alone, but rather reflected the benefit of clear incentives of government economic policy and targeted investment of the public sector over a sustained period of time.

The **fourth thesis** that needs to be recognized in accounting for the divergent development paths of East Asia and Latin America can be identified as the *"institutionalist" thesis*. This thesis is somewhat related to the "structuralist" thesis, and argues that a critical ingredient in East Asia's successful development drive and Latin America's laggard performance was the strength or weakness of the region's institutional arrangements regarding the protection of property rights, the quality of government bureaucracy, and the strength of social capital. Even in the absence of a well-developed legal framework for the protection of property rights, East Asian governments were more successful than their counterparts in Latin America in dealing with the "commitment problem" of economic development, such that private investors in the former region were generally more satisfied that the fruits of their investment activity would be protected from expropriation and that profits associated with their investment in local manufacturing could be retained, and repatriated in the case of foreign investors. There were a variety of signals and proxies for legal arrangements that East Asian governments developed to deal with the commitment problem. Two prominent examples were the export processing zone and the so-called deliberation council; the former created the legal, infrastructural, and labor conditions in a concentrated industrial space that proved to be very attractive for the development of manufacturing production by foreign investors, while the latter fostered a spirit of collaboration and trust between government officials and private businessmen in identifying and eliminating obstacles and bottlenecks in the development of new business ventures. An independent and qualified government bureaucracy was also critical for the success of these councils and for the design and implementation of a consistent economic policy framework across agencies and over time. Unlike East Asia, Latin America did not have a tradition of professionalism in its governmental bureaucratic functions to draw upon in its modern phase of development; this characteristic has only emerged over time with efforts to institutionalize more independence in the conduct of certain aspects of macroeconomic policy.

The *final of the five theses* that is relevant for understanding the comparative development of East Asia and Latin America can be called the *"political economy" thesis*, which in some ways is related to the "regionalist" thesis discussed earlier. The basic tenet of this thesis is that the nature of state–society relations played a key role in determining regional differences in governments' development efforts and the impact of industrialization drives across the two regions. Very simply put, in countries where governments were weak and poorly insulated from dominant political groups, government policy would typically be distorted in favor of particular societal interests (e.g., rural oligarchic or industrial groups) or biased toward short-term distributional concerns because of the effect of a fragmented political structure and struggles over access to public sector resources. In view of the economic and social inequalities that pervaded Latin America, political economy factors tended to focus government policy on short-term distributional concerns, and worked against the implementation of a sound development framework that could be sustained over time. It was often the case that a spell of military rule provided some coherence to economic and development policy in that region, but in an environment of brutal repression that undermined the legitimacy and durability of these governing arrangements. The political culture of East Asia also often validated an autocratic form of government, in which the state was dominant over societal forces, but it was legitimized in many instances by the improvements in general economic welfare that it promoted. Notwithstanding ethnic and sectarian differences within East Asian societies, the degree of social cohesion and social trust was still relatively high, which militated against a fragmented political culture. Notably too, in countries grounded in a Confucian culture, business relationships were imbued with certain values of reciprocity and contract fulfillment that promoted successful business ventures in both local and foreign markets, which facilitated cross-border investment and trade in the East Asian region.

The experience of East Asia raises the question of whether an autocratic form of government is conducive to, or even required for, long-term economic development. Certainly there is no general evidence across a wide spectrum of countries in support of such a proposition, as would be suggested by examining the mixed experience of Latin America as a region in this regard.[1] Nevertheless, it is remarkable that in eight of the nine countries of East Asia (all except the Philippines), as well as in the case of pre–World War II Japan, the initiation of a successful industrialization drive occurred during a period of autocratic rule. What is true in these cases is that social and political culture was tolerant of this form of government, and that strong political leadership was exhibited as regards the high strategic importance of economic development as a goal of government policy. As a period of strong economic growth was sustained and a rising middle class was formed, the balance of power between state and societal forces has shifted in such a way that the political economy of these societies has evolved toward more representative forms of government and growing popular sovereignty. China represents the most recent example of this evolutionary trend, and it remains to be seen over the medium term how the Communist Party becomes a more representative political organ in response to popular pressure and protest or allows the emergence of competing political groups in response to the demands of a growing middle class.

Each of the five theses described above contributes a different perspective to an understanding of the divergent comparative development of East Asia and Latin America, while none is sufficiently robust in and of themselves to provide a fully satisfactory explanation. In this regard, a comparative analysis of the economic development of East Asia and Latin America confirms that an interdisciplinary and multifactoral approach, which is grounded in historical forces and combines both economic and noneconomic perspectives, is essential in order to gain a satisfactory understanding of the elements that contribute to successful economic development. Moreover, each country's course of economic development is a path-dependent process, which may have certain regional commonalities, but is nonetheless rooted in a specific set of initial conditions and historical dynamic forces. In this sense, the process of economic development is not a phenomenon that can be adequately or fully represented by the neoclassical growth model, which synthesizes the economic development process into a relatively simple relationship between income per capita and capital and labor accumulation and technological development. In this respect, the model deals only with the "proximate," as distinct from the "deep" determinants of economic development.

As an extension of this summary framework, in the next section of this chapter, an attempt is made to identify, by way of a general summary, the key elements of successful economic development that can be derived from a comparative analysis of East Asia and Latin America, which reflect the interplay of the five theses just defined. A number of propositions about the nature of successful economic development can be inferred from the experience of East Asia and Latin America. These are outlined as follows:

1. While economic development entails change across many dimensions of economic and social life, it is nonetheless true that a rapid rate of growth in the pace of aggregate economic activity over a sustained period of time is required in order to make possible a

significant reduction in poverty and major gains in the level of real income per capita. The comparative economic development of East Asia and Latin America clearly shows that, unless a government can spark a sustained drive in private investment that intensifies the scale of existing economic activities or expands in new ones consistent with a country's natural and other factor endowments, workers will not experience the gains in income that will allow for real improvements in their standard of living. Nor will the public sector have the resources to establish targeted social programs that provide educational and health benefits for the extreme poor in an effort to promote growth with equity.

2. In order to experience a period of rapid economic growth, a country needs to undergo a process of significant structural transformation that results in a shift of capital and labor resources to activities of higher value added and a greater diversification in the production of goods for the domestic and external markets. In each of the successful East Asian economies, this process of structural transformation was achieved through the expansion of the manufacturing sector, which over time became strongly linked to the production of high value goods for external markets. By contrast, Latin America developed its manufacturing sector at an earlier stage than in the case of East Asia, but its share of aggregate economic activity remained less than that of East Asia and declined in relative terms over time, as the region remained highly dependent on its natural resource-based exports. The comparative economic development of the two regions also shows the importance of maintaining an appropriate balance between the production of the agricultural and manufacturing sectors. During Latin America's early post–World War II industrialization drive, many governments ignored the needs of rural workers in terms of land reform and basic educational and health requirements, with the result that bottlenecks developed in the supply of staples for the growing urban labor force and basic inputs for certain manufacturing processes. By contrast, East Asian governments early in their development efforts focused on the plight of rural workers, in part to limit the potential appeal and attraction of insurgent movements that could pose a threat to the established order.

3. Consistent with the tenets of economic growth theory, a sustained and rapid increase in real income per capita requires a significant accumulation of human and physical capital over time. The experience of East Asia clearly shows that a sustained

improvement in real income per capita can only be accomplished through a steady and continued growth in labor productivity, which, in turn, requires a major expansion in the stock of physical capital and knowledge per worker over time. For improvements in the stock of infrastructure and physical capital to be most productive, governments must ensure that technological capabilities within the industrial sector are developed and sustained over time, which require programs of labor training and improvements in industrial organization and work processes that can accommodate the fruits of technological innovation arising from locally sponsored R&D activities. Consistent with an evolutionary perspective on economic development, the experience of East Asia demonstrates that there is a significant "tacit" element in the absorption of foreign technological know-how associated with new industrial development that requires painstaking efforts on the part of local entrepreneurs and a persistent and sustained process of trial and error and "learning by doing." In this respect, industrialization is a path-dependent process in which agglomeration effects accumulate over time, and "first mover" advantages are created for those countries that can attract foreign investment at an early stage in their development and gain a foothold in global production networks.

4. The experience of East Asia and Latin America clearly shows that an environment of macroeconomic stability is required for an increase in private investment to take place and to be sustained over time. Macroeconomic stability involves not only the establishment of a sound fiscal and monetary policy framework conducive to the maintenance of relatively low inflation and a sustainable balance of payments position, but also a consistent economic policy framework across agencies and over time that inspires private sector confidence in the stability of the long-term horizon for investment planning. The design of medium-term, "indicative planning" frameworks for government policy with inputs from labor and business sector organizations can be one means of promoting a positive environment for investment, although they are certainly not a guarantee if policy implementation is poor.

5. Another essential ingredient for creating a sound investment climate is a regime that ensures the protection of property rights. Investors must be secure in their belief that the government is committed to the non-expropriation of profits and property as

regards domestic business operations. In the advanced countries, the legal basis for this system of protections developed out of a political struggle between the sovereign and private entrepreneurs that gave rise to a set of common law principles that have endured over time. Some of this legal tradition has been absorbed by many countries in East Asia and Latin America through the influence of their colonial legacy, but in practice governments have had to deal with the "commitment problem" of development through a variety of alternative devices. The experience of East Asia has shown that the institutionalization of a sound macroeconomic policy framework can serve as one such device, as can the expression of strong political leadership focused on economic development as a strategic goal of government of the highest importance. In other cases, the commitment problem has been solved by the establishment of close consultative arrangements between government officials and business leaders, noted earlier, and the promotion of an open and frank dialogue oriented to the solution of practical problems that may be frustrating the development or expansion of business operations consistent with economic priorities of the government. East Asia's experience in dealing with the "commitment problem" and China's early experiments in promoting private market-based economic activity clearly show that institutions are context specific and path dependent and need to be adapted over time. In this regard, the transfer of "best practice" institutional arrangements to developing countries may be neither feasible nor appropriate, unless they are adapted and modified to conform to local conditions and requirements.

6. The development of a sound financial sector is an important concomitant of the economic growth process. While there can be two-way interactive effects between finance and growth, the experience of East Asia and Latin America clearly demonstrates that the financial sector can be an important spur to growth by facilitating private investment, including through government action in offering development finance for promising business ventures that would not otherwise find risk capital or long-term capital resources. Conversely, problems in the financial sector, and banking crises in particular, can be an important source of variability in output and sustained losses in income. In this connection, the process of financial liberalization, both domestic and foreign, needs to be carefully

designed and monitored through effective supervision and regulation.

7. In cases of sustained economic growth, a structural change in exports is an important counterpart of the structural transformation and diversification of the domestic economy noted earlier. The cases of strong and sustained economic growth in East Asia all demonstrated a marked shift in the structure of exports away from natural-resource–based commodities toward exports of manufactured goods of increasing sophistication and value added (and of services in certain cases). The extension of domestic industries into the export market allowed countries to benefit from economies of scale more easily, while encouraging them to maintain competitiveness and upgrade over time the technological capability of the local manufacturing sector. Within the context of a stable macroeconomic environment noted earlier, the promotion of a diversified export sector requires the maintenance of a realistic exchange rate and a gradual reduction of protection toward moderate levels.

8. Industrial policy has an important role to play in facilitating the process of industrial transformation and export diversification that sustained economic growth requires. Contrary to the implicit assumptions of the neoclassical growth model, the process of economic development is rife with market failures, for example, in the form of information asymmetries among economic agents, coordination failures in investment, and missing markets for finance. These failures, in principle, call for government intervention. At one level, the case for such intervention is unambiguous and undeniable, as regards the government's role in developing basic infrastructure and logistics capabilities, increasing private sector awareness of potential export markets, and in promoting the upgrading of labor skills and domestic industrial capacity to undertake R&D and innovation. Recent experience has shown that these are critically important areas of government activity for purposes of fostering the agglomeration effects of industrial clusters and linkages with global value chains. A more controversial area of industrial policy deals with the potential role of government policy in promoting certain kinds of industrial activities in preference to others. Contrary to the heavy hand of government in guiding historic patterns of import-substitution industrialization, a more refined case can be made for government action to promote foreign direct

investment in activities that take advantage of a country's natural and other factor endowments and to create an environment where new private sector industrial ventures and entrepreneurial activity are encouraged, and the benefits of new designs of industrial processes and techniques can be fully exploited by business entrepreneurs.

9. The development of bureaucratic competence is critical to the success of a government's efforts to promote economic development. The comparative development of East Asia and Latin America clearly demonstrates the central importance of sound public administration and effective institutions of government in sustaining the process of economic development. This aspect of development is an essential institutional counterpart to the emphasis given in previous points of discussion, for example, with regard to the promotion of a sound macroeconomic policy environment, the conduct of deliberation councils, and the implementation of industrial policy. Without the existence of a government bureaucracy that is relatively insulated from political or private sector interference and that attracts a dedicated corps of competent civil servants that will accumulate over time knowledge and expertise in specific areas of policy administration, a process of sustained economic development will not take place. An additional, desirable characteristic or feature of bureaucratic effectiveness that has been demonstrated in East Asian experience is that of "embedded autonomy." This characteristic involves the capacity of government officials to inspire the trust of private sector industrialists in finding ways to foster sound investment and new business activity, while at the same time maintaining independence and professionalism in the administration, for example, of industrial policy instruments and the monitoring of mutually agreed targets and milestones of performance by favored businesses.

10. Severe inequality in income and wealth can be a major obstacle to a sound development process. In cases where there are significant cleavages by ethnic, racial, or social identity in regard to the distribution of income and wealth, it may be very difficult for governments to operate effectively. Such conditions breed social and political conflict, an emphasis on distributional rather than developmental goals in public policy, and instability and uncertainty in the policy environment. In addition, they can easily give rise to populist pressures, which are likely to lead to the use

of public employment for patronage purposes, frequent turnover in government jobs, and a low degree of bureaucratic effectiveness, not to mention problems of outright corruption. Where economic power is concentrated in certain groups, they may resist or frustrate political initiatives to strengthen government functions, especially if these would result in a higher tax burden on their resources or the empowerment of disadvantaged social groups that over time could represent a threat to their privileged position. Unfortunately, the Latin American region suffered from many of the political syndromes just mentioned during the second half of the twentieth century, which frustrated the efforts of government leaders to promote sustainable economic development. With time and effort, however, a consolidation of political power representing a balance of social forces and a strengthening of the middle class has emerged in countries such as Brazil, Chile, Peru, and Uruguay that has created a more stable political environment within which development goals can be more easily defined and pursued. Except for the Philippines, East Asia was spared much of the political and social instability associated with severe problems of inequality, although social and ethnic tensions did pose a challenge for governments at certain times in countries such as Indonesia and Malaysia. However, these and other potential problems were alleviated through policies to promote labor-intensive manufacturing and by direct government action to advance the interests of underprivileged groups, including those dependent on traditional agricultural pursuits.

The description of the development process exhibited by successful East Asian economies provided in the preceding paragraphs points to a number of obvious deficiencies and shortcomings in the Washington Consensus as a conceptual framework for development policy. In evaluating its policy prescriptions, however, one should not ignore the specific historic and regional context within which it was defined. As much as anything else, the framing of the Consensus was an attempt to identify and rationalize the range of macroeconomic policy reforms that governments in Latin America were undertaking in response to the economic disruption that had been caused by the sovereign debt crisis of the early 1980s. As noted in previous chapters, the Washington Consensus also reflected a major shift in academic and policy studies away from an emphasis on direct government action in the promotion of economic development toward a vision of greater reliance on market forces, both domestic and external, in resource allocation and the inducement of private investment and entrepreneurial activity in order to promote economic growth.

At one level, the policy prescriptions outlined in the ten principles of the Consensus represented a healthy antidote to the widespread mismanagement of macroeconomic policy that one could observe in Latin America prior to the 1980s. In this respect, the Washington Consensus is perfectly consistent with the "macro fundamentals" thesis, discussed earlier, as a mono-factoral vision of development and the natural convergence process implied by the neoclassical growth model, which is unimpeded by market failures. However, as a framework for development policy, the Consensus is very incomplete, as it ignored a number of critical dimensions or aspects of the development process in which the government has an important role to play. Most importantly, there is no recognition of the critical feature of structural transformation in the development process, which drives increases in labor productivity over time and long-term gains in income per capita, as described earlier. One also misses in the Washington Consensus any recognition of a role for government in promoting the development of technological capability and an environment supportive of innovative activity within the private sector, as well as an expanding network of telecommunications and transportation infrastructure and logistics capability to keep pace with the demands of industrial development. In this connection, there is hardly any prominence given in the Washington Consensus to the role of institutions in the development process (except for a narrow reference to the legal protection of property rights) and to the critical aspect of bureaucratic effectiveness in supporting sound policy design and implementation. On the basis of these limitations alone, the Washington Consensus must be seen as a very inadequate and incomplete framework for development policy.[2]

Of course, a major omission in the Washington Consensus, and indeed in the development debate throughout most of the period since the middle of the twentieth century, has been the issue of environmental sustainability. It is now generally recognized that the objectives of economic growth and poverty reduction must be defined within a more holistic framework of sustainable development that takes account of "planetary boundaries" and that strives to achieve sustainable consumption and production patterns, which are increasingly decoupled from the depletion of natural resources and environmental pollution. This is an immense topic (for discussion in another book) and a major challenge for the governance of the global system, which at least is being addressed in the context of the follow-up to the Millennium Development Goals that expire in 2015.[3]

Given the growing dissatisfaction with the Washington Consensus within the Latin American region, there has been an active debate on the critical elements and policy initiatives that are needed to sustain the region's drive toward convergence, which was ignited by the positive macroeconomic developments of the period since the early years of the new century. In addition, the extent to which countries in the region have been able to weather the global financial crisis without major disruption has solidified the institutional foundations that have been laid in many countries for the management of a stable macroeconomic policy framework.

One important development that has implications for Latin America's economic prospects is the growing influence of China in foreign trade, investment, and external financing. China's enormous demand for agricultural commodities and mineral resources in its recent imports from Latin America, as well as that of other Asian countries, raises the continuing risk for the region of succumbing to the perils of the natural resource "curse." The growing trade relations between China and Latin America (and South America, in particular) have, in this respect, not been the conduit for any significant technological diffusion or knowledge spillovers for Latin America, as the bilateral trade is mainly inter-industry based (e.g., grains and minerals for manufactured goods), rather than intra-industry based. Moreover, Latin America's imports from China are mainly concentrated in products reflecting unskilled-labor–intensive manufacturing. As such, the growing weight of these goods in bilateral and global trade has been a direct threat to many exports of a similar nature emanating from Central America and the Caribbean.[4] However, within this pattern of inter-regional trade, it is important to recognize that there is a distinct possibility during the remainder of this decade of some decline in the strength of China's demand for primary commodities attendant on its efforts at economic rebalancing and boosting domestic consumption. Such a structural shift in the Chinese economy could lead to a significant decline in the prices for Latin America's key natural resource-based exports and a weakening of income growth in the region.

These simple facts point to a number of important challenges for the Latin American region. One is that it must continue to expand on some of the examples arising from Chile's recent experience in diversifying the range of forest and fishing products that have been developed from its strong natural resource endowments. Among other things, these experiments point to the important role of private-public partnerships in promoting business market surveys and scientific testing and in providing "seed" finance for new product development. More generally, however, this example points to continuing deficiencies in the quality of national innovative systems and the strength of technological capabilities in Latin America, compared with those of East Asia, and the former region's lagging position in technological innovation, as reflected, for example, in the average number of patents per capita registered by each region since the late 1980s. These shortcomings also come through clearly in surveys conducted by the World Economic Forum for its 2012–2013 Global Competitiveness Index (GCI), in which Latin America lags East Asia with respect to specific qualifications of its innovative activities, in particular its "capacity for innovation," "company spending on R&D," and "the availability of scientists and engineers."

Another challenge for the Latin America region is to strengthen the quality of its basic transport infrastructure and logistics capabilities to support the expanding role of foreign trade in the region's economic activities. Anecdotal evidence of this problem is suggested by recent reports from Brazil in the Economist magazine (mid-May 2013) that trucks carrying grain for export through the main seaport city of Santos were backed up for 21 miles because of inadequate storage and loading facilities at that port, where as many as 200 ships may encounter waiting times of 54 days to unload their cargo (Talvi and Munyo 2013). Again, according to the latest GCI rankings, the quality of basic transport infrastructure is the dimension of greatest divergence between the two regions. More generally, Latin America has lost ground to other developing regions in its penetration of global export markets. As of 2010, only two countries from Latin America (Brazil and Mexico) were among the top 25 exporting countries in the global economy, whereas seven countries of East Asia (all except Indonesia and the Philippines) were represented in this group.

Building on the improvements in macroeconomic policy management that have taken place within Latin America in the past 20 years, the region needs to make further efforts to improve the business climate and the quality of government bureaucracies in order to promote the growth of investment, both domestic and foreign. In this connection, the World Bank's *Doing Business* indicators point to clear deficiencies, again with respect to East Asia, in basic areas of the business environment related to enforcing contracts, trading across borders, and protecting investors, among other things. In addition, more competition and flexibility is needed in production and labor markets, and in the regulation of business entry and exit. Again, in this connection, it is interesting to note that, within the most recent issue of the GCI, the quality of institutions is one of the three areas of greatest divergence between the two regions, along with infrastructure and innovation. Concerns related to the "incidence of crime and violence," the "diversion of public funds," and the level of "public trust in politicians" show up as areas of greatest divergence between the two regions in the surveys of business opinion that underlie the GCI.

In the area of business operations and labor market developments, the Latin America region faces a continuing challenge of reducing the size and scope of the informal sector in national economies. Within the past decade, there has been some success in reducing the size of the informal sector in certain countries such as Chile, Peru, and Uruguay, but much more needs to be done in terms of improving the quality and delivery of government social services, the facilities for job training and skills upgrading, and programs for the promotion and support of small and medium enterprises. Improvements in the business climate detailed in the previous paragraph would also have favorable spillover effects on alleviating the problem of informality.

One final consideration in defining an agenda of development challenges for Latin America relates to the role of the financial sector and the need for governments to take steps to improve its basic features, as regards access by individuals and businesses, along with the efficiency, depth, and stability of its operations, in order to provide an essential support for the expansion of private investment and business activity. Clearly, the legacy of financial crises in the region has taken a heavy toll in terms of repressing financial sector development and weakening private sector confidence in local currency banking operations. Consolidating the record of macroeconomic stability will obviously help in this regard, but more needs to be done to strengthen national systems of banking regulation and supervision.

This is far from an exhaustive list of issues relevant for the challenge of closing Latin America's development gap with respect to the advanced countries, but it is one that highlights some of the main deficiencies that emerge from a comparative analysis of the region's development in relation to that of East Asia and an understanding of the reasons for their divergent economic trajectories since the middle of the past century.

Hopefully, when the sequel to this book is written in a decade's time, Latin America will have reversed much of the economic gap that emerged with respect to East Asia (and to the advanced countries) during the second half of the twentieth century.

Notes

1 Introduction—Globalization and Economic Divergence

1. Professor Lucas's discussion of the growth convergence process can be found in a number of his writings, for example, Lucas (2007).
2. The complete data set created by Professor Maddison, which has been updated by his former colleagues at the Groningen Growth and Development Center, can be accessed at www.ggdc.net/maddison.
3. A recent chart illustrating this U-shaped curve can be found in the *Financial Times* (June 10, 2012, "The Seven Ages of Industry"), which can be accessed at www.ft.com/industrialrevolution.
4. These estimates of global income inequality can be found in Milanovic (2009). Gini coefficients range between 0 for perfect equality, that is, between successively higher shares of income and population, and 1 for perfect inequality, that is, where 1 percent of the population holds 100 percent of income.
5. The term "Washington Consensus" was coined by John Williamson of the Peterson Institute of International Economics (see Williamson 1990).
6. The ten guidelines of the Washington Consensus are examined in chapter 3 and also in chapter 10.
7. These technological forces working toward globalization have been identified and examined in a recent, provocative paper by Professor Robert Gordon (2012).
8. This second technological revolution has been called the "second unbundling" of trade, as distinct from the "first unbundling" that occurred with the development of steam power and the telegraph, as explained in Baldwin (2006).
9. The impact of the container revolution on the global transport of freight has been recently evaluated in a study by Bernhofen et al. (2013).
10. The operations of transnational or multinational corporations in the international economic system have been analyzed in various issues of UNCTAD's *World Investment Reports*. An important recent study by UNCTAD of the impact of global production networks or global value chains on global trade developments is UNCTAD (2013).

11. These data and the forces behind them are examined in Elson (2011).
12. Two benchmark studies that distil much of the literature dealing with the impact of export-oriented and import-substitution industrialization on the early post–World War II economic development of East Asia and Latin America are Gereffi and Wyman (1990) and Haggard (1990).
13. The six stylized facts of steady-state growth identified by Professor Nicholas Kaldor are as follows: (1) labor productivity grows at a sustained rate; (2) capital per worker grows at a sustained rate; (3) the real rate of interest, or return on capital, is stable over time; (4) the ratio of capital to output is stable; (5) the returns to capital and labor, as reflected in shares of national income, are stable; and (6) among the fast-growing countries of the world, there is an appreciable variation in the rate of growth on the order of 2 to 5 percent (Kaldor 1961). A recent restatement of these stylized facts can be found in Jones and Romer (2009).
14. These stylized facts of economic growth for successful developing countries during the second half of the twentieth century have been described and analyzed in a number of publications, including Ocampo (2004), Ocampo et al. (2007), and United Nations (2006).
15. The understanding of economic growth as a process of structural change was central to early post–World War II thinking about economic development (as reflected, e.g., in the writings of Alexander Gerschenkron, Simon Kuznets, and Paul Rosenstein-Rodan), but was sidelined for many years with the influence of the neoclassical growth model and its offshoots. More recently, it has featured again in the emergence of a New Structural Economics paradigm, as exemplified in the writings of Justin Lin, the former Chief Economist of the World Bank (see, e.g., Lin, 2012).
16. See, for example, Imbs and Wacziarg (2003) and Hausmann and Hidalgo (2010).
17. The stylized facts of economic development summarized here are more fully described in Rodrik (2007).
18. The existence of market failures in the development process and the role of government policy in overcoming them are examined in more detail in Chapter 3.
19. These data are presented and analyzed in Wacziarg and Welch (2008).
20. As reported in Easterly and Reshef (2009), the coefficient of correlation between manufacturing exports per capita and real income per capita for a cross section of 151 countries in 2000 was 0.88.
21. This literature is summarized and extended with new empirical results by Wacziarg and Welch (2008).
22. The positive impact of export product diversification on reducing growth volatility in developing countries is examined in Agosin (2007) and Haddad et al. (2010).
23. For a recent summary of the findings on the relationship between financial opening and economic growth, see Beck et al. (2010).

24. The data for manufactured exports from developing countries can be found on the website of the United Nations Industrial Development Organization (www.unido.org/Data1/IndStatBrief.)
25. This figure for 1980 is cited in Lall et al. (2006).
26. There is an extensive literature of the growth of global production networks or global value chains, as exemplified in the writings of Professor Gary Gereffi; see, for example, Gereffi et al. (2005).
27. A cogent analysis of the recent rapid growth in the trade of intermediate goods, or parts and components, associated with the development of global supply chains and global production networks, which has been called the "second unbundling" of globalization (see footnote 8 above), can be found in Baldwin (2011b).
28. For a recent review of the changes in the pattern of global trade summarized in the text, see IMF (2011).
29. These estimates are drawn from IMF (2011), table 1.

2 The Economic Development of East Asia and Latin America in Comparative Perspective

1. Data for FDI flows and stocks for 1990–2010 can be found in UNCTAD's World Investment Report (2012).
2. See UNECLA (2008).
3. During 1960–2010, the coefficient of variation of the average rate of growth in real GDP per capita for Latin America was double that for East Asia, while the average rate of inflation was seven times higher than for East Asia.
4. Based on the Gini coefficients compiled in the Deninger–Squire database of the World Bank (1996), which has recently been updated by UNU-WIDER and is available on its website (www.wider.unu.edu/research /Database/en_GB/database)
5. By 2010, this regional difference in Gini coefficients is estimated to have declined to around 5 percentage points, as Gini coefficients dropped in countries such as Argentina, Brazil, Colombia, Uruguay, and Venezuela, while the average Gini coefficient for East Asia increased to an estimated 45.6.
6. This important phenomenon is explored in Birdsall et al. (2011).
7. The "hukou" system, which has deep historical roots in China, is a household registration system that identifies an individual according to one's original home site (rural or urban) and limits that person's access to social benefits if s/he migrates from a rural to an urban area, for example, for purposes of work.
8. For a recent analysis of these trends in East Asia and Latin America, see Lustig et al. (2012).
9. Loayza and Rigolini (2006).

10. One of the most in-depth studies of informality in Latin America can be found in World Bank (2007).
11. These data are based on Annex Tables A.3 in UNDESA 2006.
12. "Factory Asia" is a term that is commonly used to refer to the highly integrated value chain of production for garments, electronic goods, and automobiles, in particular, that has developed throughout the nine countries of East Asia.
13. These rankings are based on data assembled by Athukorala and Hill (2010), see table 8.
14. These data are drawn from Easterly and Reshef (2009), see table A1.
15. These data are drawn from Athukorala and Hill (2010).
16. The "flying geese" theory of economic development has a long history in the discussion of the post–World War II economic development of East Asia and originated in the writings of Akamatsu (1962). It is discussed again in chapter 4.
17. The "middle-income trap" has been identified with many economies in Latin America, as exemplified recently by Felipe (2012) and Jankowska et al. (2012).
18. It is interesting to note that while the favorable terms of trade effect during the period prior to the onset of the global financial crisis in 2008 was not larger than experienced in some previous decades, the estimated income windfall of the favorable export prices was unprecedented because of the higher scale of exports. Economists at the IMF have estimated that this income windfall was equivalent to 15 percent of annual income per year from 2003 to 2012, or 100 percent of regional domestic income on a cumulative basis. In some oil export countries, such as Venezuela, the income effect was higher than just noted, whereas in some other countries such as Brazil it was lower (Adler and Magud 2013).
19. Growth accounting quantifies the contributions of growth in capital, labor, and total factor productivity to growth in real income per capita, whereas development accounting does the same exercise in terms of levels (as distinct from changes).
20. This exercise is presented in Sachs et al. (2004). The predicted or estimated growth rates for East Asia and Latin America were 7.2 and 1.2 percent, respectively, compared with actual growth rates of 6.4 and 0.4 percent.
21. TFP is required in the neoclassical growth model to offset the effects of declining marginal productivity of capital on income growth, which is ignored in the Harrod–Domar model by virtue of its assumption of a constant ICOR.
22. It is interesting to note that the basic equation of the Harrod–Domar framework ($Y=AK$, where $A=s/v$), nearly 70 years after its first introduction (1946), becomes the basic equation of the endogenous growth model in its so-called AK format ($Y=AK$), which gives rise to the phenomenon of perpetual growth. The main differences between the two frameworks

is that the definition of "A" changes from the ratio of savings to the incremental capital-output ratio (s/v) in the Harrod–Domar model to a measure of technological change or TFP in the endogenous growth framework and the definition of "K" is broadened to include human capital and the output of R&D efforts.

23. These points are persuasively developed in a study by economists at the Federal Reserve Bank of Minneapolis (Cole et al. 2006).

24. The World Bank's East Asian Miracle Study (World Bank 1993) was one of the most widely cited and extensively debated analyses of the economic development experience among its member countries during the past 25 years. Part of the study's controversy is that it downplayed the role of industrial policy in accounting for East Asia's high-growth experience.

25. This phrase most recently has been associated with the work of two World Bank research staff, David Dollar and Art Kraay, for their 2002 study titled "Growth is good for the Poor" (Dollar and Kraay 2002).

3 Changing Paradigms in Development Economics

1. The initial exposition of the neoclassical growth model was presented in Solow (1956) and later elaborated in Solow (1970). In some written contexts, the neoclassical growth model is referred to as the Solow–Swan growth model because of a similar theoretical framework that was developed by the Australian economist (Trevor Swan) and published soon after Solow's original paper.

2. A recent example of growth accounting is Caselli (2005).

3. The two economists most closely associated with the development of endogenous growth theory are Romer (1986) and Lucas (1988).

4. A more recent discussion of the results of growth accounting for East Asia and Latin America than that of Collins and Bosworth (2003) can be found in Singh and Cerisola (2006).

5. A recent study that has examined these limitations in growth accounting can be found in Acemoglu and Autor (2012).

6. The sentiment expressed in this paragraph to some extent echoes a criticism offered by Professor Jonathan Temple in his call for more attention to the role of dual economy models in the analysis of development challenges for low-income countries (Temple 2005).

7. Two extensions of the standard growth model that generate balanced growth with structural transformation can be found in Kongsamut, Rebelo, and Xie (2001) and Ngai and Pissarides (2007).

8. This view of Krugman, based on the research of Alwyn Young (1992), was popularized in an article in Foreign Affairs (1994).

9. The "evolutionist" approach to understanding the East Asian growth "miracle" is laid out in Nelson and Pack (1999).

10. These estimates are based on comments by Olivier Blanchard at a Brookings Panel discussion of a paper by Chong-en Bai et al. (2006). It is interesting to note that Richard Cooper in his comments at the same Brookings Panel discussion questioned the validity of applying a growth accounting framework to China on theoretical grounds similar to those laid out in this chapter and those of Nelson and Pack (1999). A more recent summary of research estimates of TFP growth for China, which confirms the wide range of variation cited in the text, can be found in Xu Tian and Xiaohua Yu (2012).

11. The components of TFP change are discussed in a recent study by Yusuf and Nabeshima (2012).

12. Aghion and Durlauf (2009) provide a convenient summary of recent thinking in the domain of endogenous growth models, which provides the source material for the discussion in the text.

13. See, for example, Barro and Sala-i-Martin (1995, 2003).

14. See Barro "Convergence and Modernization" (2012).

15. Easterly's critique of growth regressions can be found in his contribution to the Handbook on Economic Growth (2005).

16. For one of the first proponents of this approach, see the study by Hall and Jones (1998). A more recent and influential study is that by Rodrik et al. (2002).

17. An important statement on the role of institutions in economic development can be found in North (1994).

18. The seminal work in this field is Acemoglu et al. (2001), which pointed to the influence of colonial institutions as a long-term determinant of economic development and is examined in chapter 4. Tests on the relative importance of the three deep determinants are presented in Rodrik and Subramnaian (2003). For an opposing view defending the influential role of geography, see Sachs (2004).

19. The key studies in this area were Little, Scitovsky, and Scott (1970) and Bhagwati (1978) and Krueger (1978).

20. The pioneering work in this area is Krueger (1974). A similar approach was developed in Bhagwati (1982).

21. For an example of this school of thought, see Buchanan and Tullock (1962, 2004) and Buchanan (1987).

22. The first paper on the "Washington Consensus" was Williamson (1990). The ten principles of the Washington Consensus were defined as follows: (a) fiscal discipline; (b) the reorientation of public expenditure; (c) tax reform; (d) financial liberalization; (e) a unified and competitive exchange rate; (f) trade liberalization; (g) openness to foreign direct investment; (h) privatization; (i) deregulation; and (j) secure property rights.

23. One example of the application of the Washington Consensus to an understanding of economic development can be found in the World Bank's famous East Asia "miracle" study (1993), which essentially concluded that

a major reason for East Asia's successful economic development was because it had pursued many of the precepts identified in that framework.

24. One of the most cited articles for confirming the case that macroeconomic stability is a necessary condition for sustained economic growth is Fischer (1993).

25. For an example of this line of argumentation, see Stiglitz (1997).

26. See, for example, Krugman (1997)

27. Hausmann and Rodrik have been widely cited for their analysis of economic development as a process of "self-discovery" (2002), while Lall dedicated much of his professional life to examining the process of technological upgrading in successful developing countries and the policies that support the development of technological capability. A lucid synthesis of his views can be found in Lall (2003).

28. An important, recent contributor to the New Structuralist thinking in economic development has been Justin Lin, who was Chief Economist at the World Bank from June 2008 through June 2012 and the first economist from a developing country to hold that position. An example of his thinking can be found in Lin (2010).

29. A recent study on the experience of export upgrading in economic development can be found in Lederman and Maloney (2012).

30. A leading study in this field was Imbs and Wacziarg (2003).

31. These results are presented in Hausmann et al. (2007).

32. These changes in the global trading system are examined in UNCTAD (2013).

33. These considerations have also been raised in the context of the lens of "new geography," as summarized very usefully in Venables (2008).

34. This field is summarized in Lin (2012).

35. A seminal contribution to this perspective on development linked to the field of political economy is Evans (1995), which is elaborated upon in Kohli (2004).

36. The role of geography in accounting for differences in the economic growth paths of East Asia and Latin America is examined in Inter-American Development Bank (2000).

4 Initial Conditions for the Postwar Development of East Asia and Latin America

1. The literature on the European conquest and colonization of Mexico and Central and South America is vast. A recent study that examines the historical roots of Latin America's development problems from an institutionalist perspective is Sokoloff and Engerman (2000).

2. The Portuguese colonial regime for Brazil was somewhat less centralized and more flexible than for Spanish America, in part because of the absence of precious metals in Brazil; however, the granting of large land tracts

with rights and privileges to "donatorios" was similar to the system of "encomienda." For more information, see Boxer (1962).

3. These data are taken from Maddison (2001).

4. There is by now a long tradition of historical scholarship on Latin America that has chronicled the absence of political development and the lack of political culture in the region during the nineteenth century, which has carried over well into the twentieth century (e.g., Engerman and Sokoloff 2002, Lange et al. 2002, and Coatsworth 2008).

5. The colonial experience of Indonesia has been extensively examined by Anne Booth; see, for example, Booth (2007).

6. In the AJR study, the source used for data on settler mortality did not provide separate readings for Malaysia and Singapore, as they were part of the same British colony at the time (the Straits Settlements). Accordingly, a reading from the colonial site of Penang on the East coast of Malaysia was used for both country cases.

7. The contrasting effects of the common and civil law traditions on economic development have been examined in studies by Shleifer et al. (2008) and Shleifer and Glaeser (2002).

8. For a leading statement of the favorable effects of Japanese colonial administration on the economic development of Korea and Taiwan, see Kohli (2004).

9. Howard Wiarda has been a leading proponent of the perverse effects of Spanish cultural influences on Latin American political and historical development; see, for example, Wiarda (2001). A similar view is also expressed by a leading Latin American political and economic commentator (Vargas Llosa 2005).

10. The perverse effects of Iberian political culture on Latin America have been critically examined in a series of studies by Lawrence Harrison, who is a strong proponent of the dominant influence of culture in economic development (Harrison and Huntington 2000).

11. The views expressed here on the political implications of Confucianism are broadly consistent with those elaborated by Fukuyama et al. (2012) and Huntington (1996).

12. The expression "min-ben" is derived from the Mandarin expression "min-wei bang ben," which literally means "people are the root for government," or in more general parlance, the people's welfare should be the focus of government leaders. For a further discussion of this concept, see Murthy (2000).

13. For a recent discussion of the role of Confucian culture in the democratization of East Asia, see Shin (2011).

14. The role of trust or "social capital" as a basis for successful economic development has been highlighted by writers such as Francis Fukuyama (1996) and Robert Putnam (1995).

15. The views of Sachs on the important role of geography in economic development are presented in Bloom and Sachs (1998) and Gallup et al. (1998).

16. David Weil, the author of a leading textbook on economic growth, has summarized this evidence by stating that "Together, access to the sea and distance from major centers of economic activity help account for differences in the cost of transporting goods.... These differences in transport costs correlate well with differences in trade volume and income per capita" (Weil 2008, p. 443).

17. These results are reported in the studies cited in footnote 15 above.

18. The most widely cited book on the "dependency school," and in fact its founding document, is Cardoso and Faletto (1969), which was drafted during the time when these writers were resident scholars at the UN Economic Commission for Latin America (ECLA).

19. The strong influence of the ECLA in its early years of operation on regional thinking about economic development has been explored by Joseph Love (2007).

20. These results can be found in figures 1 and 2 (p. 210) in Coatsworth and Williamson (2004).

21. The views of Ronald Dore on East Asia's style of economic development and its "will to develop" can be found in Dore (1990).

22. Akamatsu's main outline of the "flying geese" model appeared in Japanese publications in 1935 and 1937 and in English in Akamatsu (1962). A number of later papers sought to explain the relevance of the model for understanding the East Asian economic development experience; see, for example, Kojima (2002) and Kasahara (2004). The model was also described briefly in chapter 5 of the World Investment Report for 1995 (UNIDO 1995).

23. In a recent reformulation of the "flying geese" model, Terutomo Ozawa (2009) refers to the notion of an "MPX pattern" of industrial production (M-import, P-production, and X-export) implicit in that model, which is driven by infant-industry protection.

5 Economic Policy Choices—Macroeconomic and Financial Stability

1. This calculation is described in Loayza et al. (2005).

2. Growth spells are defined as periods of at least five years in which output growth per capita exceeded 2 percent, on average (Berg et al. 2008).

3. These characteristics of the business cycle in Latin America are described in Caldentey et al. (2013).

4. A leading study that is often cited in the literature on the macroeconomic policy experience of developing countries is Fischer (1993). A more recent contribution, with particular relevance to Latin America, is Fatas and Mihov (2009).

5. One study that attempts to quantify the impact of policy variability on growth in output is Fatas and Mihov (2009).

6. The early debate between the "structuralists" of ECLA and the "monetarists" of the IMF regarding the problems of inflation and growth in Latin America was given important academic treatment in a volume by Baer and Kerstenetsky (1964).

7. The contrasting role of the agricultural sector in the economic development of the two regions is a relatively neglected topic in recent writings about the growth outcomes of East Asia and Latin America. One exception is Kay (2003).

8. These crises are described and tabulated in Sahay and Goyal (2006).

9. See, for example, the IMF *World Economic Outlook* (April 2005), Chapter 2.

10. A leading study on the nature and causes of pro-cyclical fiscal policy in Latin America was Gavin and Perotti (1997).

11. The pro-cyclicality between policy interest rates and output over the period 1960–2003 was identified in a study by Kaminsky et al. (2004).

12. These political economy issues are explored in Gavin and Perotti (1997), Alesina et al. (2008), and Cardenas and Perry (Chapter 11 in Ocampo and Ros 2011).

13. The phenomenon of the "populist business cycle" was first identified in the work of Rudi Dornbusch and Sebastian Edwards (1991).

14. According to data collected by Sturznegger and Zettelmeyer (2006), during 1824–2004, Latin America experienced more than half of all the debt crises that could be identified, and more than twice the number of any other region of the world.

15. The problem of "debt intolerance" was first attributed to Latin America in a study by Reinhart et al. (2003).

16. The problem of "original sin" was first identified by Barry Eichengreen and Ricardo Hausmann in 1999, and further developed in Eichengreen et al. (2003).

17. One of the leading scholars in this field has been Ross Levine. For a summary of the empirical work on the impact of financial sector development on economic growth, see Demirguc-Kunt and Levine (2008) and Cihak et al. (2012).

18. The tabulation of systemic banking crises around the globe can be found in Laeven and Valencia (2008).

19. This relationship was established by the empirical work of Thorsten Beck, Ross Levine, and Norman Loayza (Beck et al., 2010). A good summary of the relationship between financial deepening and economic development can be found in Wachtel (2003).

20. These issues have been explored in the writings of Rafael La Porta, Florencio Lopez de Salinas, Andrei Shleifer, and Robert Vishny (La Porta et al. 1998).

21. The mismanagement of central bank operations in the Philippines because of extensive corruption and fiscal dominance was characterized by a leading

analyst of Southeast Asia as a case of "booty capitalism" (Hutchcroft 1998).

22. The data on bank restructuring costs are taken from Barandiaran and Hernandez (1999). The Chilean financial crisis was chronicled and analyzed in an oft-cited study by Carlos F. Diaz-Alejandro titled "Good-bye Financial Repression, Hello Financial Crisis" (1985).

23. Stiglitz and Uy (1996) provide an interesting and insightful review of public policy in regard to the financial sector in Asia in the period leading up to regional financial crisis.

24. One of the most vulnerable and poorly monitored operations in the region was the Bangkok Interbank Lending Facility, which was established by the government of Thailand to encourage short-term foreign borrowing by Thai banks to support domestic credit operations.

25. The regional financial crisis of 1997–1998 has been the subject of numerous debates and controversies regarding its origins and propagating mechanisms, the role of the Fund, and the merits of capital account liberalization. For two early, insightful accounts, see Goldstein (1998) and Blustein (2003).

26. Data on dollarization can be found in various IMF publications, such as IMF (2005) and (IMF 2010).

27. These criteria and quantitative measures are fully described and examined for a range of countries across all regions of the globe in World Bank (2013).

6 Economic Policy Choices—Savings, Investment, and Industrialization

1. The role of "deliberation councils" in the economic development of East Asia has been extensively covered in Campos and Root (1996) and Evans (1995).

2. The World Bank's Doing Business indicators can be accessed at www .doingbusiness.org

3. The Global Competitiveness Index can be accessed at www.weforum.org /issues/global-competitiveness

4. These results can be found in the World Bank's Logistics Performance Index, which can be accessed at www.data.worldbank.org/data-catalog /logistics-performance-index

5. The basis for this information can be found in Calderón and Servén (2010).

6. This calculation can be found in Calderón and Servén (2010).

7. These data and calculations were presented in Rodrik and McMillan (2011), as discussed in chapter 2.

8. This finding was first identified in a path-breaking study by Imbs and Wacziarg (2003), and has since been confirmed by more recent studies.

9. The key role of national innovation systems in economic development has been highlighted in many of the writings of the evolutionist school of development economics, as exemplified by Mario Cimoli, Jorge Katz, Sanjaya Lall, and Richard Nelson.

10. Sanjaya Lall, a leading scholar of economic development at Oxford University, wrote extensively about the issue of technological capability and the role of technological absorption in the development process; see, for example, Lall (2003).

11. This quotation is from Kim (1997) and was cited in the World Bank's World Development Report of 2005, p. 29.

12. One development expert who has studied East Asian industrialization extensively (Robert Wade) has argued that East Asian governments were not involved in "picking winners," but rather in "making winners," by means of their industrial policy (see the Preface to Wade 2003).

13. A leading expert on economic development who has recently formulated an approach to industrial policy that supports the evolution of dynamic comparative advantage as a means of promoting structural change in developing economies is Justin Lin (2010, 2012). Mr. Lin, an economist based in China, was Chief Economist of the World Bank during 2008–2012.

14. Dani Rodrik and Ricardo Hausmann of the Kennedy School of Government at Harvard University are the economists most closely associated with this approach to industrial policy (see Hausmann and Rodrik 2002; Hausmann et al. 2005).

15. A succinct statement of industrial policy objectives and methods in the case of Korea that illustrates these points can be found in Westphal (1990).

16. A leading analysis of this class of studies can be found in Taylor (1998).

17. Good sources for the evaluation of Latin America's implementation of industrial policy along the lines described in the text are Fishlow (1990) and Robinson (2009).

18. One early example of the academic literature that focused on the relative merits of import substitution and export-oriented industrialization is Gereffi and Wyman (1990).

19. These data are collected by UNIDO on a regular basis for some 150 countries and are available at www.unido.org/data1/statistics/research/cip.html. One of the academic advisors for this effort at UNIDO was Professor Sanjaya Lall of Oxford University, who was an acknowledged expert on the industrialization experience of East Asia, cited in footnotes 9 and 10 above.

20. This quote is associated with the research of David Dollar and Art Kraay of the World Bank (Dollar and Kraay 2002).

21. A recent, balanced assessment of the role of exports in economic development can be found in Lederman and Maloney (2012).

22. These data comparisons are drawn from ECLA (2008), Figure II.20.

23. These data are drawn from World Bank (2007) "Tiger Economies under Stress."

24. This index can be accessed at www.weforum.org/issues/international-trade.

25. Similar findings can be found in Hesse (2007).

26. This relationship is analyzed in Papageorgiu (2013).

27. The empirical results for these results and the measures of economic complexity that Ricardo Hausmann and his colleagues have developed for a broad cross section of countries can be found in the "Atlas of Economic Complexity: Mapping Paths to Prosperity" (Harvard Center for International Development 2011), which is available online at www.atlas.media.mit.edu/media/atlas/pdf/HarvardMit_Atlas OfEconomicComplexity_Part-1.pdf

28. A good description and analysis of the first and second "unbundling" of trade can be found in Baldwin (2011b).

29. Gary Gereffi of Duke University has been a leading researcher in the field of global value chains and has produced many studies on the socioeconomic impact and governance of these operations, such as Gereffi et al. (2005).

30. Dieter Ernst and Richard Hobday have written extensively about the OEM-ODM-OBM ladder of manufacturing: see, for example, Hobday (1995) and Ernst et al. (1998).

31. These data can be found in Athukorala and Yamashita (2006), Table 1.

32. This estimate is based on data presented in Kimura (2006).

33. These data are based on UNIDO's CIP index cited in footnote 19 above.

34. As defined by UNCTAD, the GVC participation rate "measures the foreign value added used in a country's exports (upstream perspective) plus the value added supplied to other countries' exports (downstream perspective), divided by total exports" (UNCTAD 2013, p. 12).

35. These estimates of tariff protection are drawn from Berg and Krueger (2002).

36. This interpretation is based on information about the degree of restrictiveness for four types of capital controls, as calculated by the IMF in its World Economic Outlook for April 2002 (IMF 2002a).

37. This interpretation of trade and capital account openness is based on analysis of the IMF presented in its World Economic Outlook for September 2002 (IMF 2002b, ch. 3).

38. The data on black market premia for the two regions can be found in Berg and Krueger (2002).

39. The data on real effective exchange rates for East Asia and Latin America were calculated on the basis of data available in the World Bank's World Development indicators.

40. The competitive threat of China to Latin America's exports of high-tech goods is examined in Gallagher and Porzecanski (2008).

41. China's recent lending and investment activity in South America is explored in Gallagher et al. (2012).

7 The Role of Institutions and Governance

1. The role of trust in gainful economic activity and exchange has a long pedigree extending back to Adam Smith. A more recent, empirical study of its impact on economic development can be found in Hall and Jones (1998).
2. Social capital has been examined in a number of studies including Fukuyama (1996), Glaeser et al. (2000), and Knack and Keefer (1997).
3. The World Values Survey can be accessed at www.worldvaluessurvey.org
4. The role of guan-xi networks in Southeast Asia has been described in various studies, for example, Cheong (2003), Hamilton (1991), and Yeung (1999).
5. The Philippines should be included with Latin America for purposes of this discussion, because of its relatively low scores of trust according to the World Values Survey and high levels of social and economic inequality.
6. The role of "deliberation councils" in East Asian development was first highlighted in a study by Campos and Root (1996).
7. Francis Fukuyama has written insightfully on this topic and aspect of economic development. One of his most recent papers examining the role of Weberian bureaucracies in development is Fukuyama (2013).
8. Hernando de Soto created the Institute for Liberty and Democracy in 1988 to promote the reform of property rights regimes in Peru and a number of other countries in Latin America.
9. The World Bank's Governance Indicators can be accessed at www.worldbank.org/governance/wgi/index.asp
10. These rankings are presented in the International Country Risk Guide (ICRG), which can be accessed at www.prsgroup.com/icrg.aspx
11. It is also the case that institutions can be "adaptive" or "transitional," and thus less than fully formed, and still serve the needs of government at a certain phase of a country's development. This feature of institutional development is illustrated in the case of China, as noted in Box 7.1.
12. An excellent study of the informal sector in the Latin American regional economy can be found in World Bank (2007). One attempt to measure the size of the informal sector in Latin America can be found in Loayza and Rigolini (2006).
13. The case of Bolivia as an example of frustrated development in Latin America linked to problems of informality has been analyzed in Kaufman et al. (2003).

8 The Political Economy Factor in Comparative Economic Development

1. The sequential link between economic progress and political development was first expounded by Professor Seymour Lipset (1959).

2. Olson (1993) writes that the comparison between "roving" and "stationary" bandits was first suggested to him by his reading about the activities of Chinese warlords during the early part of the twentieth century.
3. This contrast between dictatorships and democracies is examined in Przeworski and Limongi (1993).
4. The "median voter" theorem was popularized by Anthony Downs in his widely read study, *An Economic Theory of Democracy* (1957).
5. The Gastil Index was developed by Raymond Duncan Gastil in 1991, and has been popularized by Freedom House in its annual surveys of political rights in countries around the world (www.freedomhouse.org).
6. The term "developmental state" was coined by Chalmers Johnson in his description of the role of the Japanese state apparatus in guiding the post–World War II economic transformation of Japan (Johnson 1982).
7. This thesis regarding the limited scope for developing state capacity in Latin America is fully developed in a paper by Mauricio Cardenas (2010).
8. Atul Kohli has invented the term "cohesive-capitalist states" as an alternative term for developmental states (Kohli 2004).
9. The description in the text of the attributes of "developmental states" follows that provided by Kohli (2004).
10. The discussion in this section follows that of Stephen Haggard in his classic comparative study of the political economy aspects of development in East Asia and Latin America (Haggard 1990).
11. This section draws on the ideas of Francisco Rodriguez who has provided an extremely illuminating analysis of political economy factors affecting Latin American economic development (Rodriguez 2001).
12. Carlos F. Diaz Alejandro has provided many examples of these political forces at work in his economic writings on Argentina; see, for example, Diaz Alejandro (1966, 1970).
13. The studies by Bela Balassa (1971), Little, Scitovsky, and Scott (1970), and Bhagwati et al. and Krueger (1978) were of particular importance in public policy debates on the early industrialization strategy in developing countries.
14. The role of the government in the development of the Chilean salmon industry is described in Izuka and Katz (2011), Katz (2004), and UNCTAD (2006).

9   Three Cross-Regional Case Studies

1. A good account of the colonial and early post-independence economic history of Jamaica and Singapore can be found in Findlay and Wellisz (1993).
2. During 1972–1977, it is estimated that public sector employment increased by 65 percent, while the contribution of general government operations to GDP rose from 10 percent to 16 percent. By conventional national accounting standards, the latter measures exclude the impact of public enterprise operations, which also expanded sharply under the Manley government (King 2000).

3. Jamaica's efforts at implementing structural adjustment and stabilization policies from the mid-1970s to the mid-1990s are examined in Handa and King (1997) and King (2000).

4. It is interesting to note that Carlos Andres Perez of Venezuela went through the same kind of transformation between his two presidential administrations as did Michael Manley, whose terms as prime minister roughly coincided with those of Perez.

5. The issues inhibiting sustained development in Jamaica are examined in Blavy (2006).

6. Jamaica's unsuccessful efforts at promoting small and medium enterprise development by means of export-processing zones and links with Global Production Networks and the problem of crime are analyzed in Acosta (2008) and Panadeiros and Benfield (2010).

7. The stages of industrialization in Singapore's economic development are succinctly explained in Ying et al. (2008).

8. The unique role of the Economic Development Board in policy making and institutional coordination in Singapore is described in Kumar and Siddique (2010).

9. Caribbean "Dependency Thinking" in the 1960s and 1970s was strongly linked to writers such as Lloyd Best, Norman Girvan, and Clive Thomas, who were affiliated with the "New World Group" at the University of the West Indies in Mona, Jamaica.

10. Lee Kuan Yew has been a strong advocate of the of the positive role of "Asian values" and Confucian culture in the economic development of East Asia, as expressed, for example, in an interview with Fareed Zakaria in *Foreign Affairs* (1994).

11. For a discussion of the agrarian reform issue in Chilean public policy, see Bellisario (2007). Agrarian reform attempts were made in the 1960s and early 1970s under the Frei and Allende administrations, respectively, but these were stymied or reversed under military rule in the 1970s and 1980s.

12. Claudio Sapelli provides a succinct assessment of Chile's experience with import-substitution industrialization during 1950–1973 (Sapelli 2007).

13. The economic reform program of Salvador Allende is evaluated in Larrain and Meller (1991).

14. The origins and early history of the New Economic Policy (NEP) are well described in Jomo (2004).

15. The monetarist experiment of the Pinochet government is discussed and evaluated in Edwards and Edwards (1987).

16. Chile's experience with financial liberalization and financial crisis in the early 1980s was famously memorialized in the title of a paper by Carlos F. Diaz-Alejandro, "Good-bye Financial Repression, Hello Financial Crash" (1985). The banking crisis and its resolution are evaluated in Barandiaran and Hernandez (1999).

17. "Bumiputera" is a Malay word that means "sons of the soil."

18. The linkage of labor market and industrial policies in Malaysia is analyzed in Chowdhury (2008).
19. Rosli and Kari (2008) provide a careful analysis of the automotive industry in Malaysia.
20. Malaysia's response to the Asian financial crisis of 1997–1998 has been the subject of many studies, in particular because of its use of capital controls and unwillingness to seek financial support from the IMF. For one report by a local observer at the time, see Sundaram (2006).
21. The institutional and political underpinnings of economic policy making in Malaysia are discussed in Yusof and Bhattasali (2008).
22. For a recent evaluation of the impact and legacy of the Pinochet era in Chile, see Solimano (2012).
23. Hal Hill has been perhaps the most prolific commentator on the economic development of Indonesia since the time of its independence; see, for example, Hill (2000).
24. For an interesting comparison of the role of the "Chicago Boys" in Chile and the "Berkeley Mafia" in Indonesia, see Shin Yasui (2002).
25. The early liberalization of capital controls in Indonesia is analyzed from a political economy perspective in Chwieroth (2010).
26. The role of political institutions in policy making in Venezuela under the *Punto Fijo* system is well described in Monadi et al. (2004).
27. Indonesia's successful macroeconomic navigation through the oil price declines of the 1980s is analyzed in Bhattacharya and Pangestu (1997).
28. The breakdown of the Venezuelan economy that began in the 1980s is well discussed and analyzed in a book by two Venezuelan economists teaching in the United States, Francisco Rodriguez (Wesleyan) and Ricardo Hausmann (Harvard), which is available on the Internet at www.frodriguez.web.wesleyan.edu (Rodriguez and Hausmann 1999).
29. The failure of Venezuela's macroeconomic adjustment program under President Perez is analyzed in Goodman et al. (1998).
30. The World Bank study referenced in the text was cited and discussed in Naim (1993).
31. The first national candidate to take advantage of this new political climate was one of Perez' long-term political rivals, Rafael Caldera, who was elected president in 1993 with the support of a new political alliance ("Convergencia").

10   Conclusions and Lessons for Development Policy

1. A very recent study that sustains the claim that Professor's Lipset's "modernization thesis" can be validated by Latin America's post–World War II experience is Bittencourt (2013).
2. The Washington Consensus has been the focus of a long stream of critiques and evaluations since the late 1990s, which convey criticisms similar

to those raised in this chapter of its suitability as a framework for development thinking. One good example of this literature is Birdsall et al. (2010). More generally, the author of this book has learned much from the critiques of mainstream development thinking since the time of the Washington Consensus offered by Dani Rodrik, formerly of the Harvard Kennedy School of Government and now at Princeton University; see, for example, Rodrik (2004).

3. One recent report that defines the challenges of sustainable development in a lucid and succinct fashion is "An Action Agenda for Sustainable Development: A Report Prepared for the UN Secretary General by the Leadership Council of the Sustainable Development Solutions Network" (Sustainable Development Solutions Network, June 15, 2013).

4. Through the end of the past decade, China's manufactured exports had been a direct threat to those of Mexico, but since then China's traditional, competitive advantage vis-à-vis Mexico in terms of relative wage costs has been eroded significantly, while Mexico has also gained access to cheap, natural gas imports from the United States for its electricity generation.

Bibliography

A. General Readings on Comparative Economic Development

Acemoglu, Daron and David Autor (2012), "What Does Human Capital Do? A Review of Goldin and Katz's the Race between Education and Technology." *Journal of Economic Literature* 50, no. 2 (June): 426–463.

Acemoglu, Daron, and James Robinson (2008), "The Role of Institutions in Growth and Development," World Bank Growth Commission Working Paper #10.

———. (2012), *Why Nations Fail: The Origins of Power, Prosperity and Poverty.* New York, NY: Crown Publishers.

Acemoglu, Daron, Simon Johnson, and James Robinson (2001), "The Colonial Origins of Comparative Development: An Empirical Examination." *American Economic Review* 91, no. 5: 1369–1401.

———. (2004), "Institutions as the Fundamental Cause of Long-Run Growth." Paper prepared for the *Handbook on Economic Growth*, April.

Acemoglu, Daron, Simon Johnson, James A. Robinson, and Pierre Yared (2009), "Reevaluating the Modernization Hypothesis." *Journal of Monetary Economics* 56, no. 8: 1043–1058.

Aditya, Anwesha, and Saikat Sinha Roy (2007), "Export Diversification and Economic Growth: Evidence from Cross-Country Analysis." Indian Statistical Institute Working Paper #317.

Agénor, Pierre-Richard, and Otaviano Canuto (2012), "Middle-Income Growth Traps." The World Bank Policy Research Working Paper #6210 (September).

Agénor, Pierre-Richard, Otaviano Canuto, and Michael Jelenic (2012), "Avoiding Middle-Income Growth Traps." World Bank Poverty Reduction and Economic Management Network #98 (November).

Aghion, Philippe (2012) "From Growth Theory to Growth Policy Design." London School of Economics, Economic & Social Research Council.

Aghion, Philippe, Julian Boulanger, and Elie Cohen (2011), "Re-thinking Industrial Policy." Bruegel Policy Brief, Issue # 2011/ 04.

Aghion, Phillipe, and Peter Howitt (2005), "Appropriate Growth Policy: A Unifying Framework." 2005 Joseph Schumpeter Lecture delivered at the 20th annual congress of the European Economic Association in Amsterdam.

Aghion, Philippe, and Steven Durlauf (2009), "From Growth Theory to Policy Design." World Bank Growth Commission Working Paper #57/2009 (April).

Agosin, Manuel (2006), "Trade and Growth: Why Does Asia Grow Faster than Latin America?" Economic and Sector Studies Series, Inter-American Development Bank (February).

Agosin, Manuel (2007), "Export Diversification and Growth in Emerging Market Economies." University of Chile Department of Economics Working Paper #233.

Aiyar, Shekkar, Romain Duval, Damien Puy, Yiqun Wu, and Longmaei Zhang (2013), "Growth Slowdowns and the Middle Income Trap." IMF Working Paper #13/17 (March).

Akamatsu, Kamame (1962), "A Historical Pattern of Economic Growth in Developing Countries." *Developing Economies* 1: 1–23.

Alesina, Alberto, Silvia Ardagna, and Francesco Trebbi (2006), "Who Adjusts and When? The Political Economy of Reforms" *IMF Staff Papers* 53, special issue: 1–29.

Alesina, Alberto, Filipe Campante, and Guido Tabellini (2008), "Why Is Fiscal Policy Often Pro-cyclical?" *Journal of European Economic Association* 6, no. 5: 1006–1036.

Amsden, Alice (2001), *The Rise of the "Rest": Challenges to the West from Late-Industrializing Economies.* New York: Oxford University Press.

Anand, Rahul, Saurabh Mishra, and Nikola Spatafora (2012), "Structural Transformation and the Sophistication of Production." IMF Working paper #12/59 (February).

Andersen, Thomas, and Finn Tarp (2003), "Financial Liberalization, Financial Development and Economic Growth in LDCs." *Journal of International Development* 15, no. 2: 189–209.

Audretsch, David B, Mark Sanders, and Lu Zhang (2012), "How Exports Matters: Trade Patterns Over Development Stages." Centre for Economic Policy Research Discussion Paper #8 815 (February).

Attanasio, Orazio and Miguel Szekely (2000) "Household Saving in Developing Countries—Inequality, Demographics and All That: How Different Are Latin America and Southeast Asia?" Inter-American Development Bank Working Paper #427 (July).

Balassa, Bela and Associates (1971), *The Structure of Protection in Developing Countries,* Baltimore, MD: Johns Hopkins University Press.

Baldwin, Richard (2006) "Globalization: The Great Unbundling" (Chapter 1 in *Globalization Challenges for Europe* Secretariat of Economic Policy, Finnish Prime Minister's Office).

———. (2011a), "21st Century Regionalism: Filling the Gap between 21st Century Trade and 20th Century Trade Rules." Centre for Economic Policy Research Policy Insight # 56.

———. (2011b), "Trade and Industrialization after Globalisation's 2nd Unbundling: How Building and Joining a Supply Chain Are Different and Why It Matters?" NBER Working Paper #17716 (December).

Banerjee, Abhijit V., and Esther Duflo (2005), "Growth Theory through the Lens of Development Economics." MIT Department of Economics Working Paper #05–01.

Barro, Robert (1998), *Determinants of Economic Growth: A Cross-Country Empirical Study*. Cambridge: MIT Press.

———. (2012), "Convergence and Modernization Revised." NBER Working Paper #18295 (August).

Barro, Robert, and Xavier Sala-i-Martin (1995, 2003), *Economic Growth*. New York, NY: McGraw Hill.

Bastagli, Francesca, David Coady, and Sanjeev Gupta (2012), "Income Inequality and Fiscal Policy." IMF Staff Discussion Note #12/08 (June).

Bayoumi, Tamim (2011), "Changing Patterns of Global Trade." IMF Policy Paper (June).

Beck, Thorsten, Ross Levine, and Norman Loayza (2010), "Finance and Sources of Growth." *Journal of Financial Economic* 58, no. (1–2): 141–186.

Beck, Thorsten (2012), "Finance and Growth—Lessons from the Literature and the Recent Crisis." Paper prepared for the LSE growth commission.

Beim, David, and Charles Calomiris (2001), *Emerging Financial Markets*. New York: McGraw-Hill.

Bénétrix, Augustín S., Kevin H. O'Rourke, and Jeffrey G. Williamson (2012), "The Spread of Manufacturing to the Periphery 1870–2007: Eight Styllized Facts." University of Oxford Department of Economic Discussion Paper Series (July).

Berg, Andrew, Jonathan D. Ostry, and Jeromin Zettelmeyer (2008), "What Makes Growth Sustained?" IMF Working Paper #08/59 (March).

Berg, Andrew, and Anne Krueger (2002), "Trade, Growth and Poverty: A Selective Survey." Paper prepared for the Annual World Bank Conference on Development Economics (ABCDE) in April.

Bernhofen, Daniel, Zouheir El-Sahli, and Richard Kneller (2013), "Estimating the Effects of the Container Revolution on World Trade." Working Paper 2013/4, Department of Economics (Lund University).

Bhagwati, Jagdish (1978), *Foreign Trade Regimes and Economic Development: Anatomy and Consequences of Exchange Control Regimes*. Cambridge: Ballinger Publishing Company.

———. (1982), "Directly Unproductive, Profit-Seeking (DUP) Activities." *Journal of Political Economy* 90, no. 5 (November): 988–1002.

Birdsall, Nancy, Augusto de la Torre, and Felipe Caicedo (2010), "The Washington Consensus: Assessing a Damaged Brand." Center for Global Development Working Paper #13 (May).

Blustein, Paul (2003), *The Chastening: Inside the Crisis That Rocked the Global Financial System and Humbled the IMF*. New York: Public Affairs Press.

Bloom, David, and Jeffrey Sachs (1998), "Geography, Demography and Economic Growth in Africa." *Brookings Papers on Economic Activity* 2: 207–265.

Bourguignon, Francois et al. (2002), "Making Sense of Globalization." Center for Economic Policy Research Policy Paper #8 (July).

Brahmbhatt, Milan, and Otaviano Canuto (2012), "Fiscal Policy for Growth and Development." World Bank Poverty Reduction and Economic Management Network Report #91 (October).

Bresser-Pereira, Luiz Carlos (2009), *Globalization and Competition: Why Some Emerging Countries Succeed While Others Fall Behind*. New York: Cambridge University Press.

Brülhart, Marius (2009), "An Account of Global Intra-industry Trade, 1962–2006." *The World Economy* 32, no. 3: 401–459.

Buchanan, James (1987) "The Constitution of Economic Policy." Nobel Prize Speech, *American Economic Review* 77, no. 3 (June): 243–250.

Buchanan, James, and Gordon Tullock (1962), *The Calculus of Consent: Logical Foundations of Constitutional Democracy*. Michigan: University of Michigan Press.

Burki, Shahid, and Guillermo Perry (1998), *Beyond the Washington Consensus: Institutions Matter*. Washington, DC: The World Bank.

Canuto, Otaviano, and Manu Sharma (2011), "Asia and South America: A Quasi-Common Economy Approach." The World Bank Poverty Reduction and Economic Management Network #65 (September).

Caputi Lélis, Marcos Tadeu, André Moreira Cunha, and Manuela Gomes de Lima (2012), "Desempeño de las exportaciones de China y Brazil hacia América Latina, 1994–2009." *Revista Cepal* #109 (April).

Carrère, Céline, Vanessa Strauss-Kahn, and Olivier Cadot (2011), "Export Diversification: What's behind the Hump?" *Review of Economics and Statistics* 93, no. 2: 590–605.

Caselli, Francesco (2005), "Accounting for Cross-Country Income Differences." Chapter 9 in P. Aghion and S. Durlauf (eds.), *Handbook on Economic Growth*. New York, NY: Elsevier.

Cattaneo, Olivier, Gary Gereffi, and Cornelia Staritz (2010), *Global Value Chains in a Postcrisis World: A Development Perspective*. Washington, DC: The World Bank.

Cattaneo, Oliver, Gary Gereffi, Sebastien Miroudot, Daria Taglioni (2013), "Joining, Upgrading and Being Competitive in Global Value Chains." World Bank Policy Research Working Paper #6406 (April).

Cibils, Alan, and Davide Gualerzi (2012), "Rethinking Development Economics." Presented at the Meeting of Historians of Economic Thought from Europe and Latin America, held in Buenos Aires, November 21–23, 2012.

Čihák, Martin, Aslı Demirgüç-Kunt, Erik Feyen, and Ross Levine (2012), "Benchmarking Financial Systems around the World." World Bank Policy Research Working Paper #6175 (August).

Cimoli, Mario, Giovanni Dosi, and Joseph Stiglitz eds. (2009), *Industrial Policy and Development: the Political Economy of Capabilities Accumulation*. New York: Oxford University Press.

Chandra, Vandana (2006), *Technology, Adaptation, and Exports-How Some Developing Countries Got It Right*. Washington, DC: The World Bank.

Chang, Ha-Joon (2009), "Industrial Policy: Can We Go beyond an Unproductive Confrontation?" Paper prepared for the Annual World Bank Conference on Development Economics.

Chen, Shaohua and Martin Ravaillon (2012), "More Relatively-Poor People in a Less Absolutely-Poor World." World Bank Policy Research Working Paper #6114 (July).

Claessens, Stijn, and Enrico Perotti (2007), "Finance and Inequality: Channels and Evidence." *Journal of Comparative Economics* 35: 748–773.

Cline, William (2010), "Exports of Manufactures and Economic Growth: The Fallacy of Composition Revisited." In *Globalization and Growth*, edited by Michael Spence and Danny Leipziger, 195–234. Washington, DC: World Bank.

Collins, Susan, and Barry Bosworth (2003), "The Empirics of Growth: An Update." *Brookings Papers in Economic Activity* 34, no. 2: 113–206.

Das, Udaibir S., Michael G. Papaioannou, and Christoph Trebesch (2012), "Sovereign Debt Restructurings 1950–2010: Literature Survey, Data, and Stylized Facts." IMF Working Paper #12/203 (August).

De Gregorio, José and John-Wha Lee (2004), "Growth and Adjustment in East Asia and Latin America." *Economía* 5, no. 1 (Fall): 69–134.

Dedrick, Jason, Kenneth L. Kraemer, and Greg Linden (2010), "Who profits from innovation in global value chains? A study of the iPod and notebook PCs." *Industrial and Corporate Change* 19, no. 1: 81–116.

Deichmann, Uwe, Somik V. Lall, Stephen Redding, and Anthony Venables (2008), "Industrial Location in Developing Countries." *The World Bank Research Observer* 23, no. 2: 219–246.

Demirguc-Kunt, Asli, and R. Levine (2008), "Finance, Financial Sector Policies and Long-Run Growth." World Bank Growth Commission Working Paper #8.

Deninger, Klaus, and Lyn Squire (1996), "A New Dataset Measuring Income Inequality." *World Bank Economic Review* 10, no. 3 (September): 565–591.

Di John, Jonathan (2008), "Conceptualising the Causes and Consequences of Failed States: A Critical Review of the Literature." Crisis States Working Paper #25 (January).

Dollar, David, and Art Kraay (2002) "Growth Is Good for the Poor." World Bank Policy Research Paper #2587 (March).

Duran Lima, Jose, Nanno Mulder, and Osamu Onodera (2008), "Trade Liberalization and Economic Performance: East Asia versus Latin America, 1970–2006." OECD Trade Policy Working Paper #70 (February).

Easterly, William (2002), *The Elusive Quest for Growth.* Cambridge, MA: MIT Press.

———. (2005), "National Policies and Economic Growth: A Reappraisal." Chapter 15 in P. Aghion and S. Durlauf (eds.), *Handbook on Economic Growth.* New York, NY: Elsevier.

Easterly, William, and Ross Levine (2003), "Tropics, Germs and Crops: How Endowments Influence Economic Development." *Journal of Monetary Economics* 50, no. 1 (January): 3–39.

Easterly, William, and Ariell Reshef (2009), "Big Hits in Manufacturing Exports and Development." New York University & University of Virginia Working Paper (March).

Eichengreen, Barry, Donghyun Park, and Kwanho Shin (2013), "Growth Slowdowns Redux: New Evidence on the Middle Income Trap." NBER Working Paper #18673 (January).

Eichengreen, Barry, Ricardo Hausmann, and Ugo Panizza (2003), "Currency Mismatches, Debt Intolerance and Original Sin." NBER Working Paper #10036 (October).

Elson, Anthony (2006), "The Economic Growth of East Asia and Latin America in Comparative Perspective: Lessons for Development Policy." *World Economics* 7, no. 2 (April–June): 97–114.

———. (2011), *Governing Global Finance: The Evolution and Reform of the International Financial Architecture.* New York, NY: Palgrave Macmillan.

Engerman, Stanley, and Kenneth Sokoloff (2005), "Colonialism, Inequality and Long-Run Paths of Development." NBER Working Paper #11057 (January).

Ernst, Dieter, and Linsu Kim (2001), "Global Production Networks, Knowledge Difussion, and Local Capability Formation: A Conceptual Framework." Paper presented at the Nelson & Winter Conference in Aalborg, Denmark, June 12–15.

Estevadeordal, Antoni, and Alan M. Taylor (2008), "Is the Washington Consensus Dead? Growth, Openness, and the Great Liberalization, 1970s–2000s." NBER Working Paper #14264 (August).

Evans, Peter (1995), *Embedded Autonomy: States and Industrial Transformation.* Princeton, NJ: Princeton University Press.

———. (2003), "Beyond 'Institutional Monocropping': Institutions, Capabilities, and Deliberative Development." *Sociologias* 9 (January): 20–63.

Evans, Peter (2004), "Development as Institutional Change: The Pitfalls of Monocropping and the Potential of Deliberation." *Studies in Comparative International Development* 38, no. 4 (Winter): 30–52.

Evans, Peter, and Patrick Heller (2012), "Human Development, State Transformation and the Politics of the Developmental State." Chapter 37 in *The Oxford Handbook of Transformations of the State*, forthcoming 2013, Oxford University Press.

Evans, Peter, and William H. Sewell (2013), "The Neoliberal Era: Ideology, Policy and Social Effects." Prepared for *Social Resilience in the Neo-Liberal Era* edited by Peter Hall and Michele Lamont forthcoming, 2013, Cambridge University Press.

Farole, Thomas (2012), "Competitiveness and Connectivity: Integrating Lagging Regions." The World Bank Poverty Reduction and Economic Management Network Report #93 (October).

Fatas, Antonio, and Ilian Mihov (2013), "Policy Volatility, Institutions and Economic Growth." *The Review of Economics Statistics* 95, no. 2: 362–376.

Fatas, Antonio, and Ilian Mihov (2009), "Macroeconomic Policy: Does It Matter for Growth? The Role of Volatility." World Bank Growth Commission Working Paper #48.

Fayad, Ghada, Robert H. Bates, and Anke Hoeffler (2012), "Income and Democracy: Lipset's Law Revisited." IMF Working Paper #12/295.

Felipe, Jesus (2008), "What Policy Makers Should Know about Total Factor Productivity." *Malaysian Journal of Economic Studies* 45, no. 1: 1–19.

———. (2012), "Tracking the Middle Income Trap: What Is it, Who Is in It, and Why?" Asian Development Bank Economics Working Paper #306 (March).

Felipe, Jesus, and Franklin M. Fisher (2003), "Aggregation in Production Functions: What Applied Economists Should Know." *Metroeconomica* 54, nos. 2&3: 208–262.

Felipe, Jesus, Utsav Kumar, and Arnelyn Abdon (2010), "How Rich Countries Became Rich and Why Poor Countries Remain Poor: It's the Economic Structure...Duh!" Asian Development Bank Working Paper No. 644 (December).

Findlay, Ronald, and Stanislaw Wellisz, eds. (1973), *Five Small Open Economies.* New York: Oxford University Press for the World Bank.

Fischer, Stanley (1993), "The Role of Macroeconomic Factors in Economic Growth." *Journal of Monetary Economics* 32, no. 3 (December): 485–512.

Fortin, Carlos (2012), "The World Bank and Industrial Policy: Hands off or Hands on?" Critical Voices of the World Bank and IMF, Bretton Woods Project (December).

Frankel, Jeffrey (2003), "The Experience of and Lessons from Exchange Rate Regimes in Emerging Economies." NBER Working Paper #10032 (February).

Fukuyama, Francis (1996), *Trust: The Social Virtues and the Creation of Prosperity.* New York: Free Press.

———. (1999), "Social Capital and Civil Society." Paper prepared for the IMF Conference on Second Generation Reforms held on October 1, 1999.

———. (2004), *State Building: Governance and World Order in the 20th Century.* Ithaca, NY: Cornell University Press.

———. (2013), "What Is Governance?" Center for Global Development Working Paper #314 (January).

Gallup, John, Jeffrey Sachs, and Andrew Mellinger (1998), "Geography and Economic Development." NBER Working Paper #6849 (December).

Gereffi, Gary (2005), "The Global Economy: Organization, Governance, and Development." *The Handbook of Economic Sociology,* 2nd edition, 160–182. Princeton, NJ: Princeton University Press and Russell Sage Foundation.

———. (2009), "Development Models and Industrial Upgrading in China and Mexico." *European Sociological Review* 25, no. 1: 37–51.

———. (2013), "Global Value Chains in a Post-Washington Consensus World." *Review of International Political Economy* 20, no. 4: 1–29.

Gereffi, Gary, and D. Wyman, eds. (1990), *Manufacturing Miracles: Paths of Industrialization in Latin America and East Asia.* Princeton, NJ: Princeton University Press.

Gereffi, Gary, John Humphrey, and Timothy Sturgeon (2005), "The Governance of Global Value Chains." *Review of International Political Economy* 12, no. 1 (February): 78–104.

Gereffi, Gary, and Olga Memedovic (2003), *The Global Apparel Value Chain: What Prospects for Upgrading by Developing Countries?* Vienna: United Nations Industrial Development Organization.

Gereffi, Gary, and Stacey Frederick (2010), "The Global Apparel Value Chain, Trade and the Crisis: Challenges and Opportunities for Developing Countries." World Bank Policy Research Working Paper #5281 (April).

Glaeser, Edward, D. Laibson, J. Scheinkman, and C. Souter (2000), "Measuring Trust." *Quarterly Journal of Economics* 65, no.3 (September): 811–846.

Goldberg, Pinelopi Koujianou, and Nina Pavcnik (2007), "Distributional Effects of Globalization in Developing Countries." *Journal of Economic Literature* XLV (March): 39–82.

Gordon, Robert (2012), "Is U.S. Economic Growth Over? Faltering Innovation Confronts the Six Headwinds." NBER Working Paper #18315.

Haddad, Mona, Jamus Jerome Lim, and Christian Saborowski (2010), "Trade Openness Reduces Growth Volatility When Countries Are Well Diversified." World Bank Policy Research Working Paper #5222 (February).

Haggard, Stephan (1990), *Pathways from the Periphery: The Politics of Growth in the New Industrializing Economies.* Ithaca, NY: Cornell University Press.

Haggard, Stephan, Andrew MacIntyre, and Lydia Tiede (2008), "The Rule of Law and Economic Development." *Annual Review of Political Science* 11: 205–234.

Haggard, Stephan, and Robert Kaufman (1995), *The Political Economy of Democratic Transitions.* Princeton, NJ: Princeton University Press.

———. (2008), *Development, Democracy and Welfare States: Latin America, East Asia and Eastern Europe.* Princeton, NJ: Princeton University Press.

Haider, Huma, and Sumedh Rao (2010), "Political and Social Analysis for Development Policy and Practice: An Overview of Five Approaches." Governance and Social Development Resource Center Report (September).

Hall, Robert, and Charles Jones (1998) "Why Do Some Countries Produce So Much More Than Others?" *Quarterly Journal of Economics* 114, no. 1: 83–116.

Hanusch, Marek (2012), "The Doing Business Indicators, Economic Growth and Regulatory Reform." World Bank Policy Research Working Paper #6176 (August).

Harrison, Ann and Andres Rodriguez-Clare (2010), "Trade, Foreign Investment, and Industrial Policy for Developing Countries." In *Handbook of Development Economics,* vol. 5, edited by Dani Rodrik and Mark Rosenzwig, 4039–4214. The Netherlands: North-Holland.

Harrison, Lawrence (2000), *Underdevelopment Is a State of Mind.* Lanham, MA: Madison Books.

Harrison, Lawrence and Samuel Huntington, eds. (2000), *Culture Matters.* New York: Basic Books.

Hausmann, Ricardo, and Cesar Hidalgo (2010), "Country Diversification, Product Ubiquity, and Economic Divergence." Center for International Development at Harvard University Working Paper #201.

———. (2011), "The Network Structure of Economic Output." *Journal of Economic Growth* 16: 309–342.

Hausmann, Ricardo, Jason Hwang, and Dani Rodrik (2007), "What You Export Matters." *Journal of Economic Growth* 12, no. 1: 1–25.

Hausmann, Ricardo, and Dani Rodrik (2002), "Economic Development as Self-Discovery." NBER Working Paper #8952 (May).

Hausmann, Ricardo, Dani Rodrik, and Andres Velasco (2005), "Growth Diagnostics." Harvard University Kennedy School of Government Working Paper (May).

Henn, Christian, Chris Papageorgiou, and Nikola Spatafora (2013), "Quality Upgrading in Developing Countries." Presentation at the IMF-DFID Conference at Washington, DC, on February 21, 2013.

Hesse, Heiko (2007), "Export Diversification and Economic Growth." Prepared for the Commission on Growth and Development Workshop on Global Trends and Challenges at Yale University, September.

Hidalgo, Cesar, Bailey Klinger, Albert-Laszlo Barabási, and Ricardo Hausmann (2007), "The Product Space Conditions for the Development of Nations." *Science* 317, no. 5837: 482–487.

Hidalgo, Cesar, and Ricardo Hausmann (2009), "The Building Blocks of Economic Complexity." *Proceedings of the National Academy of Sciences of the United States of America* 106, no. 26 (June): 1050–1075.

Humphrey, John, and Hubert Schmitz (2002), "How does Insertion in Global Value Chains Affect Upgrading in Industrial Clusters?" *Regional Studies* 36, no. 9: 1017–1027.

Huntington, Samuel (1996), *The Clash of Civilizations and the Remaking of the World Order.* New York, NY: Simon and Schuster.

Imbs, Jean, and Romain Wacziarg (2003), "Stages of Diversification." *The American Economic Review* 93, no. 1 (March): 63–86.

International Monetary Fund (2002a), *World Economic Outlook.* Washington, DC: IMF (April).

International Monetary Fund (2002b), *World Economic Outlook.* Washington, DC: IMF (September).

———. (2011a), "Changing Patterns of Global Trade." IMF Policy Paper (June 15, 2011).

Jankowska, Anna, Arne Nagengast, and José Ramón Perea (2012), "The Product Space and the Middle-Income Trap: Comparing Asian and Latin American Experiences." OECD Working Paper #311 (April).

Jomo, Kwame, and Mushtaq Khan (2000), *Rents, Rent-Seeking and Economic Development.* New York: Cambridge University Press.

Jones, Charles, and Paul Romer (2009), "The New Kaldor Facts: Ideas, Institutions, Populations and Human Capitals." NBER Working Paper #15094.

Ju, Jiandong, Justin Yifu Lin, and Yong Wang (2011), "Marshallian Externality, Industrial Upgrading, and Industrial Policies." World Bank Policy Research Working Paper #5796.

Kaldor, Nicholas (1961), "Capital Accumulation and Economic Growth." In Lutz, F. A. and Hague, D. C. (eds.), *The Theory of Capital.* New York, NY: St. Martins Press.

Kaminsky, Graciela, and Carmen Reinhart (1998), "The Twin Crises: The Causes of Banking and Balance of Payments Problems." *American Economic Review* 89, no. 3: 473–500.

Kaminsky, Graciela, Carmen Reinhart, and Carlos Vegh (2004), "When It Rains, It Pours: Procyclical Capital Flows and Macroeconomic Policies." NBER Working Paper #10780 (September).

Kay, Cristobal (2001), "Asia's and Latin America's Development in Comparative Perspective: Landlords, Peasants and Industrialization." Institute of Social Studies Working Paper #336.

————. (2003), "Why East Asia Took Over Latin America: Agrarian Reform, Industrialization and Development." *Third World Quarterly* 23, no. 6: 1073–1102.

Kimura, Fukunari, and Mitsuyo Ando (2005), "The Economic Analysis of International Production/Distribution Networks in East Asia and Latin America: The Implication of Regional Trade Arrangements." *Business and Politics* 7, no. 1: 1–36.

Klinger, Bailey, and Daniel Lederman (2004), "Discovery and Development: An Empirical Exploration of 'New' Products.'" World Bank Policy Research Working Paper #3450 (November).

Knack, Stephen, and Philip Keefer (1997), "Does Social Capital Have an Economic Payoff? A Cross Country Investigation." *Quarterly Journal of Economics* 112, no. 4 (December): 1251–1288.

Kohli, Atul (2004), *State-Directed Development: Political Power and Industrialization in the Global Periphery*. New York: Cambridge University Press.

————. (2009), "Nationalist Versus Dependent Capitalist Development: Alternate Pathways of Asia and Latin America in a Globalized World" *Studies in International Comparative Development* 44: 386–410.

Kongsamut, Pyabha, Sergio Rebelo, and Dangyand Xie (2001), "Beyond Balanced Growth." IMF Working Paper #01/85 (June).

Koopman, Robert, William Powers, Zhi Wang, and Shang-Jin Wei (2010), "Give Credit Where Credit Is Due: Tracing Value Added in Global Production Chains." NBER Working Paper #16426.

Kose, Ayhan, Esward Prasad, Kenneth Rogoff, and Shang-Jin Wei (2003), "Effects of Financial Globalization on Developing Countries." IMF Occasional Paper #220 (September).

————. (2006), "Financial Globalization: A Reappraisal." IMF Working Paper #06/189 (August).

Krueger, Anne (1978), *Foreign Trade Regimes and Economic Development: Liberalization Attempts and Consequences*. Cambridge: Ballinger Publishing Company.

Krueger, Anne (1974), "The Political Economy of the Rent-Seeking Society." *American Economic Review* 64, no. 3 (June).

Krugman, Paul (1994), "The Fall and Rise of Development Economics." *Essays Provoked by the Work of Albert Hirschman*: 39–58.

————. (1997), *Development, Geography and Economic Theory*. Cambridge, MA: MIT Press.

————. (2010), "The New Economic Geography, Now Middle-Aged." Prepared for presentation to the Association of American Geographers, April 16, 2010.

La Porta, Rafael, Francisco Lopez de Salinas, and Andrei Shleifer (1998), "Law and Finance" *Journal of Political Economy* 106, no. 6 (December): 1113–1155.

Lall, Sanjaya (2003), "Reinventing Industrial Strategy: The Role of Government Policy in Building Industrial Competitiveness." Working Paper 111 of Queen Elizabeth House, Oxford University (October).

Lall, Sanjaya, John Weiss, and Jinkang Zhang (2006), "The 'Sophistication' of Exports: A New Trade Measure." *World Development* 34, no. 2: 222–237.

Lall, Sanjaya, Manuel Albaladejo, and Jinkang Zhang (2004), "Mapping Fragmentation: Electronics and Automobiles in East Asia and Latin America." *Oxford Development Studies* 32, no. 3 (September): 407–432.

Lane, Phillip, and Gian Milesi-Ferretti (2007), "The External Wealth of Nations." *Journal of International Economics* 73, no. 2: 223–250 (November).

Lederman, Daniel, and William Maloney (2012), *Does What You Export Matter? In Search of Empirical Evidence for Industrial Policies*. Washington, DC: World Bank.

Lee, Keun, and Byung-Yeon Kim (2009), "Both Institutions and Policies Matter but Differently for Different Income Groups of Countries: Determinants of Long-Run Economic Growth Revisited" *World Development* 37, no. 3: 33–549.

Leibfried, Stephan, Frank Nullmeier, Evelyne Huber, Matthew Lange, Jonah Levy, and John D. Stephens (2013), "Human Development, State Transformation and the Politics of the Developmental State." Forthcoming (2013) as Chapter 37 in *The Oxford Handbook of Transformations of the State*, New York: Oxford University Press.

Leon, Jose Luis (2003), "The Role of the State in Economic Development." In *East Asia and Latin America: The Unlikely Alliance,* edited by Peter Smith et al. London: Rowman and Littlefield.

Levine, Ross (2004), "Finance and Growth: Theory and Evidence." In *Handbook on Economic Growth*, edited by Philippe Aghion and Steven Durlauf. Chapter 12. Elsevier

Lin, Justin Yifu (2010), "New Structural Economics: A Framework for Rethinking Development." World Bank Policy Research Working Paper #5197 (February).

————. (2012a), *New Structural Economics: A Framework for Rethinking Development and Policy*. Washington, DC: The World Bank.

Lin, Justin Yifu, and Ha-Joon Chang (2009), "Should Industrial Policy in Developing Countries Conform to Comparative Advantage or Defy It? A Debate between Justin Lin and Ha-Joon Chang." *Development Policy Review* 27, no. 5: 483–502.

Lin, Justin Yifu, and Célestin Monga (2010), "Growth Identification and Facilitation: The Role of the State in the Dynamics of Structural Change." World Bank Policy Research Working Paper #5313 (May).

Lin, Justin Yifu, and David Rosenblatt (2012), "Shifting Patterns of Economic Growth and Rethinking Development." World Bank Policy Research Working Paper #6040 (April).

Liu, Hongtao, Karen Rosel Polenske, and Joaquim J. Guilhoto (2010), "China and Brazil Productive Structure and Economic Growth Compared: 1980's to 2000's." Paper presented at the 57th Annual North American Meetings of the Regional Science Association International: Denver, CO, November 10–13, 2010.

Little, Ian, Tibor Scitovsky, and Maurice Scott (1970), *Industry and Trade in Some Developing Countries*. London and New York: Oxford University Press.

Lucas, Robert (1988), "On the Mechanics of Economic Growth." *Journal of Monetary Economics* 22, no. 1 (March): 3–42.

Lucas, Robert (2007), "Trade and the Diffussion of the Industrial Revolution." NBER Working Paper #13286 (August).

Maddison, Angus (2008), "The West and the Rest in the World Economy." *World Economics* 9, no. 2 (October–December): 75–99.

Maddison, Angus (2010), *Historical Statistics on the World Economy*. A database that is available on the website of the Maddison Project (www.ggdc.net/maddison/maddison_project).

McGuire, James (2010), *Wealth, Health and Democracy in East Asia and Latin America*. Cambridge: Cambridge University Press.

McMillan, Margaret, and Ann Harrison (2011), "Offshoring, International Trade, and American Workers." NBER Reporter Number 4: Research Summary.

McMillan, Margaret, and Dani Rodrik (2011), "Globalization, Structural Change, and Productivity Growth." NBER Working Paper #17143 (February).

Medalla, Erlinda, and Jenny Balboa (2010), "Prospects for Regional Cooperation between Latin America and the Caribbean Region and the Asia and Pacific Region: Perspective from East Asia." Asian Development Bank Working Paper Series #217 (May).

Milanovic, Branko (2009), "Global Inequality and the Global Inequality Extraction Ratio: The Story of the Past Two Centuries." World Bank Policy Research Working Paper #5044 (September).

Milanovic, Branko (2012), "Growth Inequality by the Numbers in History and Now: An Overview." World Bank Policy Research Working Paper #6259 (November).

Ngai, Rachel, and Christopher Pissarides (2007), "On the Long-Run Determinants of Industry TPP Growth Rates." CEPR Discussion Paper #6408 (July).

Narula, Rajneesh (2002), "Switching from Import Substitution to the 'New Economic Model' in Latin America: A Case of Not Learning from Asia." Maastricht Economic Research Institute on Innovation and Technology.

North, Douglas (1994) "Economic Performance through Time." *American Economic Review* 34, no. 3 (June).

North, Douglass, Daron Acemoglo, Francis Fukuyama, and Dani Rodrik (2008), *Governance, Growth and Development Decision-Making: Reflections*. Washington, DC: World Bank.

Nunn, Nathan (2009), "The Importance of History for Economic Development." *Annual Review of Economics* 1, no. 1: 65–92.

Ocampo, Jose Antonio, ed. (2004), *Beyond Reforms: Structural Dynamics and Macroeconomic Vulnerability*. Palo Alto, CA: Stanford University Press.

Ocampo, Jose Antonio, Kwame Sundaram Jomo, and Rob Vos, eds. (2007), *Growth Divergences: Explaining Differences in Economic Performance*. Hyderabad, London, and Penang: Orient Longman, Zed Books, and Third World Network.

Olson, Mancur (1965), *The Logic of Collective Action: Public Policy and the Theory of Groups*. Cambridge: Harvard University Press.

———. (1993), "Dictatorship, Democracy and Development." *American Political Science Review* 87, no. 3: 567–576.

Organization for Economic Cooperation and Development (2007), "Staying Competitive in the Global Economy: Moving up the Value Chain." OECD Report.

Pack, Howard (2010), "Industrial Policy in Historical Perspective: What Role for Industrial Policy? Perspectives from Around the World." Paper prepared for the American Economic Association Meetings in Denver, CO, January 6–9, 2010.

Pack, Howard, and Kamal Saggi (2006), "The Case for Industrial Policy: A Critical Survey." World Bank Policy Research Working Paper #3839 (February). Supplement 2: ii86–ii125.

Palma, Jose Gabriel (2006a), "Globalizing Inequality: 'Centrifugal' and 'Centripetal' Forces at Work." United Nations Department of Economics and Social Affairs Working Paper #35 (September).

———. (2006b), "Growth after Globalization: a 'Structuralist Kaldorian' Game of Musical Chairs?" Background paper for the United Nations World Economics and Social Survey.

———. (2008), "Premature De-industrialization and the Dutch Disease." In *The New Palgrave Dictionary of Economics,* Second Edition, edited by Steven N. Durlauf and Lawrence E. Blume. New York: Palgrave Macmillan.

Papageorgiou, Chris, Fidel Perez-Sebastian, and Nikola Spatafora (2013), "Structural Change through Diversification: A Conceptual Framework." Presentation prepared for an IMF's seminar delivered on February 21.

Przeworski, Adam (2004), "Democracy and Economic Development." Chapter 4 in Mansfield, E. and Sisson, R. (eds.), *The Evolution of Political Knowledge.* Columbus, OH: Ohio University Press.

Przeworski, Adam, and Fernando Limongi (1993), "Political Regimes and Economic Growth." *Journal of Economic Perspectives* 7, no. 3 (Summer): 51–69.

Putnam, Robert (1995), "Bowling Alone: America's Declining Social Capital." *Journal of Democracy* 6, no. 1 (January): 65–78.

Ranis, Gustav, and Syed Mahmood (1992), *The Political Economy of Development Policy Change*. Cambridge, MA: Blackwell.

Ravallion, Martin (2009), "A Comparative Perspective on Poverty Reduction in Brazil, China and India." World Bank Policy Research Working Paper #5080 (October).

Reinhart, Carmen, Kenneth Rogoff, and Miguel Savastano (2003), "Debt Intolerance." *Brookings Papers on Economic Activity* 1: 1–63.

Robinson, James (2009), "Industrial Policy and Development: A Political Economy Perspective." Paper prepared for the 2009 World Bank ABCDE conference in Seoul, June 22–24, 2009.

Rodrik, Dani, ed. (2003), *In Search of Prosperity: Analytic Narratives on Economic Growth*. Princeton, NJ: Princeton University Press.

———. (2004), "Industrial Policy for the 21st Century." Paper prepared for UNIDO (September).

———. (2005), "Growth Strategies." NBER Working Paper #10050.

———. (2007a) *One Economics, Many Recipes: Globalization, Institutions, and Economic Growth*. Princeton, NJ: Princeton University Press.

———. (2007b), "Industrial Development: Some Stylized Facts and Policy Directions." In *Industrial Development for the 21st Century: Sustainable Development Perspectives*, 7–28. New York: United Nations.

———. (2007c), "Normalizing Industrial Policy." Background paper prepared for the World Bank Growth Commission) September.

———. (2012), "Who Needs the Nation State?" Centre for Economic Policy Research Discussion Paper #9040 (June).

Rodrik, Dani, Arvind Subramanian, and Francesco Trebbi (2002), "Institutions Rule: The Primacy of Institutions over Integration and Geography in Economic Development." *Journal of Economic Growth* 9, no. 2 (June): 131–165.

Romer, Paul (1986), "Increasing Returns and Long-run Growth." *Journal of Political Economy* 94, no. 5 (October): 1002–1037.

Rosales, Osvaldo, and Mikio Kuwayama (2012), "China and Latin America and the Caribbean: Building an Economic and Trade Relationship." United Nations ECLAC.

Sachs, Jeffrey D. (2012), "Government, Geography and Growth: The True Drivers of Economic Development." *Foreign Affairs* September/October.

Sachs, Jeffrey D., and Andrew M. Warner (2001), "Natural Resources and Economic Development: The Curse of Natural Resources." *European Economic Review* 45: 827–838.

Sachs, Jeffrey, J. McArthur, G. Schmidt-Traub, M. Kruk, C. Bahadur, M. Faye, and G. McCord (2004), "Ending Africa's Poverty Trap." *Brookings Papers on Economic Activity* 1: 117–240.

Samen, Salomon (2010), "A Primer on Export Diversification: Key Concepts, Theoretical Underpinnings and Empirical Evidence." World Bank Growth and Crisis Unit, World Bank Institute Report.

Saslavsky, Daniel, and Ben Shepherd (2012), "Facilitating International Production Networks: The Role of Trade Logistics." World Bank Policy Research Working Paper #6224 (October).

Serra, Nancis, and Joseph Stiglitz (2008), "The Barcelona Development Agenda." In *The Washington Consensus Reconsidered: Towards a New Global Governance*, Chapter 5. New York: Oxford University Press.

Shafaeddin, Mehdi (2005), "Trade Liberalization and Economic Reform in Developing Countries: Structural Change or De-Industrialization?" United Nations Conference on Trade and Development Discussion Paper #179.

Shixue, Jiang (2008), "Cultural Factors and Economic Performance in East Asia and Latin America." Institute of Latin American Studies & Chinese Academy of Social Sciences.

Shleifer, Andrei, and Edward Glaeser (2002) "Legal Origins." *Quarterly Journal of Economics* 117, no. 4 (November): 1193–1229.

Shleifer, Andrei, Rafael La Porta, and Francisco Lopez de Salinas (2008), "The Economic Consequences of Legal Origins." *Journal of Economic Literature* 46, no. 2 (June): 258–332.

Singh, Tarlok (2010), "Does International Trade Cause Economic Growth? A Survey." *The World Economy* 33, no. 11: 1517–1557.

Solow, Robert (1956), "A Contribution to the Theory of Economic Growth." *Quarterly Journal of Economics* 70, no.1 (February): 65–94.

————. (1970), *Growth Theory—An Exposition*. New York and Oxford: Oxford University Press.

Stiglitz, Joseph (1997), "The Role of Government in Economic Development" in M. Bruno and B. Pleskovic (eds.) *Annual World Bank Conference on Development Economics 1996*, pp. 11–23.

Sturgeon, Timothy (2008), "From Commodity Chains to Value Chains: Interdisciplinary Theory Building in an Age of Globalization." MIT Working Paper Series #08–001 (January).

Sturgeon, Timothy, and Olga Memedovic (2011), "Mapping Global Value Chains: Intermediate Goods Trade and Structural Change in the World Economy." UNIDO Working Paper #05/2010.

Sturznegger, Federico, and Jeromyn Zettelmeyer (2006), *Debt Defaults and Lessons from a Decade of Crises*. Cambridge, MA: MIT Press.

Temple, Jonathan (2005), "Dual Economy Models: A Primer for Growth Economists." *Manchester School 7*, no. 4 (December): 435–478.

Temple, Jonathan, and Paul Johnson (1998), "Social Capability and Economic Growth." *Quarterly Journal of Economics* 113, no. 3 (September): 965–990.

Timmer, Marcel, and Garitzen J. De Vries (2009), "Structural Change and Growth Accelerations in Asia and Latin America: A New Sectoral Data Set." *Cliometrica* 3, no. 2: 165–190.

UNCTAD (2006), *Global Partnerships and National Policies for Development: Trade and Development Report*. New York and Geneva: United Nations.

————. (2008), *Transnational Corporation* 17, no. 3: 1–152.

————. (2013), *Global Value Chains and Development: Investment and Value Added Trade in the Global Economy—A Preliminary Analysis*. Geneva: United Nations.

UNIDO (2002), "Competition through Innovation and Learning," *Industrial Development Report*.

————. (2004), "Inserting Local Industries into Global Value Chains and Global Production Networks: Opportunities and Challenges for Upgrading with a Focus on Asia." *Industrial Development Report*.

————. (2005), "Capability Building for Catching-up." *Industrial Development Report*.

———. (2009), "Breaking up and Moving up: New Industrial Challenges for the Bottom Billion and the Middle-Income Countries," *Industrial Development Report*.

United Nations (2006), "World Economic and Social Survey 2006: Diverging Growth and Development." United Nations Economic and Social Affairs.

———. (2008), *Structural Change and Productivity Growth 20 Years Later: Old Problems, New Opportunities*. Santiago: United Nations.

———. (2010), "Industrial Development for the 21st Century: Sustainable Development Perspectives." United Nations Department of Economics and Social Affairs.

Venables, A. (2008), "Rethinking Economic Growth in a Globalized World: An Economic Geography Lens." World Bank Growth Commission Working Paper #18.

Wachtel, Paul (2003), "How Much Do We Really Know about Growth and Finance?" *Economic Review,* Federal Reserve of Atlanta 88, no. 1: 33–47.

Wacziarg, Romain, and Karen Horn Welch (2008), "Trade Liberalization and Growth: New Evidence." NBER Working Paper #10152 (September).

Westphal, Larry (2002), "Technology Strategies for Economic Development in a Fast Changing Global Economy." *Economics of Innovation and New Technology* 11, no. 4–5: 275–320.

Williamson, Jeffrey (2011), "Industrial Catching Up in the Poor Periphery 1870–1975." NBER Working Paper #16809 (February).

Woo-Cumings, Meredith, ed. (1999), *The Developmental State*. Ithaca, NY: Cornell University Press.

Wood, Adrian (1997), "Openness and Wage Inequality in Developing Countries: The Latin American Challenge to East Asian Conventional Wisdom." *World Bank Economic Review* 11, no. 1: 33–57.

Woolcock, Michael, Simon Szreter, and Vijayendra Rao (2011), "How and Why Does History Matter for Development Policy?" *Journal of Development Studies* 47, no. 1 (January): 70–96.

World Bank (2012), *Doing Business in a more Transparent World*. Washington, DC: The World Bank and the IFC.

———. (2013) *Rethinking the Role of the State in Finance: Global Development Finance Report*. Washington, DC: World Bank.

World Bank Growth Commission (2008), *The Growth Report: Strategies for Sustained Growth and Inclusive Development*. Washington, DC: The World Bank.

Yasui, Shin (2002), "How Was the Market Mechanism Implanted in Developing Countries: The Cases of Chile and Indonesia." Paper presented at a MDT Workshop in Tokyo, July.

Yusuf, Shahid, and Kaoru Nabeshima (2012), *Some Small Countries Do It Better: Rapid Growth and Its Causes in Singapore, Finland and Ireland*. Washington, DC: The World Bank.

Zak, Paul J., and Stephen Knack (2001), "Trust and Growth." *The Economic Journal* 111, no. 470: 295–321.

B. Readings on the Economic Development of East Asia

Ahston, David, F. Green, J. Sung, and D. James (2002), "The Evolution of Education and Training Strategies in Singapore, Taiwan and South Korea: A Development Model of Skill Formation." *Journal of Education and Work* 15, no. 1: 5–29.

Akyüz, Yılmaz (2011), "Export Dependence and Sustainability of Growth in China." *China & World Economy* 19, no. 1: 1–23.

Anderson, Benedict (1988), "Cacique Democracy in the Philippines: Origins and Dreams." *New Left Review* 169, no. 3: 3–31.

Ando, Mitsuyo, and Fukunari Kimura (2005), "The Formation of International Production and Distribution Networks in East Asia." NBER Working Paper Series #10167.

———. (2009), "Fragmentation in East Asia: Further Evidence." ERIA Discussion Paper Series (October), #1347.

Asian Development Bank (2011), *Asia 2050: Realizing the Asian Century*. Singapore: Asian Development Bank.

Athukorala, Prema-chandra (2010), "Production Networks and Trade Patterns in East Asia: Regionalization or Globalization?" Asian Development Bank Working Paper Series on Regional Economic Integration #56 (August).

Athukorala, Prema-chandra, and Hal Hill (2010), "Asian Trade: Long-Term Patterns and Key Policy Issues." *Asia Pacific Economic Literature* 24, no. 2 (November): 52–82.

Athukorala, Prema-chandra, and Nobuak Yamashita (2006) "Production Fragmentation and Trade Integration: East Asia in a Global Context." *The North American Journal of Economics and Finance, Elsevier* 17, no. 3 (December): 233–256.

Baldwin, Richard (2008), "Managing the Noodle Bowl: The Fragility of East Asian Regionalism." *The Singapore Economic Review* 53, no. 3: 449–478.

Bhattacharya, Amar, and Mari Pangestu (1997), "Indonesia: Development Transformation and the Role of Public Policy." In *Lessons from East Asia*, edited by D. Leipziger, Chapter 7. Ann Arbor: University of Michigan Press.

Bloom, David, and Jeffrey Williamson (1998), "Demographic Transition and Economic Miracles in Emerging Asia." *World Bank Economic Review* 12, no. 3: 419–456.

Booth, Anne (2005), "Did It Really Help to be a Japanese Colony? East Asian Economic Performance in Historical Perspective." Asia Research Institute Working Paper Series #43.

———. (2007), "Night Watchman, Extractive or Developmental States: Some Evidence from South East Asia." *Economic History Review* 60, no. 2 (May): 241–266.

Bulman, David, and Aart Kraay (2011), "Growth in China 1978–2008: Factor Accumulation, Factor Reallocation, and Improvements in Productivity." World Bank Report.

Campos, Jose Edgardo, and Hilton Root (1996), *The Key to the Asian Miracle: Making Shared Growth Credible*. Washington, DC: Brookings Institution Press.

Capannelli, Giovanni, and See Seng Tan (2012), "Institutions for Asian Integration: Innovation and Reform." Asian Development Bank Institute Working Paper Series #375 (August).

Chandra, Vandana, Israel Osorio-Rodarte, and Carlos A. Primo Braga (2009), "Korea and the BICs (Brazil, India and China): Catching Up Experiences." World Bank Policy Research Working Paper #5101 (October).

Chang, Yongsung, and Andreas Hornstein (2011), "Transition Dynamics in the Neoclassical Growth Model: The Case of South Korea." Federal Reserve Bank of Richmond Working Paper #11–04 (July).

Cheong, Young Kok (2003), "Chinese Business Networks and Their Implications for South Korea." In *The Korean Diaspora in the World Economy*, edited by C. Bergsten and I. Choi. Washington, DC: Petersen Institute for International Economics.

Chong-en Bai, Chang-Tai Tsieh, and Yingyi Qian (2006), "The Return to Capital in China." *Brookings Panel on Economic Activity* 2006, no. 2 (Fall): 61–101.

Chowdhury, Anis (2008), "Labor Market Policies as Instruments of Industrial Policy: What Can Europe Learn from Southeast Asia?" *American Journal of Economics and Sociology* 67, no. 4 (October): 661–681.

Chwieroth, Jeffrey M. (2010) "How Do Crises Lead to Change? Liberalizing Capital Controls in the Early Years of New Order Indonesia." *World Politics* 62, no. 3 (July): 496–527.

Corden, W. Max (2009), "China's Exchange Rate Policy, Its Current Account Surplus, and the Global Imbalances." *Economic Journal* 119, no. 541: 103–119.

Defever, Fabrice, and Alejandro Riaño (2012), "China's Pure Exporter Subsidies." Center for Economic Performance Discussion Paper #1182 (December).

Deyo, Frederic, ed. (1987), *The Political Economy of the New Asian Industrialism*. Ithaca, NY: Cornell University Press.

Doner, Richard F., Bryan K. Ritchie, and Dan Slater (2005), "Systemic Vulnerability and the Origins of Developmental States: Northeast and Southeast Asia in Comparative Perspective." *International Organization* 59, no. 2 (April): 327–361.

Dore, Ronald (1990), Chapter 3 in G. Gereffi and D. Wyman (eds.), *Manufacturing Miracles: Paths of Industrialization in Latin America and East Asia*. Princeton, NJ: Princeton University Press.

Ernst, Dieter (2009), "A New Geography of Knowledge in the Electronics Industry? Asia's Role in Global Innovation Network." East-West Center Policy Studies #54.

Ernst, Dieter, Tom Ganiatsos, and Lynn Mytelka (1998), *Technological Capabilities and Export Success in Asia*. London: Routledge Studies in the Growth Economies of Asia.

Faustino, Jaime, and Raul V. Fabella (2011), "Engendering Reform." In *Built on Dreams, Grounded in Reality: Economic Policy Reform in the Philippines*. Makati City, the Philippines: Asia Foundation.

Felipe, Jesus (2010), "Industrial Policy, Capabilities and Growth: Where does the Future of Singapore Lie?" Paper presented at the Singapore Economic Policy Forum, October 22, 2010, Singapore.

Feng, Wang (2011), "The End of 'Growth with Equity'? Economic Growth and Income Inequality in East Asia." *Asia Pacific Issues (East-West Center)* 101 (July): 1–8.

Fukuyama, Francis, Minxin Pei, Yunhan Chu, and Larry Diamond (2012), "China and East Asian Democracy." *Journal of Democracy* 23, no. 1 (January): 14–26.

Gill, Indermit, and Homit Kharas (2007), *An East Asian Reinassance: Ideas for Economic Growth.* Washington, DC: The World Bank.

Goldstein, Morris (1998), *The Asian Financial Crisis: Causes, Consequences and Systemic Implications.* Washington, DC: Petersen Institute for International Economics.

Gong, Yooshik, and Wonho Jang (1998), "Culture and Development: Reassessing Cultural Explanations on Asian Economic Development." *Development and Society* 27, no. 1 (June): 77–97.

Guthrie, Douglas (1998), "The Declining Significance of Guanxi in China's Economic Transition." *The China Quarterly* 154 (June): 254–282.

Haddad, Mona (2007), "Trade Integration in East Asia: The Role of China and Production Networks." World Bank Policy Research Paper #4160 (March).

Haggard, Stephan (2004), "Institutions and Growth in East Asia." *Studies in Comparative International Development* 38, no. 4 (Winter): 53–81.

Hamanaka, Shintaro (2012), "Anatomy of South–South FTAs in Asia: Comparisons with Africa, Latin America, and the Pacific Islands." Asian Development Bank Working Paper Series on Regional Economic Integration #102 (September).

Hamilton, Gary, ed. (1991), *Business Networks and Economic Development in East and Southeast Asia.* Hong Kong: University of Hong Kong Press.

Heckman, James J., and Junjian Yi (2012), "Human Capital, Economic Growth, and Inequality in China." Institute for the Study of Labor Discussion Paper #6550 (May).

Hernandez, Zenaida (2004), "Industrial Policy in East Asia: In Search for Lessons." A Background Paper for the World Development Report 2005.

Hill, Hall (2000), *The Indonesian Economy.* New York: Cambridge University Press.

Hill, Hal, and Arsenio Balisacan (2002) "The Philippines Development Puzzle." In *Southeast Asian Affairs 2002*, edited by D. Singh and A. J. Smith. Singapore: Singapore Institute of Southeast Asian Studies.

Hiratsuka, Daisuke (2008), "Production Fragmentation and Networks in East Asia Characterized by Vertical Specialization" In *Vertical Specialization and Economic Integration in East Asia*, edited by Hiratsuka and Uchida, 91–116. IDE-JETREO.

Hobday, Michael (1995), *Innovation in East Asia: The Challenge of Japan.* Brookfield, VT: Edward Elgar.

Horn, John, Vivien Singer, and Jonathan Woetzel (2010), "A Truer Picture of China's Export Machine." *Mckinsey Quarterly* (September).

Huang, Yasheng (2012), "How Did China Take Off?" *Journal of Economic Perspectives* 26, no. 4 (Fall): 147–170.

Huang, Yukon, and Alessandro Magnoli, eds. (2009), *Reshaping Economic Geography in East Asia*. Washington, DC: The World Bank.

Hutchcroft, Paul (1998), *Booty Capitalism: The Politics of Banking in the Philippines*. Ithaca, NY: Cornell University Press.

Hutchcroft, Paul, and Joel Rocamora (2003), "Strong Demands and Weak Institutions: The Origins and Evolution of the Democratic Deficit in the Philippines." *Journal of East Asian Studies* 3: 259–292.

International Monetary Fund (2011b), "Implications of Asia's Regional Supply Chain for Rebalancing Growth." IMF Regional Economic Outlook (April).

Johnson, Chalmers (1982), *MITI and the Japanese Miracle: The Growth of Industrial Policy*. Stanford, CA: Stanford University Press.

Jongwanich, Juthathip (2010) "Determinants of Export Performance in East and Southeast Asia." *The World Economy* 33, no. 1: 20–41.

Jorgenson, Dale W., and Khuong M. Vu (2011) "The Rise of Developing Asia and the New Economic Order." *Journal of Policy Modeling* 33: 698–745.

Kasahara, Shigehisa (2004), "The Flying Geese Paradigm: A Critical Study of Its Application to East Asian Regional Development." UNCTAD Discussion Paper #169.

Kenny, Charles (2008), "What's Not Converging? East Asia's Relative Performance in Income, Health and Education." *Asian Economic Policy Review* 3, no. 1: 19–37.

Kharas, Homi, Albert Zeufack, and Hamdan Majeed (2010), *Cities, People & The Economy: A Study on Positioning Penang*. Kuala Lumpur: Khazanah Nasional Berhad & The World Bank.

Kim, Linsu (1997), *Imitation to Innovation: The Dynamics of Korea's Technological Learning*. Cambridge, MA: Harvard Business Review Press.

Kimura, Fukunari (2006), "International Production and Distribution Networks in East Asia: Eighteen Facts, Mechanics, and Policy Implications." *Asian Economic Policy Review* 1: 326–344.

Kojima, Kiyoshi (2002), "The Flying Geese Model of Asian Economic Development: Origins, Theoretical Extensions and Regional Policy Implications." *Journal of Asian Economies* 11: 365–401.

Kotschwar, Barbara, Theodore Moran, and Julia Muir (2012), "Chinese Investments in Latin American Resources: The Good, the Bad, and the Ugly." Peterson Institute for International Economics Working Paper #12–3 (February).

Krugman, Paul (1994), "The Myth of Asia's Miracle." *Foreign Affairs*, November–December.

Kumar, Sree, and Sharon Siddique (2010), *The Singapore Success Story: Public-Private Alliance for Investment Attraction, Innovation and Export Development*. Santiago, Chile: ECLAC.

Kwame, Jomo (2004), "The New Economic Policy and Inter-Ethnic Relations in Malaysia." Identity, Conflict and Cohesion Program paper #7 (September), UN Research Institute for Social Development (UNRISD).

———. (2006), "Pathways through Financial Crisis: Malaysia." *Global Governance* 12, no. 4: 489–505.

Kwon, Jene K., and Jung Mo Kang (2011), "The East Asian Model of Economic Development." *Asian- Pacific Economic Literature* 2, no. 2: 116–130.

Lee, Il Houng, Murtaza Syed, and Liu Xueyan (2012), "Is China Over-Investing and Does it Matter?" IMF Working Paper #12/277 (November).

Leipziger, Danny ed. (1997), *Lessons from East Asia*. Ann Arbor: University of Michigan Press.

Li, Hongbin, Lei Li, Binzhen Wu, and Yanyan Xiong (2012), "The End of Cheap Chinese Labor." *Journal of Economic Perspectives* 26, no. 4 (Fall): 57–74.

Liang, Ming-Yih (2010), "Confucianism and the East Asian Miracle." *American Economic Journal: Macroeconomics* 2, no. 3 (July): 206–234.

Lim, Linda (2008), "Singapore's Economic Growth Model—Too Much or Too Little?" Paper prepared for the *Singapore Economic Policy Conference* on October 24, 2008.

Lin, Justin Yifu (2012b), "China's Rise and Leaving the Middle-Income Trap in Latin America and the Caribbean Countries." Paper presented at a Conference of the Chief Economist of the World Bank at the UN Economic Commission for Latin America and the Caribbean, May 14.

———. (2012c), "Demystifying the Chinese Economy." Paper presented at the London School of Economics on December 18, 2012.

Lin, Justin Yifu, and Volker Treichel (2012), "Learning from China's Rise to Escape the Middle- Income Trap: A New Structural Economics Approach to Latin America." World Bank Policy Research Working Paper #6165.

Meng, Xin (2012), "Labor Market Outcomes and Reforms in China." *Journal of Economic Perspectives* 26, no. 4 (Fall): 75–102.

Moran, Theodore (2011), "Foreign Manufacturing Multinationals and the Transformation of the Chinese Economy: New Measurements, New Perspectives." Peterson Institute for International Economics Working Paper #11–11.

Murthy, Viren (2000), "The Democratic Potential of Confucian 'Minben' Thought." *Asian Philosophy* 10, no. 1: 33–47.

Nelson, Richard, and Howard Pack (1999), "The Asian Miracle and Modern Growth Theory." *Economic Journal* 109 (July): 416–436.

Nelson, Robert (2007), "The Philippine Economic Mystery." *The Philippine Review of Economics* 44, no. 1 (July):1–32.

Noland, Marcus (2011), "Korea's Growth Performance: Past and Future." East West Center Working Papers #123 (November).

Noland, Marcus, and Howard Pack (2003), *Industrial Policy in an Era of Globalization: Lessons from Asia*. Washington, DC: Institute for International Economics.

Noland, Marcus, Donghyun Park, and Gemma B. Estrada (2012), "Developing the Services Sector as Engines of Growth for Asia: An Overview." Asian Development Bank Working Paper (October). #12–18

Ozawa, Terutomo (2009), *The Rise of Asia: The "Flying Geese" Theory of Tandem Growth and Regional Agglomeration*. Cheltenham: Edward Elgar.

Pack, Howard (2001), "The Role of Acquisition of Foreign Technology in Taiwanese Growth." *Industrial and Corporate Change* 10, no. 3: 713–734.

Palma, José Gabriel (2009), "Flying geese and Waddling Ducks: the Different Capabilities of East Asia and Latin America to 'Demand-adapt' and 'Supply-upgrade' their Export Productive Capacity." In *Industrial Policy and Development: the Political Economy of Capabilities Accumulation.* 203–238. Oxford: Oxford University Press.

Park, Donghyun, and Kwanho Shin (2012), "The Services Sector in Asia: Is It an Engine?" Asian Development Bank Working Paper #12–21 (October).

Qian, Yingyi (2003), "How Reform Worked in China." Chapter 11 in Rodrik, D. (ed.), *In Search of Prosperity: Analytic Narratives on Economic Growth.* Princeton, NJ: Princeton University Press.

Quimpo, Nathan Gilbert (2007), "The Philippines Political Parties and Corruption" *Southeast Asian Affairs* 2007: 277–294.

Rauch, James E., and Vitor Trindade (2002), "Ethnic Chinese Networks in International Trade." *Review of Economics and Statistics* 84, no. 1 (February): 116–130.

Rosli, Mohamad, and Fatimah Kari (2008), "Malaysia's National Automotive Policy and the Performance of Proton's Local and Foreign Vendors." *Asia Pacific Business Review* 14, no. 1 103–118.

Rowen, Henry, ed. (1998), *Behind East Asian Growth: The Political and Social Foundations of Prosperity.* London: Routledge.

Saich, Anthony, Dwight Perkins, David Dapice, Vu Thanh Tu Anh, Nguyen Xuan Thanh, and Huynh The Du (2008), "Choosing Success: The Lessons of East and Southeast Asia and Vietnam's Future." Harvard Vietnam Program: Harvard University.

Shin, Doh Chull (2011), *Confucianism and Democratization in East Asia.* New York: Cambridge University Press.

Shi, Tianjian, and Jie Lu (2010), "The Shadow of Confucianism." *Journal of Democracy* 21, no. 4 (October): 123–130.

Stiglitz, Joseph, and Marilou Uy (1996), "Financial Markets, Public Policy and the East Asian Miracle." *World Bank Research Observer* 11, no. 2: 249–276.

Stiglitz, Joseph E., and Shahid Yusuf, eds. (2001), *Rethinking the East Asian Miracle.* New York: Oxford University Press & The World Bank.

Stubbs, Richard (2009), "What Ever Happened to the East Asian Developmental State? The Unfolding Debate." *The Pacific Review* 22, no. 1: 1–22.

Sundaram, Jomo Kwame (2006), "Pathways through Financial Crises: Malaysia." *Global Governance* 12, no. 4 (October–December): 489–505.

Tao Yang, Dennis (2012), "Aggregate Savings and External Imbalances in China." *Journal of Economic Perspectives* 26, no. 4 (Fall): 125–146.

Thorbecke, Willem, and Nimesh Salike (2011), "Understanding Foreign Direct Investment in East Asia." Asian Development Bank Institute Working Paper Series #290 (June).

Tolo, Willa Boots J. (2011), "The Determinants of Economic Growth in the Philippines: A New Look." IMF Working Paper #11/288.

United Nations (2011), *People's Republic of China and Latin America and the Caribbean: Ushering in a New Era in the Economic and Trade Relationship.* Santiago: United Nations.

Wade, Robert (2003), *Governing the Market: Economic Theory and the Role of the Government in East Asian Industrialization.* Princeton, NJ: Princeton University Press.

Wang, Zhi, and William Powers (2009), "Value Chains in East Asian Production Networks—An International Input-Output Model Based Analysis." U.S. International Trade Commission, Office of Economics Working Paper (October).

Weil, Roman (2008), *Economic Growth.* Englewood Cliffs: Prentice Hall.

Weiss, John (2005), "Export Growth and Industrial Policy: Lessons from the East Asian Miracle Experience." Asian Development Bank Institute Discussion Paper #26 (February).

Westphal, Larry (1990), "Industrial Policy in an Export-Propelled Economy: Lessons from South Korea's Experience." *Journal of Economic Perspectives* 4, no. 3 (Summer): 41–59.

Woo, Wing Thye (2009), "Getting Malaysia Out of the Middle-Income Trap." Economics Department of the University of California (Davis) Working Paper.

———. (2010), "Indonesia Economic Performance in Comparative Perspective and a New Policy Framework for 2049." *Bulletin of Indonesian Economic Studies* 46, no. 1: 33–64.

———. (2012), "The Changing Ingredients in Industrial Policy for Economic Growth: The Over- Selling of Market Fundamentalism ('Get the Prices Right') and Institution Fundamentalism ('Get the Institutions Right'." Paper presented at the Asia-Pacific Research and Training Network Symposium Towards a Return of Industrial Policy? July 25–26, 2011, United Nations Economic and Social Commission for Asia and the Pacific, Bangkok.

World Bank (1993), *The East Asian Miracle: Economic Growth and Public Policy.* Washington, DC: World Bank.

———. (2007), "Malaysia and the Knowledge Economy: Building a World Class Higher Education System." World Bank Report # 40397 (March).

———. (2012), *China 2030: Building a Modern, Harmonious, and Creative High-Income Society,* by the Development Research Center of the State Council, the People's Republic of China & The World Bank. Washington, DC: The World Bank.

Xu Tian, and Xiaohua Yu (2012), "The Enigma of TFP in China: A Meta-Analysis." Courant Research Centre (Gottingen, Germany) Discussion Paper #113 (June).

Yang, Mayfair Mei-hui (2002), "The Resilience of Guanxi and Its New Deployments: A Critique of Some New Guanxi Scholarship." *The China Quarterly* 170 (June): 459–476.

Yeung, Henry (1999), "The Internationalization of Ethnic Chinese Business Firms from Southeast Asia: Strategies, Processes and Comparative Advantage." *International Journal of Urban and Regional Research* 23, no. 1: 103–127.

Ying, Tan Yin, Alvin Eng, and Edward Robinson (2008), "Perspectives on Growth: A Political Economy Framework (Lessons from the Singapore Experience)." World Bank Growth Commission Working Paper #1.

Young, Alwyn (1992), "A Tale of Two Cities: Factor Accumulation and Technical Change in Hong Kong and Singapore." In Blanchard, O. and Fischer, S. (eds.) *NBER Macroeconomics Annual 1992* vol. 7: 13–64.

Yusof, Zainal Aznam, and Deepak Bhattasali (2008), "Economic Growth and Development in Malaysia: Policy Making and Leadership," World Bank Commision on Growth and Development Working Paper #27.

Yusof, Shahid, M. Anjum Altaf, and Kaoru Nabeshima (2004), *Global Production Networking and Technological Change in East Asia*. Washington, DC: World Bank.

Yusuf, Shahid, and Kaoru Nabeshima (2009), *Tiger Economies under Threat: A Comparative Analysis of Malaysia's Industrial Prospects and Policy Options*. Washington, DC: World Bank.

Yusof, Zainal, and Deepak Bhattasali (2008), "Economic Growth and Development in Malaysia: Policy Making and Leadership." World Bank Growth Commission Background Paper #27.

Zakaria, Fareed (1994), "An Interview with Lee Kuan Yew." *Foreign Affairs* 73, no. 2: 109–126.

Zhu, Xiaodong (2012), "Understanding China's Growth: Past, Present and Future." *Journal of Economic Perspectives* 26, no. 4: 103–124.

C. Readings on the Economic Development of Latin America

Adler, Gustavo, and Nicolas Magud (2013), "Four Decades of Terms-of-Trade Booms: Savings and Investment Patterns and a New Metric of Income Windfall." IMF Working Paper #13/03 (May).

Adrogue, Ricardo, Martin Cerisola, and Gaston Gelos (2006), "Brazil's Long-term Growth Puzzle: Trying to Explain the Puzzle." IMF Working Paper #06/282.

Agosin, Manuel, Christian Larrain, and Nicolas Grau (2010), "Industrial Policy in Chile." Inter-American Development Bank Working Papers Series # 170 (December).

Agosin, Manuel, Eduardo Fernandez-Arias, and Fidel Jaramillo (2009), *Growing Pains: Binding Constraints to Productive Investment in Latin America*. Washington, DC: Inter-American Development Bank.

Aizenman, Joshua (2005), "Financial Liberalisations in Latin-America in the 1990s: A Reassessment." NBER Working Paper #11145 (February).

Ardanaz, Martín, Carlos Scartascini, and Mariano Tommasi (2010), "Political Institutions, Policymaking, and Economic Policy in Latin America." Inter-American Development Bank Working Paper Series #158 (March).

Arza, Valeria (2005), "Technological Performance, Economic Performance and Behavior: A Study of Argentine Firms during the 1990s." *Innovation: Management, Policy and Practice* 7, nos. 2–3 (April): 131–165.

Astorga, Pablo, and Ame R. Berges (2011), "Productivity Growth in Latin America over the Long Run." *Review of Income and Wealth* 5, no. 2 (June): 203–223.

Barandiaran, Edgardo, and Leonardo Hernandez (1999), "Origins and Resolution of a Banking Crisis: Chile 1982–86." Central Bank of Chile Working Paper #57.

Baer, Werner, and Isaac Kerstenetsky (1964), *Inflation and Growth in Latin America*. Homewood, IL: Richard T. Irwin.

Bates, Robert H, John H. Coatsworth, and Jeffrey G. Williamson (2006), "Lost Decades: Lessons from Post-Independence Latin America for Today's Africa." NBER Working Paper #12610 (October).

Bellisario, Antonio (2007), "Chilean Agrarian Transformation: Agrarian Reform and 'Partial' Counter-Agrarian Reform, 1964–80." *Journal of Agrarian Reform* 7, no. 1: 1–34.

Bello, Omar D., Juan S. Blyde, and Diego Restuccia (2011), "Venezuela's Growth Experience." *Latin American Journal of Economics* 48, no. 2 (November): 199–226.

Berg, Andrew G., and Jonathan D. Ostry (2011), "Inequality and Unsustainable Growth: Two Sides of the Same Coin?" IMF Staff Discussion Note #11/08 (April).

Birdsall, Nancy, Augusto De La Torre, and Rachel Menezes (2008), *Fair Growth: Economic Policies for Latin America's Poor and Middle-Income Majority*. Washington, DC: Center for Global Development.

Birdsall, Nancy, Nora Lustig, and Darryl McLeod (2011), "Declining Inequality in Latin America: Some Economics, Some Politics." Center for Global Development Working Paper #251 (May).

Bittencourt, Manoel (2013), "Yet another Look at the Modernization Hypothesis: Evidence from South America." ERSA Working Paper #342 (March) Economic Research Southern Africa, which is sponsored by the National Treasury of South Africa.

Blanco, Carlos, Ramon Espinasa, Keving Ghallager, Ann Helwege, Silvia Inclan, Thomas Kunz, David Palmer, Dylon Robbins, and Riordan Roett (2011), "Latin America 2060: Consolidation or Crisis?" Boston University Pardee Center Task Force Report (September).

Blavy, Rodolphe (2006), "Public Debt and Productivity: The Difficult Quest for Growth in Jamaica." IMF Working Paper #06/235 (October).

Blyde, Juan, and Christian Volpe Marticunus (2011), "Trade and the International Organization of Production: Prospects for Latin America and the Caribbean." *IADB Integration and Trade*, 15, no. 32 (January–June): 1–4.

Boianovsky, Mauro (2009), "Furtado and the Structuralist-Monetarist Debate on Economic Stabilization in Latin America." Document presented in the Brazilian Economic Association meeting.

Boxer, Charles (1962), *The Golden Age of Brazil 1695–1750: Growing Pains of a Colonial Society*. Berkeley: University of California Press.

Brink, Rogier van den, Arshad Sayed, Steve Barnett, Eduardo Aninat, Eric Parrado, Zahid Hasnain, and Tehmina Khan (2012), "South-South Cooperation: How Mongolia Learned from Chile on Managing a Mineral-Rich Economy." World Bank Poverty Reduction and Economic Management Network (September).

Calderón, César, and Luis Servén (2010), "Infrastructure in Latin America." World Bank Policy Research Working Paper #5317 (May).

Calvo, Guillermo, Carmen Reinhart, Eduardo Fernandez, and Ernesto Talvi (2001), "Growth and External Financing in Latin America." Inter-American Development Bank Working Paper #457 (August).

Canales-Kriljenko, Jorge Iván, Luis I. Jácome, Ali Alichi, and Ivan Luís de Oliveira Lima (2010), "Weathering the Global Storm: The Benefits of Monetary Policy Reform in the LA5 Countries." IMF Working Paper #10/292.

Cárdenas, Mauricio (2010), "State Capacity in Latin America." *Economia* 10, no. 2 (Spring): 1–45.

Cárdenas, Mauricio, and Ariana Krugler (2011), "The Reversal of the Structural Transformation in Latin America after China's Emergence." Brookings Working Paper (August 2, 2011).

Cardoso, Eliana, and Vladimir Kuhl Teles (2010), "A Brief History of Brazil's Growth." In *Growth and Sustainability in Brazil, China, India, Indonesia and South Africa*, 19–50. OECD.

Cardozo, Fernando Henrique, and Enzo Faletto (1969), *Dependencia y Desarrollo en America Latina*. Buenos Aires: Siglo XXI Editores, S.A.

Casanova, Lourdes, Jeff Dayton-Johnson, Nils O. Fonsta, and Anna Pietikainen (2012), "Innovation from Emerging Markets: The Case of Latin America." INSEAD Working Paper #2012/76/ST.

Cesa-Bianchi, Ambrogio, Mohammad Hashem Pesaran, Alessandro Rebucci, and Teng Teng Xu (2011), "China's Emergence in the World Economy and Business Cycles in Latin America." Discussion Paper for the Institute for the Study of Labor #5889.

Centennial Group (2011), *Latin America 2040: Breaking Away from Complacency*. New York: Sage Press.

Cimoli, Mario, and Jorge Katz (2003), "Structural Reforms, Technological Gaps and Economic Development: A Latin American Perspective." *Industrial and Corporate Change* 12, no. 2: 387–411.

Cimoli, Mario, Marcio Holland, Gabriel Porcile, Annalisa Primi, and Sebastián Vergara (2006), "Growth, Structural Change and Technological Capabilities: Latin America in a Comparative Perspective." Sant'Anna School of Advanced Studies LEM Working Paper Series (May).

Cirera, Xavier, Anabel Marin, and Ricardo Markwald (2012), "Firm Behaviour and the Introduction of New Exports: Evidence from Brazil." Institute of Development Studies Working Paper #390 (March).

Coatsworth, John (2008), "Inequality, Institutions and Economic Growth in Latin America." *Journal of Latin American Studies* 40, no. 3: 545–569.

Coatsworth, John, and Oliver Williamson (2004), "Always Protectionist? Latin American Tariffs from Independence to the Great Depression." *Journal of Latin American Studies* 36, no. 2: 205–232.

Cole, Harold, Lee Ohanian, Alvaro Riascos, and James Schmitz (2006), "Latin America in the Rear-view Mirror." *Federal Reserve Bank of Minneapolis Quarterly Review* (September).

Damill, Mario, and Roberto Frenkel (2012), "Macroeconomic Policies, Growth, Employment, and Inequality in Latin America." UNU-Wider Working Paper #2012/23 (February).

Daude, Christian (2010), "Innovation, Productivity and Economic Development in Latin America & the Caribbean." OECD Development Centre Working Paper #288 (February).

Dayton-Johnson, Jeff, Juliana Londoño, and Sebastián Nieto-Parra (2011), "The Process of Reform in Latin America: A Review Essay." OECD Development Center Working Paper #304 (October).

De Ferranti, David, Guillermo Perry, Francisco Ferreira, Michael Walton, David Coady, Wendy Cunningham, Leonardo Gasparini, Joyce Jacobsen, Yasuhiko Matsuda, James Robinson, Kenneth Sokoloff, and Quentin Wodon (2003), *Inequality in Latin America: Breaking with History?* Washington, DC: World Bank.

De La Mora, Luz Maria, and Dora Rodriguez (2011), "Why Is It Worth Rethinking Latin America Integration?" *IADB Integration and Trade Journal* 15, no. 33 (July–December): 7–15.

Devlin, Robert, and Graciela Moguillansky (2011), *Breeding Latin American Tigers: Operational Principles for Rehabilitating Industrial Policies.* Washington, DC: World Bank.

———. (2012), "What's New in the New Industrial Policy in Latin America?" World Bank Policy Research Working Paper #6191 (September).

Diaz-Alejandro, Carlos F. (1966), *Exchange Rate Devaluation in a Semi-Industrialized Economy: The Experience of Argentina, 1955–61.* Cambridge: MIT Press.

———. (1970), *Essays on the Economic History of the Argentine Republic.* New Haven, CT: Yale University Press.

———. (1985) "Good-bye Financial Repression, Hello Financial Crash." *Journal of Development Economics* 19, no. 1–2: 1–24.

DiJohn, Jonathan (2004), "The Political Economy of Economic Liberalisation in Venezuela." Crisis States Programme, London School of Economics and Political Science Working Paper #46 (June).

Dornbusch, Rudiger, and Sebastian Edwards, eds. (1991), *Macroeconomics of Populism in Latin America.* Cambridge: MIT Press.

Duprenit, Gabriela, and Jorge Katz (2005), "Introduction: Innovation, Growth and Development in Latin America: Stylized Facts and Policy Agenda." *Innovation, Management, Policy and Practice* 7, no. 2–3: 105–135.

ECLA (2002), "The Integration of Latin America and the Caribbean in Global Trade and Production Circuits." Chapter 6 in *Globalization and Development,* UNECLA.

———. (2011), *Forum for East Asia-Latin America Cooperation (FEALAC).* Santiago: United Nations.

Edwards, Sebastian (1996), "Why Are Latin America's Savings Rates So Low? An International Comparative Analysis." *Journal of Development Economics* 51, no. 1 (October): 5–44.

———. (2009), "Forty Years of Latin America's Economic Development: From the Alliance for Progress to the Washington Consensus." NBER Working Paper #15190 (July).

———. (2009), "Latin America's Decline: A Long Historical View." NBER Working Paper #15171 (July).

Edwards, Sebastian, and Daniel Lederman (1998), "The Political Economy of Unilateral Trade Liberalization." NBER Working Paper #6510 (April).

Edwards, Sebastian, and A. Cox Edwards (1987), *Monetarism and Liberalization: The Chilean Experiment.* Cambridge, MA: Ballinger.

Engerman, Stanley L., and Kenneth L. Sokoloff (2002), "Factor Endowments, Inequality, and Paths of Development among New World Economies" *Economia* 3, no. 1 (Fall): 41–88.

Ferranti, David, Guillermo Perry, Francisco Ferreira, and Michael Walton (2004), *Inequality in Latin America: Breaking with History.* Washington, DC: World Bank.

Ferreira, Francisco H.G., Phillippe G. Leite, and Julie A. Litchfield (2006), "The Rise and Fall of Brazilian Inequality: 1981–2004." World Bank Policy Research Working Paper #3867 (March).

Fishlow, Albert (1990), "The Latin American State." *Journal of Economic Perspectives* 4, no. 3 (Summer): 61–74.

Frankel, Jeffrey (2011), "A Solution to Fiscal Procyclicality: The Structural Budget Institutions Pioneered by Chile." NBER Working Paper #16945 (April).

Frenkel, Roberto, and Martín Rapetti (2012), "External Fragility or Deindustrialization: What Is the Main Threat to Latin American Countries in the 2010s?" *World Bank Economic Review* 1, no. 1: 37–56.

Freyre, Gilberto (1946), *The Masters and the Slaves: A Study in the Development of Brazilian Civilization.* New York: Knopf.

Fukuyama, Francis, ed. (2010), *Falling Behind: Explaining the Development Gap between Latin America and the United States.* New York: Oxford University Press.

Gallagher, Kevin, and Roberto Porzecanski (2008), "Climbing Up the Technology Ladder? High-Technology Exports in China and Latin America." University of California, Berkeley Working Paper (January).

———. (2010), *Dragon in the Room: China and the Future of Latin America.* Palo Alto: Stanford University Press.

Gallagher, Kevin, Amos Irwin, and Katherine Koleski (2012), "The New Banks in Town: Chinese Finance in Latin America." Inter-American Dialogue Report (March).

Gasparini, Leonardo, Guillermo Cruces, and Leopoldo Tornarolli (2009), "Recent Trends in Income Inequality in Latin America." Society for the Study of Economic Inequality Working Paper #2009–132.

Gavin, Michael. and Roberto Perotti (1997), "Fiscal Policy in Latin America." *NBER Macroeconomics Annual* 12: 11–72.

Goodman, Louis, Johanna Mendelson Forman, Moises Naim, and Joseph Tulchin (1998), *Lessons of the Venezuelan Experience.* Washington, DC: Woodrow Wilson Center Press.

Gros, Daniel, Cinzi Alcidi, and Alessandro Giovannini (2013), "Brazil and the European Union in the Global Economy." CEPS Working Document #371 (February).

Guerrero, Pablo, Krista Lucenti, and Sebastián Galarza (2010), "Trade Logistics and Regional Integration in Latin America and the Caribbean." Inter-American Development Bank Working Paper Series # 233 (August).

Handa, Sudhanshu, and Damien King (1997), "Structural Adjustment Polices, Income Distribution and Poverty: A Review of the Jamaican Experience." *World Development* 25, no. 6: 831–1002.

Hanson, Gordon H. (2010), "Why Isn't Mexico Rich?" NBER Working Paper #16470.

Hanushek, Eric A., and Ludger Woessmann (2009), "Schooling, Cognitive Skills, and the Latin American Growth Puzzle." Institute for the Study of Labor Discussion Paper #4576 (November).

Hausmann, Ricardo, and Michael Gavin (1996), "Securing Stability and Growth in a Shock Prone Region: The Policy Challenge for Latin America." IADB Office of the Chief Economist Working Paper #315 (January).

Heinrich Böll Foundation (2012), "Inside a Champion: An Analysis of the Brazilian Development Model." Heinrich Böll Stiftung: Publication Series on Democracy.

Huber, Evelyne (2005), "Inequality and the State in Latin America." Conference of the APSA Task Force on Difference and Inequality in the Developing World, University of Virginia, April 22–23, 2005.

Iizuka, Michiko, and Jorge Katz (2011), "Natural Resources Industries, 'Tragedy of the Common Commons' and the Case of Chilean Salmon Farming.'" *International Journal of Institutions and Economies* 3, no. 2: 259–286.

Inter-American Development Bank (2000), "Latin America at the Turn of a New Century." In *Development beyond Economics,* Chapter 1 in Economic and Social Progress in Latin America Annual Report.

International Monetary Fund (2005), "Stabilization and Reform in Latin America: A Macroeconomic Perspective on the Experience of the 1990s." IMF Occasional Paper #238.

———. (2010), "Dollarization Decline in Latin America." *Finance and Development* 47, no. 1: 57.

———. (2012), "Macroeconomic Policy Frameworks for Resource-Rich Developing Countries." IMF Policy Paper (August 14).

Izquierdo, Alejandro, and Ernesto Talvi (2008), *All that Glitters May Not be Gold: Assessing Latin America's Recent Economic Performance.* Washington, DC: Inter-American Development Bank.

———. (2011c), *One Region, Two Speeds? Challenges of the New Global Economic Order for Latin America & the Caribbean.* Washington, DC: Inter-American Development Bank.

Johnston, Jake, and Juan A. Montecino (2012), "Update on the Jamaican Economy." Center for Economic and Policy Research (May).

Kalter, Ellio, Steven Phillips, Marco A. Espinosa-Vega, Rodolfo Luzio, Mauricio Villafuerte, and Manmohan Sing (2004), "Chile: Institutional Policies Underpinning Stabilization and Growth." IMF Occasional Paper #231.

Katz, Jorge (2000), "Structural Change and Labor Productivity Growth in Latin American Manufacturing Industries 1970–96." *World Development* 28, no. 9: 1583–1596.

——. (2004), "Market-oriented Reforms, Globalization and the Recent Transformation of Latin American Innovation Systems." *Oxford Development Studies* 32, no. 3 (September): 375–387.

Kaufman, Daniel, Massimo Mastruzzi, and Diego Zavaleta (2003), "Sustained Macroeconomic Reforms, Tepid Growth: A Governance Puzzle in Bolivia?" Chapter 12 in Dodrik, D. (ed.) *In Search of Prosperity: Analytical Narratives of Economic Growth.* Princeton, NJ: Princeton University Press.

Kehoe, Timothy J., and Felipe Meza (2011), "Catch-up Growth Followed by Stagnation: Mexico, 1950–2010." Federal Reserve Bank of Minneapolis Research Department Working Paper #693 (December).

Kehoe, Timothy, and Kim Ruhl (2010), "Why Have Economic Reforms in Mexico Not Generated Growth?" NBER Working Paper #16580 (December).

Keifman, Saúl N., and Roxana Maurizio (2012), "Changes in Labour Market Conditions: Their Impact on Wage Inequality." UNU WIDER Working Paper #2012/14 (February).

King, Damien (2000), "The Evolution of Structural Adjustment and Economic Policy in Jamaica." Economic Reform Study #65. Santiago, Chile: ECLA.

Kotschwar, Barbara (2012), "Transportation and Communication Infrastructure in Latin America: Lessons from Asia." Peterson Institute for International Economics Working Paper #12–6 (April).

Kuwayama, Mikio (2009), "Quality of Latin American and Caribbean industrialization and Integration into the Global Economy." CEPAL Serie Comercio Internacional #92 (September).

Lall, Sanjaya, Manuel Albaladejo, and Mauricio Mesquita Moreira (2004), "Latin American Industrial Competitiveness and the Challenge of Globalization." Institute for the Integration of Latin America and the Caribbean Occassional Paper SITI—05 (June).

Lange, Mathhew, James Mahoney, and Matthias Vom Hau (2002), "Colonialism and Development: A Comparative Analysis of Spanish and British Colonies." *American Journal of Sociology* 111, no. 5: 1412–1462.

Larrain, Felipe, and Patricio Meller (1991), "The Socialist-Populist Chilean Experience, 1970–73." In *Macroeconomics of Populism in Latin America,* edited by Rudiger Dornbusch and Sebastian Edwards. Chicago: University of Chicago Press.

Larrain, Felipe, Luis F. Lopez-Calva, and Andres Rodriguez-Clare (2000), "Intel: a Case Study of Foreign Direct Investment in Central America." Center for International Development Working Paper #58.

Lederman, Daniel (2010), "Does What You Export Matter? In Search of Empirical Guidance for Industrial Policies." Study of the Office of the Chief Economist for Latin America and the Caribbean of the World Bank.

Loayza, Norman V., and Jamele Rigolini (2006), "Informality: Trends and Cycles." World Bank Policy Research Working Paper #4078 (December).

Loayza, Norman, P. Fajnzylber, and C. Calderon (2005), "Economic Growth in Latin America and the Caribbean: Stylized Facts, Explanations and Forecasts." World Bank Policy Research Working Paper #7315 (September).

Love, Joseph (2007), "The Latin American Contribution to Center-Periphery Perspectives: History and Prospect." Technology, Governance and Economic Dynamics, The Other Canon Foundation and Tallinn University of Technology Working Papers in Technology Governance and Economic Dynamics #10 (January).

Lustig, Nora, Luis F. Lopez-Calva, and Eduardo Ortiz-Juarez (2012), "Declining Inequality in Latin America in the 2000s: The Cases of Argentina, Brazil, and Mexico." Center for Global Development Working Paper #307 (October).

Mahoney, James (2000), "Was Latin America Too Rich to Prosper?" In *Modern Political Economy in Latin America,* edited by J. Frieden et al., 165–172. Boulder, CO: Westview Press.

———. (2003), "Long-Run Development and the Legacy of Colonialism in Latin America." *American Journal of Sociology* 109, no. 1 (July): 51–106.

Maurizio, Roxana (2012), "Labour Informality in Latin America: The Case of Argentina, Chile, Brazil and Peru." Brooks World Poverty Institute Working Paper #165 (April).

McGuire, James W. (2011), "Social Policies in Latin America: Causes, Characteristics, and Consequences." Allbrinton Center for the Study of Public Life Working Paper Series (September), Vol. 1, Article 1.

Mejia Acosta, Andres (2008), "The Policy-making Process in Jamaica: Fiscal Adjustment and Crime Fighting in Jamaica." Inter-American Development Bank Conference Report (February).

Mishkin, Frederic (2006), *The Next Great Globalization: How Disadvantaged Nations Can Harness Financial Systems to Get Rich.* Princeton, NJ: Princeton University Press.

Monadi, Franciso, Rosa Amelia Gonzalez, Richard Obuchi, and Michael Penfold (2004), "Political Institutions, Policy-making Processes, and Policy Outcomes in Venezuela." Latin American Research Network Working Paper.

Moschella, Manuel (2010), "Mexico and the IMF in the 1990's: Old and New Issues on Capital Account Liberalization and Emerging Market Economies." *Comparative Economic Studies* 52, no. 4: 589–609.

Mulder, Nanno (2009), "Weak Links Between Exports and Economic Growth in Latin America and the Caribbean." CEPAL—Serie Comercio Internacional #91 (February).

Naim, Moises (1993), *Paper Tigers and Minotaurs: The Politics of Venezuela's Economic Reforms.* Washington, DC: Carnegie Endowment for International Peace.

North, Douglass, William Summerhill, and Barry R. Weingast (2000), "Order, Disorder and Economic Change: Latin America vs. North America." In *Governing for Prosperity,* 1–58. New Haven, CT: Yale University Press.

Ocampo, Jose Antonio (2012), "The Development Implications of External Integration in Latin America." UNU-Wider Working Paper #2012/48 (May).

Ocampo, Jose Antonio, and Jaime Vos, eds. (2011), *The Oxford Handbook of Latin American Economics.* New York: Oxford University Press.

Pages, Carmen, ed. (2010), *The Age of Productivity: Transforming Economies from the Bottom Up.* Washington, DC: Inter-American Development Bank.

Palma, Jośe Gabriel (2010), "Why Has Productivity Growth Stagnated in Most Latin-American Countries Since the Neo-liberal Reforms?" Cambridge Working Papers in Economics #1030 (May).

Panadeiros, Monica, and Warren Benfield (2010), "Productive Development Policies in Jamaica." Inter-American Development Bank Working Paper #128 (March).

Paus, Eva, Nola Reinhardt, and Michael Robinson (2003), "Trade Liberalization and Productivity Growth in Latin American Manufacturing, 1970–1998" *Policy Reform* 6, no. 1 (March): 1–15.

Peres, Wilson (2011), "Industrial Policies in Latin America." UNU-Wider Working Paper No.2011/48 (September).

Pérez Caldentey, Esteban, and Matías Vernengo (2008), "Back to the Future: Latin America's Current Development Strategy." The IDEAs Working Paper Series Paper #07/2008.

Pérez Caldentey, Esteban, Daniel Titelman, and Pablo Carvallo (2013), "Weak Expansions: A Distinctive Feature of the Business Cycle in Latin America and the Caribbean." Levy Economics Institute of Bard College Working Paper #749.

Perry, Guillermo, William Maloney, Omar Arias, Pablo Fajnzylber, Andrew Mason, and Jaime Saavedra-Chanduvi (2007), "The Informal Sector: What Is It, Why Do We Care, and How Do We Measure It?" In *Informality: Exit and Exclusion*, 215–248. Washington, DC: World Bank.

Pietrobelli, Carlo, and Roberta Rabellotti (2004), "Upgrading in Clusters and Value Chains in Latin America: The Role of Policies." IADB Sustainable Development Department Best Practices Series (January).

Rasiah, Rajah, and Jebamalai Vinanchiarachi (2012), Review of "Drivers of Technological Upgrading and Economic Synergies: Evidence from Four Dynamic Clusters in Latin America and Asia." World Economic Review.

Restuccia, Diego (2011), "The Latin American Development Problem." University of Toronto Department of Economics Working Paper #432 (June).

Rodriguez, Francisco (2001), "The Political Economy of Latin American Economic Growth." Working Paper available at Prof. Rodriguez webpage at Wesleyan University (January) www.frodriguez.web.weslayan.edu

Rodriguez, Francisco, and Ricardo Hausmann, eds. (1999), *Venezuela: Anatomy of a Collapse*. www.frodriguez.web.wesleyan.edu

Roett, Riordan (1999), *Brazil: Politics in a Patrimonial Society*. Westport, CT: Praeger.

Rojas-Suarez, Liliana (2010), "The International Financial Crisis: Eight Lessons For and From Latin America." Center for Global Development Working Paper #202 (January).

Rosales, Osvaldo, and Mikio Kuwayama (2012), *China and Latin America and the Caribbean: Building an Economic and Trade Relationship*. Santiago: ECLAC.

Sachs, Jeffrey (1989), "Social Conflict and Populist Policies in Latin America." NBER Working Paper #2897 (March).

Sahay, Ratna, and Rishi Goyal (2006), "Volatility and Growth in Latin America: An Episodic Approach." IMF Working Paper 06/287 (December).

Sapelli, Claudio (2007), "The Political Economics of Import Substitution Industrialization." Catholic University of Chile Department of Economics Working Paper #257 (December).

Scartascini, Carlos, Ernesto Stein, and Mariano Tommasi (2010), *How Democracy Works: Political Institutions, Actors and Arenas in Latin America Policy Making.* Washington, DC: Inter-American Development Bank.

Schmidt-Hebbel, Klaus (2012), "The Political Economy of Distribution and Growth in Chile." Pontificia Universidad Catolica de Chile, Department of Economics Working Paper #417.

Segura-Ubiergo, Alex (2012), "The Puzzle of Brazil's High Interest Rates," IMF Working Paper #12/62 (February).

Singh, Annop (2006), "Macro Volatility: The Policy Lessons from Latin America." IMF Working Paper #06/166 (July).

Singh, Annop, and Martin Cerisola (2006), "Sustaining Latin America's Resurgence: Some Historical Perspectives." IMF Working Paper #06/252 (November).

Sokoloff, Kenneth, and Stanley Engerman (2000), "Institutions, Factor Endowments and Paths of Development in the New World." *Journal of Economic Perspectives* 14, no. 3 (Summer): 217–232.

Solimano, Andres (2012), *Chile and the Neoliberal Trap: The Post-Pinochet Era.* New York: Columbia University Press.

Spar, Debora (1998), "Attracting High Technology Investment: Intel's Costa Rica Plant." Foreign Investment Advisory Service Ocassional Paper #11 (April).

Stein, Ernesto, and Mariano Tomassi (2008), *Policymaking in Latin America: How Politics Shapes Policies.* Washington, DC: Inter-American Development Bank.

Talvi, Ernesto, and Ignacio Munyo (2013), "Latin American Macroeconomic Outlook: A Global Perspective—Are the Golden Years Over?" Brookings Institution LAC regional report (June).

Taylor, Alan (1998), "On the Costs of Inward-Looking Development: Price Distortions, Growth and Divergence in Latin America." *Journal of Economic History* 58, no 1 (March): 1–28.

———. (2003), "Foreign Capital in Latin America in the 19th and 20th Centuries." NBER Working Paper #9580 (March).

Thorpe, Rosemary (1998), *Progress, Poverty and Exclusion: An Economic History of Latin America.* Washington, DC: Inter-American Development Bank.

UNESCO (2008), "Structural Change and Productivity Growth 20 years later: Old Problems, New Opportunities." Report for 32nd Annual Conference of UNECLA.

Vargas Llosa, Alvaro (2005), *Liberty for Latin America: How to Undo Five Hundred Years of State Oppression.* New York, NY: Farrar, Straus and Giroux.

Volpe Martincus, Christian (2010), "Odyssey in International Markets: An Assessment of the Effectiveness of Export Promotion in Latin America and the

Caribbean." Special report prepared by the Integration and Trade Sector at the Inter-American Development Bank.

Wiarda, Howard (2001), *The Soul of Latin America: The Cultural and Political Tradition*. New Haven, CT: Yale University Press.

Williamson, Jeffrey G. (2010), "Latin America Growth-Inequality Trade-offs: The Impact of Insurgence and Independence." NBER Working Paper #15680 (January).

Williamson, John, ed. (1990), *Latin American Adjustment: How Much Has Happened?* Washington, DC: Petersen Institute for International Economics.

Williamson, John (2010), "Exchange Rate Policy in Brazil." Peterson Institute for International Economics Working Paper #10–16 (December).

Williamson, John, and Pedro Pablo Kuczynski (2003), "After the Washington Consensus: Restarting Growth and Reform in Latin America." Washington, DC: Peterson Institute for International Economics.

World Bank (2004), "Inequality and Economic Development in Brazil." World Bank Country Study Series.

———. (2006), "The Impact of Intel in Costa Rica: Nine Years after the Decision to Invest." In *Investing in Development Series*, World Bank Multilateral Investment Guarantee Agency.

———. (2009), "Reshaping Economic Geography in Latin America and the Caribbean." A companion volume to the 2009 World Development Report of the World Bank.

———. (2011), "Latin America and the Caribbean's Long Term Growth: Made in China?" World Bank LAC regional semi-annual report (September).

Zettelmeyer, Jeromin (2006), "Growth and Reforms in Latin America: A Survey of Facts and a Conjecture." IMF Working Paper #06/210 (September).

Index

Note: a page number followed by "n" indicates a reference in the Notes section of the book.

Printed in the United States of America